the Teen VOGUE HAND BOOK

An Insider's Guide to Careers in Fashion

razOr bill

RAZORBILL

Published by the Penguin Group
Penguin Young Readers Group
345 Hudson Street, New York, New York 10014, USA
Penguin Group (USA) Inc., 375 Hudson Street, New York, New York 10014, USA
Penguin Group (Canada), 90 Eglinton Avenue East, Suite 700, Toronto, Ontario,
Canada M4P 2Y3 (a division of Pearson Penguin Canada Inc.)
Penguin Books Ltd, 80 Strand, London WC2R 0RL, England
Penguin Ireland, 25 St. Stephen's Green, Dublin 2, Ireland (a division of Penguin Books Ltd.)
Penguin Group (Australia), 250 Camberwell Road, Camberwell, Victoria 3124, Australia
(a division of Pearson Australia Group Pty. Ltd.)
Penguin Books India Pvt. Ltd., 11 Community Centre, Panchsheel Park, New Delhi–
110 017, India
Penguin Group (NZ), 67 Apollo Drive, Rosedale, North Shore 0632, New Zealand
(a division of Pearson New Zealand Ltd.)

Penguin Books (South Africa) (Pty.) Ltd., 24 Sturdee Avenue, Rosebank, Johannesburg
2196, South Africa

Penguin Books Ltd., Registered Offices: 80 Strand, London WC2R 0RL, England
10 9 8 7 6 5

Library of Congress Cataloging-in-Publication Data

The teen vogue handbook : an insider's guide to careers in fashion.
        p. cm.
Includes bibliographical references and index.
ISBN 978-1-59514-261-0
1. Fashion merchandising—Juvenile literature. 2. Vocational guidance—Juvenile literature.

HD9940.A2T44 2009
746.9'2023—dc22
                              2009010626

Printed in China

CONTENTS

READERS' QUESTIONS

HERE ARE SOME QUESTIONS, FROM *TEEN VOGUE* READERS LIKE YOU, THAT HELPED TO INSPIRE THIS BOOK.

HOW DO I GET *an internship* AT A *magazine?*

I want TO WORK IN *fashion.* WHAT SHOULD I *major* IN DURING *college?*

WHAT *should I wear* TO A JOB *interview?*

I LOVE TAKING *pictures.* IS THERE A COMMON *career path* FOR PHOTOGRAPHERS *that I* SHOULD KEEP IN *mind?*

I'M A *sophomore* IN *high school* AND *live* IN THE *Midwest.* DO I *need* TO MOVE TO NEW YORK CITY TO *get* A JOB IN *fashion?*

Do I HAVE TO GO TO *art school* TO BE A FASHION *designer?*

DO *TEEN VOGUE editors* REALLY *travel* TO *places* LIKE PARIS TO ATTEND *fashion shows* AND PARTIES, *the way* THEY *do* ON *"The Hills"?*

Amy Astley

EACH OF THESE QUESTIONS, AND MORE, IS ADDRESSED IN THIS BOOK.

Nearly every *Teen Vogue* reader I have come in contact with has asked me at least one of the questions at left, or some combination of several of them! I have always been impressed with how career-focused these young women (and men) are, and I eventually realized that we needed to create a book addressing the basic query: How do I break in to the fashion industry?

The truth is, becoming a stylist, a designer, a model, a fashion critic, or a photographer is not like becoming a doctor or a lawyer. One does not attend a specific sort of school, follow a prescribed course of study, and emerge ready to be employed. While concentrating on the fashion arenas where *Teen Vogue* has the most expertise—design, styling, photography, and journalism—the talents profiled in our handbook (from industry legends to up-and-comers) describe very idiosyncratic paths to success, and yet common threads of advice and experience emerge to provide an invaluable road map for young people. As such, the book is a useful, practical reference guide: How to build a portfolio, dress for an interview, and land an internship. But it is also a visual record of work by *Teen Vogue*'s most treasured collaborators. It is our world, and we invite you to join it and find your own path to living a creative life.

Question:
I want to he a fash Where do I begin?

Answer:
Legends and newco how to break in to

ion designer.

mers alike reveal
the business.

The Dream Weavers

Rodarte

THE MULLEAVY SISTERS EMERGED FROM A SLEEPY NORTHERN CALIFORNIA TOWN TO TAKE THE FASHION WORLD BY STORM WITH THEIR MAGICAL GOTHIC DESIGNS.

Mulleavy sisters Kate, 30, and Laura, 29—better known as the design duo behind the ethereal cult-favorite label Rodarte—don't seem, on paper, to be the likeliest style stars: They grew up in a fashion-challenged California town called Aptos, and they eschewed Parsons the New School for Design and Pratt Institute in favor of their botanist father's alma mater, University of California, Berkeley (where Kate majored in art history and Laura studied English lit). Post-college, they prepared for their future careers by reading books about couture sewing and by watching, as Kate puts it, "a year's worth of horror films."

Unlikely origins notwithstanding, the Mulleavys became darlings of the design set almost as soon as they brought their first ten-piece collection to New York, in February 2005, landing on the cover of the must-read industry rag *Women's Wear Daily* within days of their arrival. In 2006 and 2007, they were nominated for the CFDA Swarovski Award for Womenswear, and in 2008, they won it. Today the sisters work in a downtown Los Angeles studio decorated with strange-looking stuffed animals and shelves full of oversize art books, all carefully organized according to the color of their spines.

Your mother and father are, respectively, an artist and a scientist. How did you become interested in fashion?
Laura Mulleavy: Well, we grew up in a world where people looked at things in a microscopic way. And even though we were in a town where people weren't exactly dressing as a lifestyle, we were always among the redwoods or in tide pools, and I think all that had an impact.
Kate Mulleavy: We often went to the Monterey Bay Aquarium, and some of those underwater environments look like a beautiful Chanel couture show—everything ruffles and there are all these incredible colors. We were also influenced by the aesthetics of the skaters, punks, and hippies living in Santa Cruz at the time.
LM: It was like that movie *The Lost Boys.* And actually, I think the first time we were really exposed to fashion was through film and costume design.
KM: Film projects a fantasy that we had about what a garment could do, how it could transform someone's life.

So why didn't you go to fashion-design school?
KM: I thought about it, but I wasn't sure—there were so

KATE: *"Working with someone you connect with can be more fun than going it alone, because when it comes to challenging or tedious tasks, you'll have someone to do them with."*

LAURA: *"As a designer you need to have a library of visual references, so ask for fashion and art books for your birthday. The Kyoto Costume Institute and the Metropolitan Museum of Art both have amazing titles."*

THE MULLEAVYS (LAURA, LEFT, AND KATE) TRADE THEIR USUAL DRESSED-DOWN UNIFORMS OF T-SHIRTS, JEANS, AND NEW BALANCE SNEAKERS FOR TWO RUNWAY SIGNATURES FROM THEIR FALL 2008 COLLECTION—DRAMATIC TIE-DYE AND A WEBBY KNIT.

DISSECTING THE LOOK

The Mulleavy sisters share their process for designing a runway ensemble.

"Our fall 2008 collection was about Japanese horror films, so we wanted the models to have a black-red lip and moonshine eyes. The hair was inspired by the film *Ladies and Gentlemen, the Fabulous Stains* and streaked bleach-white down the back."

"We tried to illustrate with the knits what we see in our favorite Eva Hesse sculptures. Our knits are done like broken spider webs—delicately unraveled. They're tightly wound in some places and very loose in others. Most of the yarns are mohair and different wools. We dyed them to have veins of color that at some points look as though they're bleeding or covering a seeping wound."

"The blouse is made of a silk screen that is dyed what we call horror gray. It's meant to look like fog on the skin."

"We imagined that our pant would be cropped and would need to be worn with a tattered sweater. Each model in the show wore tights, so it was natural to pair the pants with knit kneesocks as well."

"The shoe finalizes a silhouette. It affects everything from the hem of a pant or dress to the gait of the model. We always dream of the shoe alongside the clothing. We sketch out all the details of it before we even draw the clothing. This shoe has spikes and studs. We wanted it to be fierce."

many things I was interested in: writing, fine art. We didn't get the technical training, but we did take all these amazing classes on, you know, nineteenth-century Venice and French photography. It gave us a foundation.

LM: In a liberal arts education, the subjects you're studying are pretty broad, but they can help you form a way of analyzing things and looking at visual culture. You need reference points outside of fashion.

KM: For the clothes we make, visual knowledge is the most important thing.

LM: We thought about fashion school again once we graduated, but we already had all these college loans, so we decided to try and see if we could make it work by ourselves.

Where did you begin?

LM: We moved back home. We had planned a trip to Italy with a friend and backed out, so we had a little money. I got a job as a waitress, and Kate sold her record collection.

KM: We had been sewing our whole lives.

LM: Our mother taught us. But I didn't really make too many of my own clothes after a certain point. I've never really had the urge to design for myself.

Even now?

LM: If I designed what I wanted to wear, I would only ever design pants and T-shirts! It's funny: I enjoy beautiful things, but I don't want to hoard them. I create, and then I let it go.

KM: So we began experimenting. We would make things, and then we'd be like, Okay, we made this, but what's the point of making it for us? We were finding our voice. Eventually we did a small, ten-piece collection, but we weren't sure what to do with it. We didn't know how to sell the clothes. We wrote a letter to Cameron Silver [the owner of L.A. vintage couture boutique Decades] and asked him what he thought, and he told us to go to New York.

LM: I remember at the time it felt like this life-or-death situation—like, this is everything we've been working on and this is all the money we have. We went to New York and stayed with a friend, and we met with stores like Barneys New York and Bergdorf Goodman. The only reason that even happened is because we called them all a zillion times, until they gave us appointments. But they were amazing—so willing to offer advice. And then *WWD* called and we landed on the cover. It happened very quickly.

What's a typical day like for you now?

LM: We do everything, every day: production, shipping, dealing with stores, PR, designing the next collection. You have to be good at bouncing back and forth.

KM: We have a team in-house: a sewer whom we've worked with since the beginning, someone who can do samples, a knitter, and a production person. But it's still

ABOVE: A RODARTE DRESS ON THE COVER OF *VOGUE*, OCTOBER 2008. RIGHT: RODARTE'S DREAMY DESIGNS ARE FAVORITES OF HOLLYWOOD RISK-TAKERS SUCH AS NATALIE PORTMAN, SEEN HERE AT A 2008 FILM PREMIERE.

a very hands-on process. If we need to embroider, we embroider. We don't send it to Italy.

Do you divvy up the work?

LM: Day to day we do, but there's no true division between what she does and what I do. We're both creative and we're both business-minded.

Is it difficult to balance the commercial and the creative concerns?

LM: There's a misconception that if you do something that's creative and personal, then you're less aware of the commercial side. For me, the way to create a brand that people will be invested in long-term is to do something very creative.

KM: It's an interesting dynamic. You have to live and breathe both the creative and the business parts—it's not like being a musician, where you can go off to India and do your "experimental" album. In fashion, you can be experimental, but it still has to be popular. If you have a connection to what you're doing, like we do, then the route you take really doesn't matter. You're going to do it. ★

The King of Cool

Marc Jacobs

COVETED CLOTHES, CUTTING-EDGE ADS, AND CELEB-PACKED FRONT ROWS ENSURE THIS STYLE PIONEER'S HOLD ON THE THRONE.

Marc Jacobs was only sixteen when he started working as a stock boy at the influential Upper West Side boutique Charivari. It was there that he first met Perry Ellis—the designer who, Jacobs says, encouraged him to apply to Parsons the New School for Design and mentored him while he was a student. Eight years later, Jacobs produced his infamous grunge collection for the Perry Ellis label. It was also at Charivari that Jacobs sold his first pieces, a collection of oversize, hand-knit sweaters that he designed while at Parsons (his grandmother made the original samples), the popularity of which he still refers to as "kind of my first big break."

Today Jacobs is one of the most well-known and closely watched designers in the world, helming his own signature label, a diffusion line, and the French luxury brand Louis Vuitton. But he shies away from offering explicit advice to anyone looking to duplicate his success: "I hate the word *advice*," he explains. "It's not a mathematical situation. I'm happy to share my experience, but everybody has a different path."

How did you first become interested in fashion?
As far back as I can remember, I had an interest in fashion. I used to go to sleepaway camp, and they'd provide a list of things that you had to bring, and I always wanted to be a bit more creative than the list allowed. Like, if they required chinos, I wanted to hand-paint them. Even then I thought of clothes as a way to express oneself, as a kind of theater. I was also really into making Halloween costumes and stuff like that. So I guess I saw fashion as a way to bring fantasy into my everyday reality. I never had enough money to do what I wanted to do when I was a teenager, but it was never really a problem—it pushed me to be more resourceful. I'd go to a uniform store and buy an air-conditioner-repairman jumpsuit and then customize it. I'd buy carpenter's pants and overdye them, or a sweatshirt and cut off the sleeves. That way I could achieve the look I wanted.

Even at sixteen I knew that I wanted to be a fashion designer. I met Perry Ellis at Charivari and asked him what he thought I should do about it. He said that if I was serious, I should go to Parsons. And that was that.

Do you think that design school is important for an aspiring designer?
I don't think there's anything wrong with getting an education. There are plenty of designers with no fashion background,

JACOBS TAKES A BREAK IN HIS
SOHO, NEW YORK, STUDIO.

MODELS IN LOOKS FROM JACOBS'S FALL 2006 GRUNGE REVIVAL COLLECTION, WHICH WAS SAID TO BE INSPIRED BY FRIEND AND FAN MARY-KATE OLSEN'S HOBO-CHIC STYLE.

but it probably helps in terms of being recommended for your first job. It helps you get your foot in the door at certain places.

For my senior show I made these oversize sweaters, and one of the owners of Charivari noticed and loved them so much that she asked if she could produce them for her store. Then *The New York Times* ran a number of photographs of women wearing the sweaters in its Street Style column, which got people asking, "Who's Marc Jacobs?" That was, for me, kind of the beginning. I was 21 years old, and it showed me that something I made was sellable. The experience made me realize that something I'm feeling may speak to somebody else, too. And all it takes is someone who believes in you. So I thought, Well, if I can do that with one sweater, then I can do it with a small collection—and things evolved from there.

Seeing strangers in your designs must be an everyday occurrence for you now. Is it still exciting?
Yes! To me, it's the greatest compliment. Even when I see

a copy, something that's inspired by something I've done, it's a rewarding feeling. Because that's why I do what I do. It was never my desire to revolutionize fashion, to make clothes that could be in a museum. I want to create clothes that have a certain style, but I want to see them used. I want to see people enjoy the things I've made.

What does your job consist of now?
Actually, I do two jobs. I work for my own company and I work for Louis Vuitton, but my position at both companies is the same. I'd describe it as being part of a team—a very big team—of creative people: designers, sewers, pattern-makers, salespeople. We put on shows, we do lots of press, and I work on shoes, handbags, perfume ... all sorts of things. But it's always the same process: coming up with an idea, working through the colors, the materials, the sensibility, the spirit, and having that idea realized in a three-dimensional form. Then you check it, correct it, tweak it, and get it as close as you can—within the time that you have—to what the initial thought was.

TEEN VOGUE TIP Get your stuff out there! When Jacobs created his first line of sweaters, his pals wore them all around town. Photos of the knits ended up in the newspaper, which generated buzz about the designer.

JACOBS'S MUSES

The effortlessly quirky-cool girls who inspire the designer.

FROM KITSCHY CAMPAIGN GIRLS LIKE VICTORIA BECKHAM TO CLOTHES-OBSCURING SHOPPING BAGS, JACOBS LOVES TO PLAY WITH CONVENTION IN HIS ADS.

THE DESIGNER NAMED A STYLE OF THE LACE-TRIMMED LOUIS VUITTON DENTELLE PURSE "KIRSTEN," IN HONOR OF ACTRESS KIRSTEN DUNST, PHOTOGRAPHED HERE BY MUTUAL PAL SOFIA COPPOLA.

JACOBS'S NUMBER ONE MUSE, DIRECTOR SOFIA COPPOLA—WHO HAS STARRED IN ADS FOR BOTH MARC JACOBS AND LOUIS VUITTON—DESIGNED A LINE OF SHOES AND BAGS FOR VUITTON.

ACTRESS WINONA RYDER (HERE IN A MARC JACOBS JACKET) POSED FOR THE SPRING 2003 CAMPAIGN, ONE YEAR AFTER HER HIGH-PROFILE TRIAL FOR SHOPLIFTING, FOR WHICH SHE FAMOUSLY WORE A SERIES OF DEMURE MARC JACOBS ENSEMBLES. THE ADS CHEEKILY REFERENCED THE INCIDENT.

JACOBS CAST THEN-12-YEAR-OLD ACTRESS DAKOTA FANNING IN HIS SPRING 2007 ADS. THE LABEL HAD TO CUSTOM-MAKE THE CLOTHES TO FIT HER SMALL SIZE.

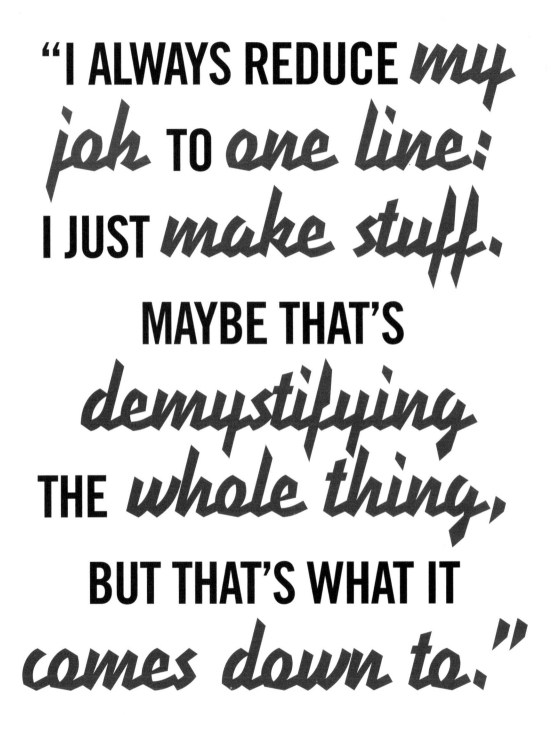

"I ALWAYS REDUCE *my job* TO *one line:* I JUST *make stuff.* MAYBE THAT'S *demystifying* THE *whole thing,* BUT THAT'S WHAT IT *comes down to."*

—MARC JACOBS

JACOBS'S SPRING 1993 GRUNGE
COLLECTION FOR PERRY ELLIS WAS A
CRITICAL SENSATION BUT LED TO THE
DESIGNER'S DISMISSAL FROM THE
COMPANY. STILL, "IT'S MY FAVORITE,"
JACOBS HAS SAID. "I LIKE THE IDEA
OF MAKING SOME VISUAL NOISE
THROUGH CLOTHING."

ZOE CASSAVETES AND SOFIA COPPOLA

MARY-KATE AND ASHLEY OLSEN

MANDY MOORE

KATE BOSWORTH

EACH SEASON, JACOBS HAS MADE HIS FRONT ROW THE ONE TO WATCH FOR ITS CAREFULLY CULTIVATED MIX OF GUESTS, FROM CHIC ACTRESSES AND ARTSY FRIENDS TO OVER-THE-TOP POP STARS AND COUNTERCULTURAL ICONS.

And where do the ideas come from in the first place?
Everywhere. Everywhere and anywhere. They come from other people, they come from me, they come from people I see on the streets. Sometimes they come from a movie I saw the night before, and sometimes it's as simple as wanting a big, soft sweater because I'm cold that day.

Is it challenging to work on so many different lines?
Yes. But it's not only me here—there's a bunch of other people. That's one of the things I think is so great about us as a com-

pany. Robert [Duffy, Jacobs's business partner] and I have created an environment that really allows the people we've chosen to express themselves. We don't have a totalitarian dictatorship of watching over everyone's shoulder as they sketch, and nobody is waiting around for me to tell them what to do. They just get on with it. They make stuff. I always reduce my job to that line: I say, "You know, I just make stuff." And that's what everybody here does. We make stuff, we look at it, we add to it, we edit it, we change it. Maybe that's demystifying the whole thing, but that's what it comes down to. ★

ARTIST COLLABORATIONS

TAKASHI MURAKAMI'S EYE LOVE MONOGRAM.

STEPHEN SPROUSE'S MONOGRAM GRAFFITI.

RICHARD PRINCE'S MONOGRAM JOKES.

JACOBS HAS MASTERMINDED WAIT LIST–INDUCING BAG COLLABORATIONS FOR LOUIS VUITTON BY BRINGING IN COOL TALENT LIKE POP ARTIST TAKASHI MURAKAMI, PUNKY DESIGNER STEPHEN SPROUSE, AND CONCEPTUAL ARTIST RICHARD PRINCE TO RIFF ON THE CLASSICS.

The Prince of Prints

Thakoon Panichgul

THIS BUDDING STAR IS RISING FAST, THANKS TO WITTY PRINTS THAT APPEAL TO EVERYONE FROM HIP YOUNG THINGS TO THE FIRST LADY.

"My mother was a seamstress, so, in a sense, I grew up in the industry. But for her it was a way to put food on the table. We moved from Thailand to Omaha when I was eleven years old, and she got a job sewing coats and blankets at a company called Pendleton Woolen Mills. It wasn't very glamorous, especially in Nebraska.

Nevertheless, I have always been interested in fashion. I remember being intrigued by the way people put together their clothes, even when I was still in Bangkok. I had a green Adidas soccer outfit that my mom got me—

sort of a casual take on a uniform, with a matching top and bottom—which I thought had to be matchy, not mix-and-matchy. I was very particular. I had to wear my socks a certain way. And after we moved to the United States, I became a fashion-magazine freak.

When the time came to go to college, I applied to a business program at Boston University because that's what my mom wanted me to do. I won a scholarship and accepted it for my family's sake, but I resolved to pursue a career in fashion once I graduated.

THE DESIGNER, PHOTOGRAPHED FOR *VOGUE* WITH ACTRESS AND FAN KATE BOSWORTH. SHE IS WEARING A DRESS FROM HIS SPRING 2008 COLLECTION, WHICH FEATURES BLOWN-UP AND DIGITIZED FLORALS.

THAKOON'S DEBUT COLLECTION

PANICHGUL'S ARTFULLY EXECUTED DEBUT PRESENTATION FOR SPRING 2005, WHICH HE STAGED AT AN ART GALLERY IN NEW YORK CITY'S CHELSEA, IMMEDIATELY CAUGHT THE ATTENTION OF FASHION EDITORS AND BUYERS.

MICHELLE OBAMA'S CHOICE TO WEAR A THAKOON PRINTED DRESS THE NIGHT HER HUSBAND ACCEPTED THE DEMOCRATIC NOMINATION FOR PRESIDENT BOOSTED THE DESIGNER ONTO A GLOBAL PLATFORM.

I got a summer internship at Showroom Seven, a press and sales showroom in New York City, and the experience taught me that there are little niches in fashion, different paths you can take. After graduation I worked in production for J. Crew, as a liaison among the designers, the merchandisers, and the factories that produce the clothes. A lot of coordination was involved. I would have to say, 'Okay, we want this shirt, but we want it at this price point, so you need to source the cotton at a lower price and finish it this way.' After a little while, I was promoted to the merchandising department, where the designers would present the clothes to us and we would pick and choose which items would be made and sold.

Eventually I realized it was time to move on to something more creative. I became an assistant in the fashion features department at *Harper's Bazaar,* which really allowed me to learn about fashion from the top down. I started taking design classes at Parsons the New School for Design on nights and weekends; I took an apparel-construction class, a pattern-making class, and a sketching class, and then I decided to give designing a whirl.

I had a book of sketches and ideas I had been collecting, and at *Bazaar* I met with a lot of designers who had started on a whim and got things going, so I thought, I can do that! I made maybe eight pieces and took them to stores, where I met with people I knew through the magazine.

Barneys New York and Bergdorf Goodman liked the collection, but they couldn't work with so few pieces, so I sold it to Ikram in Chicago and Kirna Zabête in New York. It was crazy because I didn't exactly have a plan—I just had the samples—so then I was like, What do I do now? I convinced the guy who had made the sample patterns to help me produce the clothes; I had to go to Hold Everything to buy boxes to ship them in.

I realized I needed to do some kind of presentation for the next collection. I rallied friends to help me get a space for cheap and people to do hair and makeup. I didn't think anyone was going to come, but every editor of every magazine was there. Later, people told me there was a buzz that day at fashion week, like, 'Are you going to see Thakoon?' It was such a cool feeling. I was picked up by 15 or 20 stores, and things have been building ever since.

Now a typical day for me consists of juggling all the various production and sales issues that arise in regard to the current collection—for example, if deliveries are delayed—while designing and producing samples for the next collection. I'll do my rough little sketches—I call them chicken scratches—and then the designers who work for me, who illustrate beautifully, take the sketches to the next level. We go back and forth a few times about the way a piece is supposed to be draped, how it will hang on the body, and then it goes to the pattern-maker and a sample is made. And, of course, I have to coordinate each show, confirm the space, and hire a casting person. So it's all over the place. But it's exciting and fun at the same time, because I get to do everything." ★

*teen*VOGUE TIP "You have to look at fashion from the perspective of high-end editors and publications. Read all the magazines—commercial and underground—and your voice will evolve from what you see there." —THAKOON PANICHGUL

Lee Anderson, PANICHGUL'S INTERN
AGE 23 COLLEGE PARSONS THE NEW SCHOOL FOR DESIGN HOMETOWN CHICAGO, ILLINOIS

"I'm originally from Chicago, and while I was studying fashion at Savannah College of Art and Design in Georgia, I worked at the store Ikram when I was home on break. The owner let me spend mornings on the floor, helping with sales, and afternoons in the alterations department, learning to sew. It was an amazing opportunity.

After two years, I decided to transfer to Parsons, so I started looking for a New York designer to intern with. I focused on designers Ikram carried because I knew more about them (including how to get in touch with them), and Thakoon seemed like the best fit for me.

My duties change daily, but they include research, sourcing, getting fabrics and trims from factories, working with samples and pattern-makers, and discussing finishings—the little decisions about the garments, which is one of my favorite parts. Working at a small company allows me a more hands-on view of the business than I would get if I worked at a big house. I see every angle, even if it's just through conversations with salespeople or the accounting team. And I've been here quite a while, so I've been able to watch the brand progress.

The best advice I can offer someone who wants to intern is to just get out there. Don't be too picky: I lucked out, but you can learn from whatever situation you're in. The important thing is to be active in the design world, because that's how you build momentum. As for the dress code, fashion is actually a very casual environment, but it's important to be aware of the distinction between comfortable and sloppy: I almost always wear flats instead of sneakers, and I dress up my T-shirts with scarves and necklaces."

Dylan Kawahara, PANICHGUL'S INTERN
AGE 22 COLLEGE PARSONS THE NEW SCHOOL FOR DESIGN HOMETOWN LOS ANGELES, CALIFORNIA

"I started working for Thakoon the summer before my junior year at Parsons. In high school, I saw one of his dresses hanging in the closet of a friend's mom and—even though Thakoon didn't advertise and I didn't know who he was—I was instantly drawn to it. I e-mailed him about an internship, and I remember being surprised that he interviewed me himself. We chatted for 20 minutes about my portfolio, and our personalities just clicked.

I did a lot of grunt work, but I got a good sense of the industry. I matched fabrics and found trimmings; I never had to get coffee. On my first day, the very first thing Thakoon asked me to do was to get a toggle. I spent hours at M&J Trimming, sourcing toggles, and when I got back I realized that what he really wanted was a cord pull, which is something totally different. It was funny. He always knows what he wants, but sometimes the hardest part of working with a design team is explaining it to someone else.

If I had to pick the single day of my internship from which I learned the most, I would say it was when the fit model and the production manager came in with a garment made of this amazing fabric; it looked totally finished, and Thakoon took a Sharpie and started drawing all over it. I was shocked. The garment looked perfect to me, but he knew exactly what he wanted. You expect fashion design to be so simple, but it's not.

The internship also taught me that I need more time after graduation to learn from someone else. School's not enough; there's more to this industry than you think. It's an old-fashioned system, but you learn a lot by apprenticing."

The Earth Ambassador

Stella McCartney

THIS ANIMAL-RIGHTS ACTIVIST CREATES INFLUENTIAL FASHION THAT IS ALSO ECO-FRIENDLY.

Stella McCartney first sent ripples through the fashion world when, as a senior at Central Saint Martins School of Art & Design in London, she showcased her graduation collection with the help of her supermodel best friends Kate Moss and Naomi Campbell. The designer's lineage may already have been legendary (her father is former Beatle Sir Paul McCartney, and her late mother, Linda, was a photographer and animal-rights activist), but determined to become a success in her own right, she spent her teenage years tirelessly training on London's Savile Row. McCartney made a name for herself with a blockbuster stint as chief designer at Chloé, then launched her own label in 2001 as part of Gucci Group. She eschews fur and leather and has orchestrated innovative approaches to earth-friendly design—not only with her signature collection, but through a successful organic beauty line, Care, and with the Stella McCartney Eco-Collection for Barneys New York. "The natural environment has always been a huge inspiration," she says. "I try to design in harmony with it."

McCARTNEY GOES FOR A RIDE ON HER HORSE FLO JO AT HER ESTATE IN GLOUCESTSHIRE, ENGLAND. THE ANIMAL-LOVING DESIGNER HAS BUILT A BRAND ON VEGAN FASHION THAT DOESN'T SACRIFICE STYLE.

McCARTNEY IS MOBBED BY FANS AFTER A FASHION SHOW SHE STAGED TO RAISE MONEY FOR AN ARTS SCHOOL COFOUNDED BY HER FATHER, BEATLE PAUL McCARTNEY, IN HIS NATIVE LIVERPOOL. THE MUSICIAN IS A FREQUENT FRONT-ROW GUEST AT HIS DAUGHTER'S PARIS RUNWAY SHOWS.

What made you decide to launch your label?
I guess I always felt that I had it in me and that I had a place in the industry. I felt I had a valid voice and, if given the opportunity to house that voice, I had a good chance of success.

What is your central philosophy?
To make clothes that allow women to reflect their inner confidence, help them to be different and be noticed but in a subtle, attractive kind of way.

You have advocated against the use of leather and fur in your collections from day one. Can you explain your stance on animal products in fashion?
I don't understand why beautiful creatures should have to die for someone's coat—it's medieval and barbaric. More than a billion animals are killed every year, 25 million of them for the sake of fashion. That's a lot, and it has a big impact on the environment. I will never use leather or fur, ever! For me, it's the principle. There are plenty of alternatives. Our label isn't perfect, but we are trying. Something is better than nothing.

What challenges have you faced in building a fashion business that adheres to your personal ethics?
My first job is to be a fashion designer and to make desirable, luxurious, beautiful clothing that women want to buy. If that is hugely sacrificed by being 100 percent organic, then I will put my job first. But I always take any opportunity I can to use a beautiful, organic fabric. My first decision is always, Can I do this in a more environmental way? It's just a way of thinking. If only we all could think like that.

In addition to your eponymous label, you've launched an organic skin-care line, two fragrances, and collaborations with Adidas and H&M. What does an average workday entail for you?
I feel incredibly privileged: I get to dip into many different things and dabble in all trades. One minute I'm directing an advertising campaign, the next I'm thinking about hair and makeup for a fashion show. Then I'm designing shoes before working on the interior of one of my shops. Or I get to think about perfumes and become a chemist for a second while I work on a body scrub. I also do public relations, marketing, and turn on the lights in my shop. It's hard work and very demanding, but it's incredible.

What would you be if you weren't a designer?
I grew up in the arts. Before I decided I wanted to be a fashion designer, I thought I might become a photographer or perhaps do landscape gardening or something along those lines.

What is your advice to aspiring designers?
Believe in yourself and be prepared to work hard. ★

teenVOGUE TIP Fashion doesn't have to be superficial. In addition to creating clothes that are animal- and Earth-friendly, McCartney uses her brand as a platform to draw attention to causes that she cares about.

SINGER RIHANNA WEARS A STELLA McCARTNEY DRESS ON THE NOVEMBER 2007 *TEEN VOGUE* COVER.

THE DESIGNER WITH LONGTIME FRIEND KATE MOSS. MOST RECENTLY, McCARTNEY CAST MOSS IN HER SPRING 2009 AD CAMPAIGN.

STARTING IN 2004, McCARTNEY TEAMED UP WITH SPORTS BRAND ADIDAS. MODEL KASIA STRUSS WEARS A JACKET FROM THE LINE IN A 2007 ISSUE OF *TEEN VOGUE*.

THE BACKDROP FOR MCCARTNEY'S SPRING 2008 SHOW WAS A VERTICAL GARDEN, WHICH SHE AFTERWARD DONATED TO A HOUSING PROJECT.

FOR SPRING 2009, McCARTNEY'S SHOW FEATURED A MASSIVE FELT MURAL MADE BY BRITISH ARTISTS JAKE AND DINOS CHAPMAN. THE DESIGNER SAID SHE HOPED TO PLACE IT IN A SCHOOL OR AUCTION IT OFF FOR A CHILDREN'S CHARITY.

THE SCENE BACKSTAGE AT ALEXANDER
WANG'S SPRING 2009 SHOW. THE
DESIGNER (WEARING A WHITE T-SHIRT)
CREATES A RUNWAY SHOW THAT
HAS BECOME ONE OF THE HOTTEST
TICKETS AT NEW YORK FASHION WEEK.

The Next Big Thing
Alexander Wang

EDGY, CHIC DESIGNS AND A MODEL FAN CLUB CONFIRM THIS UP-AND-COMER'S COMMAND OF COOL.

Ask Alexander Wang what exactly a designer does all day, and the 25-year-old laughs. "I used to ask myself that same question," he admits. "My first season, when I was still just doing sweaters, I was finished after, like, one day. I picked my fabrics, picked my colors, and then I thought, Now what? What does everyone else do, just sit around? I took a lot of walks." Only a few years later, Wang—who dropped out of Parsons the New School for Design to launch his eponymous line at the tender age of 20—no longer needs to wonder what "real" designers do, because his days are filled with the business of being one of fashion's favorite new stars. "It's insane," he says. "We do six deliveries a year, we recently launched handbags, we're working on shoes, and every couple of months—before you know it—it's time for another show. I'll have to fly overseas to look at a factory that I'm considering for production, to London for a press tour, or to Miami for a photo shoot. And I never turn my brain off. I'm working all that time."

Not that he's complaining. In fact, Wang's current career, demanding as it may be, is nothing less than the culmination of a long-held dream. He started subscribing to fashion magazines when he was in grade school, and as a teenager he attended summer sessions at Otis College of Art and Design in Los Angeles and Central Saint Martins in London. He secured an internship at Marc Jacobs before he'd even begun classes at Parsons. And subsequent stints at *Teen Vogue, Vogue,* and Derek Lam convinced the budding designer that there was a hole in the market, an opportunity for someone who wanted to make clothing that was "contemporary and exciting but not too expensive," Wang says. With the help of his mother and sister-in-law and the encouragement of his former boss, *Teen Vogue* fashion director Gloria Baume, he created a small collection of modern, oversize, unisex cashmere sweaters.

"We didn't know anything about line sheets or market dates," he says, "so we had to figure it all out through trial and error. But because I didn't know anything, I could just do what I wanted, and I was free to think a little more openly."

There were some, Wang says, who told him that he wasn't ready, that he should give up and go back to school. "I think it's very important to be open and listen to other people's advice," he says. "But you have to make a judgment about what makes sense for you. You have to go with your instincts."

Starting small, with just knits, paid off, and it wasn't long before the designer was able to develop a full-fledged fashion line—which, he explains, was always the goal. "There was more demand than supply," he says, "and we like to keep it that way. But I also wanted to show people my vision, and I realized that the only way to do that was to design a complete collection. Before that, I don't think most people knew who the 'Alexander girl' really was."

"Each season is an evolution," Wang continues, "but everything is based on the idea of classics with a fresh, modern take, basics that a girl can make her own. There's a thematic inspiration—for example, evening-wear, but instead of doing something obvious like a ball gown or a cocktail dress, we do a sick beaded vest paired with a tank top. I like the idea of a girl running through the streets at night, splashing in puddles and ripping her nylons, understanding that it makes the outfit that much cooler. Next year, the line will probably take another turn, but there's always something that I'm chasing after." Which, according to Wang, is a good thing: "It's nice to feel that energy, that motivation to take it to the next level—every single day." ★

RUNWAY SIGNATURES

DISTRESSED DENIM

BOYFRIEND BLAZER

GRUNGE-GLAM

WANG'S WORLD
Take a peek into the designer's career.

WANG, WITH FRIEND AND BRITISH SCENESTER ALICE DELLAL IN ONE OF THE DESIGNER'S DRESSES, CELEBRATES TAKING HOME THE NIGHT'S TOP HONOR AT THE 2008 CFDA/*VOGUE* FASHION FUND AWARDS.

"IN THE *beginning,* WE DIDN'T *know anything* ABOUT *line sheets* OR MARKET DATES, SO WE HAD TO *figure it all out* THROUGH *trial and error.* BUT *because* I DIDN'T KNOW ANYTHING, I COULD JUST *do what I wanted,* AND I WAS *free to think* A LITTLE MORE *openly.*"

—ALEXANDER WANG

WANG'S MUSE, MODEL ERIN WASSON (CENTER), HELPS HIM STYLE A LOOK BACKSTAGE BEFORE THE SPRING 2008 SHOW.

WANG POSING FOR *VOGUE* ON A MANHATTAN ROOFTOP WITH MODEL CAROLINE TRENTINI, WHO WEARS A DRESS AND SHOES FROM SPRING 2009, THE SEASON THE DESIGNER DEBUTED HIS FOOTWEAR LINE.

The Brand Master

Tory Burch

WITH A WILDLY POPULAR BALLET FLAT AND UBIQUITOUS LOGO, THIS SOCIETY PRESENCE HAS PARLAYED HER PERSONAL STYLE INTO A FASHION EMPIRE.

"Growing up in Philadelphia, I wasn't really interested in fashion—I was much more of a tomboy. But my mother always had great style, and I used to love watching her get ready to go out at night. When I went away to school, at the University of Pennsylvania, my interest in fashion grew. After graduation I got a job in New York, assisting the minimalist designer Zoran. The company was basically just Zoran and me, so I got a real crash course in the industry.

I moved on to Ralph Lauren, where I worked first as a PR assistant and later as an advertising copywriter. After six years there I went on to run the PR and advertising departments for Vera Wang, when she was just breaking out of bridal and in to ready-to-wear, and followed that with a stint at Spanish leather-goods brand Loewe, which was then designed by Narciso Rodriguez. I decided to leave work for a while to spend time with my three little boys, and that's when I began thinking about starting my own company.

It was definitely scary to start over at that stage in my career. For a long time I didn't want to use my own name, and I tried—without success—to get the rights to several other names. I wanted to revive a clothing brand called Jax, which was a great line of easy basics from the sixties and seventies,

but I couldn't get permission. By then I had already started putting together an inspiration book, and it evolved into the vision for my own label.

I didn't have any design experience, but working with Ralph, Vera, and Narciso was great training. At Ralph Lauren, especially, I learned the enormous value of having a cohesive brand identity. We introduced Tory by TRB in 2004 (shortened to just Tory Burch in 2006) with fifteen categories—from candles and umbrellas to beach towels—so it was a lifestyle concept from day one. We also worked hard on the logo, trying to come up with one that would really resonate.

Instead of launching our line the conventional way, wholesaling it out to department stores and boutiques, we dove right in and opened our own shop in downtown Manhattan, where we sold the designs exclusively. This was, for me, the only way to ensure the consistency of the brand's image. At the time, store design had gone in a direction that was very minimal and clean, but we wanted ours to be lush—like you were walking into my living room—so that when you entered the store you would immediately understand what the label was about. We spent an incredible amount of time on each detail, including the orange lacquer doors and brass doorknobs,

BEFORE SHE HIT IT BIG, BURCH DID STINTS WITH DESIGNERS RALPH LAUREN, VERA WANG, AND NARCISO RODRIGUEZ.

A BAG FROM FALL 2008 (ABOVE) DISPLAYS BURCH'S SIGNATURE DOUBLE T'S, ONE OF THE MOST COPIED DESIGNER LOGOS IN AMERICA. IT WAS INSPIRED BY THE GEOMETRIC STYLE OF SIXTIES INTERIOR DESIGNER DAVID HICKS. BURCH'S METICULOUSLY DECORATED STORES, LIKE THIS ONE IN MANHATTAN'S MEATPACKING DISTRICT (CENTER), CONVEY HER VISION VIA DETAILS SUCH AS MIRRORED WALLS AND PLUSH GREEN CARPETING.

the lighting, the flowers, and what kind of music we would play.

We scheduled an opening-day event from 10:00 A.M. to 6:00 P.M. But the night before, the store still wasn't ready. I think one of my greatest strengths is that I don't get frazzled under pressure; if something goes wrong I just think about how to fix it, because it's never the end of the world. My stepdaughters and I worked straight through the night, running home at 9:30 in the morning to shower and getting back to the store by 10:05. The day turned out to be amazing—we sold out of all our merchandise. People were yanking clothes off racks and changing right in the middle of the store!

Events like that are a big part of my job, and because I'm a very private person, they're something I've had to get used to. But I am the face of the brand, and the social aspect really does make a difference. Our company has grown rapidly since those early days. We now have seventeen stores. When we first started, we were just two people working out of my apartment on the Upper East Side, and in the last five years we've moved offices three times. We've definitely been fortunate to have a lot of people in the industry helping and advising us. That's another thing I think I'm good at: surrounding myself with great people.

Then there are the things that you can't take credit for, like the *Oprah* incident. One of Oprah Winfrey's producers gave her a Tory Burch sweater for Christmas, and she liked it so much that she invited us to be on her "Next Big Thing" special in 2005. The impact of appearing on her show was immeasurable—it changed our entire company. One day we were getting 10,000 hits on our Web site, and the next day it was 8 million. That episode really put us on the map!

Of course, the pieces themselves deserve credit too. Our tunic, our tote, and especially our Reva ballet flat, which is named for my mother (she's one of my muses), have all been phenomenal hits. Because I don't have a design background, it's easier for my brain to work on both the creative and the business levels. I think about the bottom line—I'm not tied to anything that won't sell, but I don't want products that are just commercial either.

When I interview designers for jobs, I look for candidates with portfolios that don't channel us. I want to hire people who have a point of view and can bring something new to our team, because I want an interesting mix. I think that's why our collection is so successful and why so many different types of girls wear our clothes.

People always ask me when I realized that I had made it—whether it was the *Oprah* episode or the success of the Reva flat. But I don't think I'll ever necessarily feel that way. It's just not my nature. I am always going to feel like I can do more, to keep evolving the brand." ★

teenVOGUE TIP Have a clear idea of what you'd like to offer visually. "When I started this company, I asked myself what was going to make it stand apart. You've got to have a point of view." —TORY BURCH

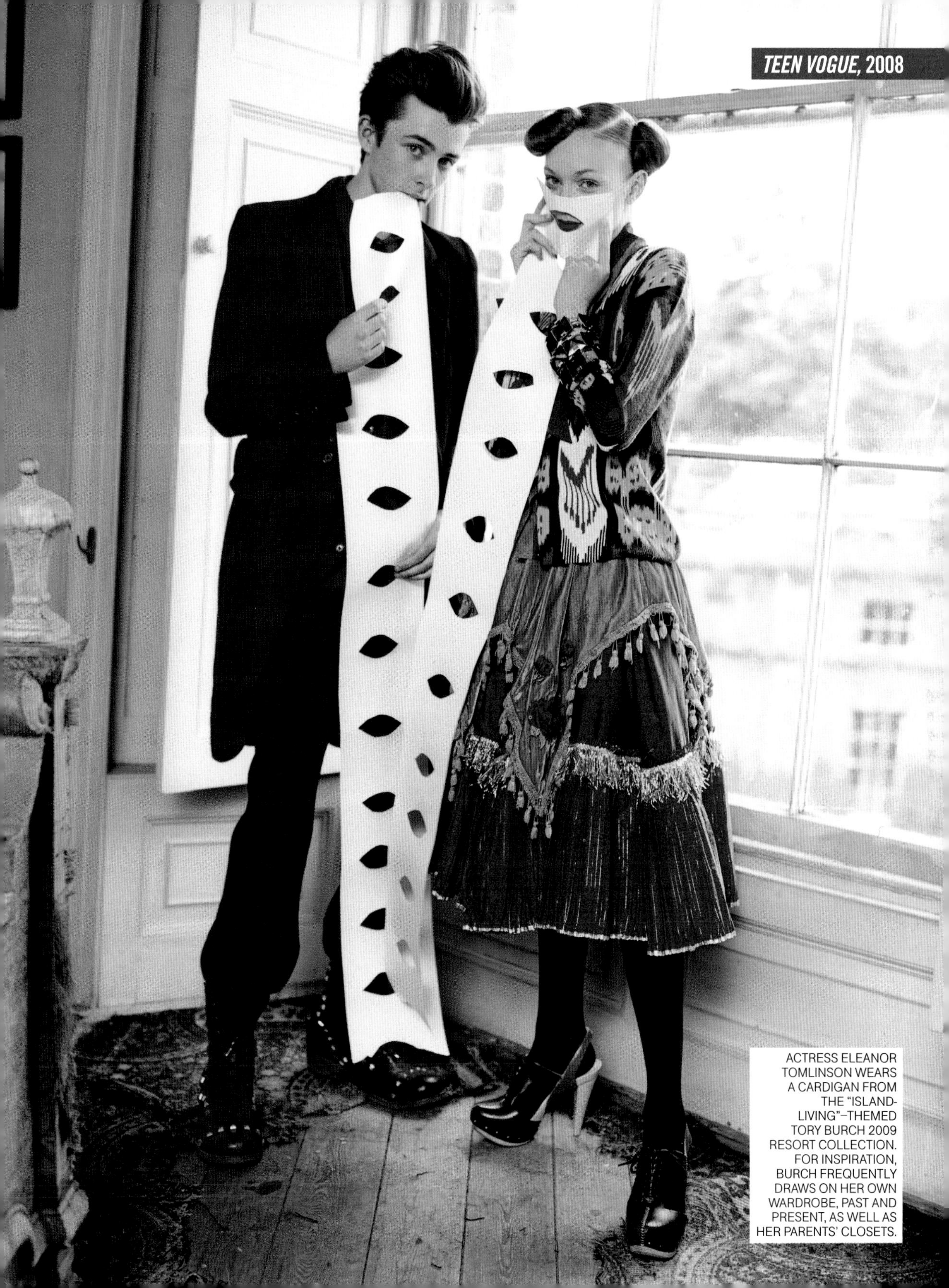

TEEN VOGUE, 2008

ACTRESS ELEANOR TOMLINSON WEARS A CARDIGAN FROM THE "ISLAND-LIVING"–THEMED TORY BURCH 2009 RESORT COLLECTION. FOR INSPIRATION, BURCH FREQUENTLY DRAWS ON HER OWN WARDROBE, PAST AND PRESENT, AS WELL AS HER PARENTS' CLOSETS.

The Fan Favorite
Phillip Lim

BY DROPPING OUT OF BUSINESS SCHOOL AND STARTING FROM SCRATCH, THIS SUCCESS STORY FOLLOWED HIS HEART INTO FASHION.

"You cannot teach design. You can teach techniques and procedures, but design is inherent. I don't care what anyone says—you either have it or you don't. Don't get me wrong: It's great to study fashion and to know the basics, like how to sew and make patterns. You should know about textiles, and you should go to school for that, to hone in on your interests. But if you never have the privilege of going to design school, yet you feel that fashion is what you should do, don't let a lack of education prevent you. There is more than one way.

Growing up with a traditional Chinese background, there were three options for me: be a physician, a lawyer, or a businessperson. I chose to study business [at California State University at Long Beach] because it seemed like the most general subject. I did that for about three years, until one day I was sitting in accounting class, and I had an epiphany—like a panic attack—and I realized, I can't do this. I'm miserable. I can't do this for another hour, let alone a lifetime.

So I went over to what was then called the Home Economics Department and started taking classes in fashion merchandising, design, sewing, draping, and window dressing. I thought, Wow, this is really fun and, though not exactly easy, it's natural to me. I didn't see it as something I was studying; it was something I was curious about. My parents were heartbroken, especially my mother, who was a seamstress while I was growing up. She said, 'We brought you here to try to give you a good life, and you are studying to become me?' I had to explain to her that it wasn't just about sewing.

While I was in college, I started working at Barneys New York, which was my first exposure to smaller, independent labels. I remember unpacking merchandise from a new company called Katayone Adeli and liking the sensibility of it. I called 411 and they told me the office was in Los Angeles, then put me through over the phone. When an assistant answered, I asked if they needed an intern. I didn't even have a portfolio, just a résumé and some Polaroids of a few things I had been working on. It was so hokey. When I look back, I think that being a little naive was actually a positive thing, because I had no fear. Sometimes, when you know too much, you can overdo it.

On my first day at Katayone Adeli, I had no idea what to expect. I thought it was going to be some beautiful atelier and everything would be fancy and glamorous. But it was reality, and people had jobs that they needed to get done. My job had nothing to do with design; it was more about getting coffee and making copies. Still, observing the entrepreneurial spirit

LIM CUSTOM-MADE THIS GOWN FOR MODEL CHANEL IMAN, HIS DATE FOR THE 2008 METROPOLITAN MUSEUM COSTUME INSTITUTE GALA. THE DRESS WAS INSPIRED BY THE EVENING'S THEME, "SUPERHEROES: FASHION AND FANTASY." "WE WANTED TO PLAY WITH THE IDEA OF SUPERNATURAL POWERS," LIM SAYS. "WE CHOSE FIRE—WE DYED ORGANZA FLAME GOLD, THEN CRAFTED SWIRLS TO LOOK AS IF THEY WERE GIVING OFF HEAT." THE FROCK WAS TOPPED WITH A WONDER WOMAN–STYLE BELT AND CUFFS, AND LIM DONNED A MATCHING GOLD TIE FOR THE PARTY.

I did that for about five years, then decided to take some time off. And at that moment, my present business partner asked me to come to New York. I got here thinking I was just taking a break—again, it was me being naive, because when I arrived, she was like, 'We're going to start a business together!' I had fifteen minutes to come up with the name—we decided on 3.1 because we were both 31 years old at the time. We had two months to register the company, get a license, put the collection together, and go to market. That was fall 2005, and here we are now!" ★

of the company taught me so much. Two weeks later they asked me to work for them full-time. I was still in school, but I didn't tell them that because I didn't want to let them see me sweat. Say yes and figure out the details later.

So I became a design assistant. When people hear that, they think it means I was sketching all day. But design is more than that. It's making sure the door is locked every night and confirming shipments with UPS. I get a lot of interns who are jaded and say, 'This is not what I learned in school.' I tell them, 'But this is how it is.' Every time I talk to young people, I say, 'All those things you think you are going to do? You're not. Instead, you're going to do a whole set of other things that will eventually set you up to do what you want to do.' The most important things I learned at Katayone Adeli were how to manage time and how to turn a no into a yes. I look back now and think I could have been a lawyer three times over!

After two years there I was approached by some friends starting a fashion company, and they asked me to be the designer. I thought, You have the wrong person! But then I figured, Why not? I have nothing to lose. We called the company Development, and the first season we worked out of a garage. We decided that if our first order was for more than $3,000, we'd quit our day jobs. It ended up being around $30,000.

A 3.1 PHILLIP LIM JACKET FROM THE FALL 2007 COLLECTION. THE DESIGNER IS KNOWN FOR HIS COOL, TAILORED OUTERWEAR AND EASY, PRETTY DRESSES.

ACTRESS CAMILLA BELLE WEARS A 3.1 PHILLIP LIM SEQUINED MINIDRESS TO THE OPENING OF THE DESIGNER'S STORE IN HIS NATIVE LOS ANGELES.

ONE OF THE DESIGNER'S TRADEMARK ROSETTE-ADORNED DRESSES FROM THE SPRING 2007 RUNWAY SHOW.

LIM TEAMED UP WITH TATAMI, A GERMAN SHOE BRAND OWNED BY BIRKENSTOCK (FAMOUS FOR ITS STURDY HIPPIE SANDALS), TO DESIGN A LINE OF CHIC YET PRACTICAL FOOTWEAR, MODELED HERE IN THE MAY 2008 ISSUE OF *TEEN VOGUE*.

Asia Ragland, LIM'S STUDIO COORDINATOR AGE 25 COLLEGE CALIFORNIA STATE UNIVERSITY, LONG BEACH HOMETOWN SAN DIEGO, CALIFORNIA

"I double-majored in fashion design and merchandising at Cal State Long Beach, and every year the school runs a trip to New York City for the fashion students, where they attend workshops and seminars with designers and stylists. That's how I met Phillip. I was organizing a fashion show at my school and asked him if he would be willing to judge it. He wasn't able to, but we started corresponding via e-mail. After graduation, I got a job with the denim label Habitual, where I had interned, but I wanted to move to New York, so I contacted Phillip to set up an interview. I worked on my portfolio until, literally, two hours before our meeting, but I still got the job. In my current role at the company, I help with the development of graphics, embellishments, and embroidery and assist with sample development. After Phillip sketches something, it's given to the pattern-maker, who creates the pattern. Then I help order the fabric, cut it, buy the trim, and get everything ready to be sewn.

If you're interested in working in fashion, read magazines and stay culturally aware. It's good to know what's going on in the rest of the world, in terms of politics and economics, because we deal with other countries all the time. Sketch and study fabrics and colors, then once you get to college, intern as much as you can. Education is important because it teaches you the necessary skills, but, honestly, interning and building relationships are the best ways to get a job."

The All-American

Patrick Robinson

AS GAP'S HEAD DESIGNER, THIS HIGH-FASHION VETERAN SPREADS RUNWAY-CALIBER STYLE ACROSS AMERICA.

"I'm good at fixing things," Patrick Robinson says when asked to make sense of his varied career in fashion. "I enjoy working for a company, getting into its mind-set, and bringing it back to what I think it should be." Starting with his first big job, helming Giorgio Armani's Collezioni line—a gig he got when he was only 24—the designer has spent almost two decades doing just that, working for Anne Klein, Perry Ellis, Paco Rabanne, and now Gap. Robinson also spent a few years operating an eponymous label. Although this is a position many young designers would consider the ultimate dream job, Robinson says that "having my own business wasn't the biggest joy I've ever had." Instead, he likens his line of work to that of an actor's: "I enjoy playing different characters."

You're a doctor's son from Southern California— what first attracted you to fashion?
From the age of nine, I surfed pretty much every day and became fascinated by the clothing of that culture— the way it allowed you to express your personality and

VOGUE

MAY

SPRING TIME!
75 Perfect Picks
SWIMWEAR TO EYE-POPPING PRINTS

The World's Next Top Models ...

Fashion's 10 New Superstars

LIKE MOTHER, LIKE DAUGHTER
Is the HPV Vaccine Right for All Women?

SKIN SPECIAL
Sunscreen Myths and the Anti-Tan

THIS SPECIAL MAY 2007 *VOGUE* FOLDOUT COVER FEATURED TEN TOP MODELS WEARING SHIRTS FROM GAP'S DEBUT DESIGN EDITIONS COLLECTION. THE HONOREES OF 2006'S CFDA/*VOGUE* FASHION FUND AWARD— THAKOON, RODARTE, AND DOO.RI—EACH PUT THEIR STAMP ON THE CLASSIC WHITE BUTTON-DOWN.

GAP'S FALL 2008 CAMPAIGN INCLUDED RISING STARS AND FASHION INSIDERS LIKE MODEL LILY DONALDSON, ABOVE.

show the world exactly who you were. As I got older, I started admiring designers like Perry Ellis, Jeffrey Banks, and Calvin Klein, so I decided to study fashion at Parsons the New School for Design in Paris and New York.

My parents helped me pay for school, but I still needed a job, and I wanted to learn my craft. So I began to work for designers Patrick Kelly and Albert Nipon. I don't remember exactly how I got the positions—I know it sounds easy when I talk about it now—but I do recall that there were far more nos than yeses. Fashion is a tough field, and there are only so many jobs, so you have to know what you want and really go after it. You can't give up.

What if you've been persistently pursuing your dream job and things still aren't happening for you? Should you adjust your approach?

Opportunity doesn't always come dressed exactly the way you fantasize it will: It comes dressed as something unexpected, something maybe you don't even want—unless you're smart enough to see how it could lead you down a different path. I've interviewed many young people, and I can always tell who the smart ones are because they're unafraid to embrace a challenge that's a little different from what they were looking for. They'll take a job in accessories, even though they really want a job in womenswear, because they can see that if they prove themselves, they'll move forward.

That's what I did in my first job. I wanted to be a designer, not an assistant, but I was hired to assist the designer at a small company. I saw it as an opportunity: I worked my behind off, and within a few months I had her job.

Some people caution against going out on your own too early, but you had a big job at a young age. Do you think, under certain circumstances, it's okay to skip a long apprenticeship? And how do you compensate for it?
Yes. Look at Proenza Schouler: Those guys totally have a grasp of their craft, but they're still learning, and you can see it in the way they push themselves every season. Zac Posen is the same way. There's nothing wrong with being young and successful, and young people sometimes have a better way of looking at the world.

I think that I got the Armani job because I believed in myself to an almost obnoxious degree—I had that youthful drive, that feeling that I could fix everything just by touching it. But I also studied: I went to the stores, looked at the product, and knew exactly what I wanted to do with the brand.

And, as it turns out, that's what you've done in most of the jobs you've had since. But Gap isn't the sort of company you were accustomed to working for.
No, it's better. But again, it goes back to seeing the opportunities when they come. This wasn't what I was used to doing; it wasn't on my radar. But I saw it for what it was and went after it with everything I had.

What are the challenges you face now, designing for a large, lower-priced brand?
It's hard because it's huge. It's global! But I cope by picturing it as just one store, one perfect Gap. If I design everything for that one store and fix that one store, then I can fix them all. That's an extension of what I tell my designers: I want them to make clothes they want to wear. And I have lots of brilliant designers working for me; I'm not the only one who makes it happen. In truth, designing is a very small part of my job. My focus now is to give ideas and concepts, to approve colors, to oversee everything, and to push people to do things better.

What do you look for when interviewing designers for your team?
You must have your own personality. I often ask designers simple, straightforward questions about what they want to do with their lives or what their dreams are. And I'm more interested in hiring people who can really answer those questions than people who just say what they think I want them to say. I'm looking for individuals, because individuals make the best designers.

Does it matter to you what someone wears to an interview?
Well, you need to dress in a style that works for the brand

ROBINSON, HERE IN *VOGUE* WITH MODEL CAROLYN MURPHY, BOTH WEARING GAP, IS THE FIRST BIG NAME TO STEP IN TO THE ROLE OF HEAD DESIGNER FOR THE CLASSIC BRAND.

you're interviewing for. If you're going into the Gap, you should look like the Gap. But don't come in dressed like one of the ads. You need to express your own style as well.

And are there any important resources—books, movies, magazines—that you recommend all aspiring designers examine for inspiration?
No. If one more person brings me a picture of Ali MacGraw in *Love Story,* I'll jump out a window. Who cares? I'm not big on worshipping others, so it drives me nuts when people get so caught up in one thing and think everyone needs to follow it. Like that's the best movie of all time? Boring.

Instead, I think the most important thing is really to be in the world. Look at what's going on outside, in the street, and be a part of that. That's fascinating. When we all look at the same books, read the same magazines, and watch the same movies, that's when fashion gets dull. You can admire people, but don't study them. Of course I have books that I am inspired by, but you need to figure out your own favorite books. When people who are young really pop out in the fashion world, it's because they're telling a different story. ★

KRAKOFF STYLED
AND PHOTOGRAPHED
THIS FALL 2007 AD
CAMPAIGN FOR COACH
BAGS, WHICH SHOWS
THE DESIGNER'S
VIBRANT DIRECTION
FOR THE TIME-
HONORED BRAND.

The Success Story

Reed Krakoff

COACH'S MAIN MAN COMBINED BUSINESS SAVVY AND DESIGN MOJO TO REVIVE A CLASSIC BRAND WITH YOUTHFUL FLAIR.

"I think that anyone who wants to be in the fashion industry needs to start by working in retail. My first jobs in New York City were at the Valentino and Versace boutiques. While at the time I was just trying to pay my bills and maybe get some clothes out of it, I actually found retail to be a fantastic experience. When you work in a store, you get to see the whole operation: how they sell, how they dress the windows, how they order inventory. And you basically learn why people shop—why they buy things and why they don't. It's important to understand these mechanics, because no matter what you do in fashion, you're going to be involved in selling. Understanding what the customer sees and experiences is critical.

From the time I was in high school, I knew that fashion was something I might want to pursue as a career. I wanted to go to design school, but my parents urged me to get a liberal arts education instead. So I studied economics and art history at Tufts University [in Boston]. After graduation, I moved to

LIFE
Picasso

KRAKOFF HAS A CORKBOARD IN HIS OFFICE ON WHICH HE PINS PHOTOS, SKETCHES, AND CLIPPINGS THAT INSPIRE HIM, FROM ALBUM COVERS TO PICTURES OF ARTWORK BY SCULPTOR HENRY MOORE.

New York and got another degree, in fashion design, from Parsons the New School for Design. It was a good mix, and over the years I've been surprised by how well my education has served me—and it has, because at Coach I'm involved in so many different aspects of the business.

When I was finishing up my degree at Parsons, I applied for a design job but learned very quickly that it can be tough to get a job when you don't have any experience. And, of course, you can't get any experience if you don't have a job. It's like a riddle. I remember being at an interview and saying, 'I'll make you a deal: If you give me a job, I'll get some experience.' What I ended up doing—and what I recommend doing—is getting an internship. I interned for Narciso Rodriguez, who at the time was the design director of Anne Klein. It may be difficult not making any money, but people will line up to work for free at most of the truly desirable places, so you really don't have a choice. I got to hang around with one of the most talented designers in the industry, and that's not a paying job. You can wait tables at night to pay your bills.

Another critical part of making it in the industry is being willing to do anything. I'm always amazed at how many people don't understand that. When you're just out of school, it's really a privilege to work for a prestigious company— you may be working for free, but they're almost doing you a favor by letting you. And it pays off in the long run to be with a company that has an image and a reputation that

you truly want to learn from. At Anne Klein, I did anything they asked: I xeroxed sketches, picked up the dry cleaning, swept, and clipped news articles. But I also got to see how a real, talented designer works. By watching Narciso, I was able to understand so much about how a line comes together. I learned a lot just by being in the same room with him. Having a boss like Narciso also taught me what I *couldn't* be. I knew that I didn't have his talent—I couldn't sketch like him, I couldn't drape like him. And it's helpful to have an experience like that early in your career; it helped me to understand that I needed to embrace what I was good at. People who are successful are not always the most creative, the most artistic, but they're honest with themselves about what they can do.

Narciso helped me with my sketching, and when I went to my next interview and was asked about my experience, I was able to say I had worked for him. I ended up joining the art department at Ralph Lauren, which wasn't ideal—I wanted to be a designer—and it paid less than some of the other jobs I had been offered. But I felt that it was a place where I could have a career, and as soon as the right job opened up, I moved to design.

Again, I started at the very bottom. I remember one day a woman asked me to clean up a sweater closet—thousands of Fair Isle sweaters were all over the floor—and I said, 'I'm not very good at folding sweaters.' And she just looked at me

Teen VOGUE TIP Invest in your future. "Get a job at a company you love, even if it can only offer you a part-time position and you have to do something else to make money. The experience will be worth it in the long run." —REED KRAKOFF

AN AVID PHOTOGRAPHER, KRAKOFF SHOOTS AND STYLES ALL OF COACH'S AD CAMPAIGNS AND RECENTLY RELEASED A BOOK OF UFC FIGHTER PORTRAITS.

TRADITIONALLY, THE CLUTCH IS CONSIDERED AN EVENING BAG. BUT COACH TRANSFORMED IT INTO AN AROUND-THE-CLOCK ESSENTIAL VIA HEAVY HARDWARE AND A BIGGER, BOXIER SHAPE. HERE, MODEL SASHA PIVOVAROVA WORKS A COACH CLUTCH FOR DAY WITH JEANS, A BLOUSE, AND A BLAZER.

and said, 'You better learn fast,' and then walked out of the room. You have to put in your time. If you work hard and do a good job, then you'll succeed.

I stayed at Ralph for five years, moving from freelance assistant to assistant to associate to a designer-level position. When my boss went on maternity leave, I got to be the acting director of design, and I actually created and presented a collection. After she came back, I knew it was time for me to move on. I got a call from Tommy Hilfiger, which was then just a teeny-tiny business. People thought I was crazy to consider it—but when you get in on the ground level, if you're flexible, you can do a lot of different things. I worked on photo shoots and fashion shows, I styled clothing for the showroom, and, ultimately, I became more of a creative director than a designer. I worked on advertising and media campaigns, and I learned how to evolve a brand and to carry an idea into children's clothing, swimwear, pajamas, home design—every category you can imagine. It was a good example of what can happen if you take a chance.

After five years there, I felt like it was time to try something else again. I briefly worked for Trussardi, in Milan, but while I was back in New York, literally packing up my apartment to move to Italy, I got a call from Coach. Like most people from the East Coast, I had grown up with the brand—and was intrigued by the idea of working with the company.

Coach was one-seventh of the size it is today, and as I checked out the stores, I thought about what it could be. The job, as executive creative director, seemed perfectly tailored to all my different experiences. It just felt right. Once you're a bit further into your career, looking for a job can be a lot like looking for a girlfriend or a boyfriend. You can't really control it, and you need to stay open. This job came out of nowhere, and the company wasn't even on the list of companies I had imagined working for. But I saw it as an opportunity for me to grow.

Now I'm the president as well as executive creative director of Coach. I think it's easier to organize the company this way than if there were separate people heading marketing, design, and PR. I'm able to go to a design meeting and come up with a shoe that we need for spring based on a conversation I had a few minutes before in an advertising meeting. All the things I work on build off one another. There's an amazing connection between the business and creative sides of this company. Everyone works in the same direction, and everyone understands what needs to be accomplished.

But I always say that my first job is to keep people a little bit uncomfortable with where we're going. If you're too comfortable, then what you're doing probably isn't different enough from what you did last year. You have to have an environment in which you're able to experiment, because the key is to keep the customer excited about the brand.

My career has moved along organically, and that's true for a lot of people in fashion. It's not about doing any one thing. You need to be flexible because you don't know where you're going to end up. My advice boils down to a few simple things: Stay open, work hard, do a good job, and be nice." ★

The Dynamic Duo

Proenza Schouler

FASHION'S ORIGINAL BOY WONDERS SHOT TO STARDOM WHEN BARNEYS NEW YORK SNAPPED UP THEIR ENTIRE SENIOR THESIS COLLECTION—AND THEIR COOLLY SOPHISTICATED CLOTHES HAVEN'T STOPPED TURNING HEADS SINCE.

JACK McCOLLOUGH (FAR LEFT) AND LAZARO HERNANDEZ FITTING DEMI MOORE INTO ONE OF THEIR SIGNATURE BUSTIER DRESSES FOR JULY 2003 *VOGUE*. MARIO TESTINO PHOTOGRAPHED THE SCENE.

Neither of you started out studying fashion in college. What made you decide to transfer to Parsons the New School for Design?

Lazaro Hernandez: I had a whole different life before! I was doing premed at University of Miami, where I'm from. Then the summer before my second year, I went to New York with friends and randomly met some fashion people. My mom had a beauty salon when I was growing up, and I always looked at fashion magazines there, but it wasn't until the trip to New York that I realized fashion could actually be a career. I wasn't happy in premed, so I decided to go for it and apply to Parsons. I enrolled in some art classes on the side and put together a portfolio. I didn't tell anyone I was applying. I thought, If I get accepted, I'll go. If not, I'll just stay in Miami and do premed.

Jack McCollough: I was studying glassblowing at San Francisco Art Institute. I grew up on the East Coast; I transferred to Parsons because I wanted to be back in New York. I didn't initially know that I would go into fashion. I just wanted to get back to the East Coast! But then I met Lazaro; we'd sneak into fashion shows, and it all seemed very exciting.

Studying in a place like New York definitely allows you exposure to the industry. How important do you think location should be in determining a school?

LH: If you're going to do fashion, there's really only one city in the States where you can do it. I've never understood the idea of a design school outside New York. What's the point? All the magazines are here, the press is here—everyone is here. I mean, the Rodarte girls in Los Angeles proved that you can do fashion in other places, but it makes it a lot easier to be here.

You both took advantage of interning while you were in school [McCollough at Marc Jacobs, and Hernandez at Michael Kors]. How did those experiences add to your fashion education?

SPRING 2004

JM: It's such a different type of learning experience than school. You get to know the fabric mills where the textiles are made and how fittings and castings for the shows operate. Marc has a small design team, so I was in the room with everyone, seeing the process. It was very hands-on in that way.

LH: The best thing I learned was a taste for fabrics. Michael has a really good eye for simple but rich luxury fabrics, things like cashmere that I had never been exposed to growing up in Miami. Michael always said, "If you're going to use camel, why dye something else camel? It should be cashmere." It was the idea of keeping things honest and finishing them beautifully. And just the environment of a design room—school is one thing, but the real world is much more practical.

When did you decide to start collaborating together?

LH: We had every class together, so we would informally bounce ideas off each other, and by senior year we said, "Why don't we ask if we can do something together?"

JM: We're together 24-7, so we have a lot of the same sets of references. When we're doing colors, I can say, "Remember that beautiful color we saw on the side of that building when we were traveling?" and Lazaro will know exactly what I'm talking about.

What initially set your clothes apart from others'?

LH: Our senior collection came out in 2001, a time when everyone was ripping up T-shirts and throwing studs on them. Everything was deconstructed and downtown. What we did was react against that. We didn't think every young designer had to do street.

JM: We were learning how to construct clothes in school, and we were into fit and old-world designers like Christian Dior, Coco Chanel, and Cristobal Balenciaga. So we were feeling a return to something a bit more polished.

LH: I think it was more extreme to go in a sophisticated direction than if we had done punk, because that's almost what's expected of a young designer. We were looking at rarefied images by Irving Penn, and that felt more rebellious to us.

SPRING 2007

JM: We grew up in the nineties, so that sense of effortless dressing is something that is always with us. But I think it's a combination of the two that makes us unique.

You sold your entire senior thesis collection to Barneys New York, which was pretty much unheard of for a student collection. How did you figure out production?

LH: We had worked with local factories through our internships, so we had those connections. But Michael [Kors] had donated all the fabric for our thesis collection, so we had to call him up and say, "You know that fabric you gave us? Where did you get it, because we need 50 more yards!" I think the biggest thing, though, was figuring out sizing and fit issues. We did the whole bustier, which is the most body-conscious thing ever. How can you standardize something like that? How big are the cups? Are they a C, a B, or an A? Who is our customer? We also had to figure out delivery and price. Our first season we delivered on the last day of the window, so Barneys had only one or two months to sell the clothes at full price. And because we weren't producing many of each design, they cost a fortune. Now we have a little more volume, so we can keep the prices down. All that stuff comes with experience.

You have been with your business partner, Shirley Cook, since the very beginning. What is the role of a CEO?

JM: It's a huge role. Basically, everything that isn't design falls on Shirley. The three of us talk constantly. You don't really learn anything business-wise in an internship. It's more the creative process. So we had to figure that out on our own. Shirley helps us find investors. She keeps the business afloat.

Can you explain what purpose investors serve?

LH: They are so important because there are orders you have to front up, and stores don't pay until after you ship. But it's a fine line. As a designer, you want to have creative control. You don't want someone telling you to design pink sweater sets because he or she thinks they're a trend. We've always kept more than a 50 percent stake in our company so that we're the majority owners. We're the bosses. And thankfully, all our partners are in Europe, so there's an ocean between us!

You entered into a financial partnership with Valentino Fashion Group recently. Aside from monetary support, what has that enabled you to do?

LH: What's good about Valentino is that the company has connections that are specific to our needs. It has amazing factories for handbags, shoes, and knitwear. It has perfumes and stores. Everything we want to do, it has already done.

JM: And Valentino has never diluted the brand. It has always been geared toward high fashion and couture.

LH: Also, we didn't want to be one brand among zillions. We wanted a partner who was small enough to be psyched about Proenza Schouler and give it the attention it deserves.

You recently launched shoes and bags. What other plans for growth do you have?

IN 2004, HERNANDEZ AND McCOLLOUGH TOOK HOME TOP PRIZE IN THE FIRST CFDA/*VOGUE* FASHION FUND—THE EXPERIENCE WAS CAPTURED ON FILM IN THE DOCUMENTARY *SEAMLESS*. HERE THEY POSE AT THEIR CHINATOWN STUDIO WITH MODEL NATASHA POLY, WHO WEARS A GOWN FROM THEIR COLLECTION.

LH: Our primary concern has always been the clothing. Of course we wanted shoes, to complete the look, but we never make plans. Everything has just fallen into place organically. Stores and a fragrance are on our wish list. But it's not so much a business thing as it is that we get bored with what we have and want to do something else.

What qualities does a designer need to have?

LH: A thick skin! Know that you can't please everyone every single time. There are a lot of different people with a lot of different tastes in this industry. You need to design for yourself because the minute you start thinking about other people's needs is the minute you begin to limit your own thing.

What do you look for when hiring assistants?

LH: It sounds shallow, but it's really the way people present and carry themselves. You need to have taste. Taste and education. It's as simple as that. It's important to have a broad knowledge of both fashion history and contemporary fashion. You need to be aware of what's happening and what other brands are doing. At the same time, you have to be able to separate yourself from that and stay true to yourself.

JM: We ask them about clothes, their sketches, what they get inspired by. You want someone who can draw. But like Lazaro said, it's also just a matter of who fits in. If someone walks in wearing a suit, we know this isn't the right place for him. Lazaro and I live in jeans and T-shirts! ★

The Craftsman
Justin Giunta

THIS JEWELRY DESIGNER STRUCK GOLD WITH A MIX OF COMMERCIAL APPEAL AND FINE-ART FINESSE.

It requires a true visionary to take a tangled mass of chains that looks "as though you picked up your jewelry box, and everything inside was in a knot," according to designer Justin Giunta's description, and turn it into one of his company's best-selling pieces. Yet that's exactly what the Pittsburgh native has done. A multilayered background in the arts (from still-life painting to fabricating more functional objects such as chandeliers) has helped Giunta craft beautiful couturelike necklaces, cuffs, and rings that have widespread appeal. Not long after its launch in 2003, his line of one-of-a-kind, handwrought creations—named Subversive Jewelry, in part for its juxtapositions of components like Grecian leaves with hip-hop bling—was taking up real estate alongside luxe baubles at Bergdorf Goodman and Barneys New York. Next came runway collaborations with labels such as DKNY and then CFDA nominations for accessory design in 2007 and 2008. But one of his most anticipated collaborations was a partnership with megastore Target, for which Giunta translated Subersive's intricate one-off jewels into an afforable collection capable of being mass-produced—once again blurring the line between art and commerce.

GIUNTA APPROACHES MAKING NECKLACES AS THOUGH HE WERE PAINTING. HE LAYS OUT ALL THE MATERIALS (SOURCED FROM HIS NATIVE PITTSBURGH AND SUCH FAR-FLUNG LOCALES AS ARGENTINA, GERMANY, AND MOROCCO) ON THE TABLE LIKE PAINTS ON A PALETTE, THEN PULLS TOGETHER DIFFERENT PIECES INTO A COMPOSITION, CAREFULLY BALANCING COLORS AND TEXTURES.

You started your career as an artist. What made you decide to segue from art to jewelry design?
I wanted to diversify my craft, so I started exploring charms and jewelry. I made a bracelet with gun charms, and so many women obsessed over it that it became the launching point for my jewelry.

What do you think initially set your designs apart?
If you look at magazines from the early 2000s, when I started, the designs of that time were all very minimal. On the other hand, I was working with found objects and raw materials. I think the industry was ready to see something different.

You didn't go the traditional designer route of fashion design school. Instead, you received a degree in Fine Art from Carnegie Mellon University in Pittsburgh. What are the advantages or disadvantages of a liberal arts education?
I spent my whole life wanting to be an artist, but I went to Pratt Institute for a year and hated it. The liberal arts structure at Carnegie Mellon gave me an intellectual background. I found it more engaging and stimulating than just rearticulating imagery. Art is about ideas, and ideas are only as good as they can be expressed.

For those who don't live in a big metropolis, what advice would you give them for exploring and honing their craft?
Just get busy and delve into the materials that are accessible to you. Innovation does not necessarily require technology or big-city resources. In fact, design from reclaimed, or reappropriated, materials is both innovative and green.

Did you work any odd jobs while trying to build your company?
I once worked as the assistant to an interiors painter. A big turning point for me was when I took a job at a restaurant for one night. I thought to myself, You should be eating at a restaurant, not cleaning one. It was a benchmark moment because I learned that I had to work harder at what I really wanted to do. So for two years I went around to stores, selling chandeliers and T-shirts that I had made. I needed to earn money, and making things was a natural form of income that allowed me to hone my craft at the same time. It worked—since then I've been able to support myself through my creative efforts.

What would you suggest to young designers looking to sell their pieces to stores?
You may have 95 doors close on you before two open. You must be willing to walk out of a store that doesn't want your stuff with the confidence that your work *is* good and someone *will* buy it. ★

MODEL ARLENIS SOSA
WEARING A SUBVERSIVE
CRATER NECKLACE.

The Good Sole

Blake Mycoskie

A TRIP TO ARGENTINA INSPIRED THE FOUNDER OF TOMS TO CRAFT COLORFUL SHOES WITH A CONSCIENCE.

What was the inspiration behind TOMS?

I was in Argentina on vacation in January 2006, and I noticed that a lot of local farmers and polo players were wearing these slip-ons called alpargatas. I bought a pair and really enjoyed wearing them. Around the same time, I met some people doing volunteer work in the area, and they told me about a shoe drive they were running for the local kids who couldn't afford shoes. I went with them and heard stories I'll never forget—one was about two brothers and one sister, and they had only one pair of shoes, so the kids would alternate every third day to go to school. I thought, This is crazy. As an entrepreneur, when you see something that seems broken, your brain immediately goes to "How can we fix this?" I didn't feel like a straight charity was the most sustainable way to do it, because then I would have to ask my friends and family for money year after year. And what happens when they get bored of my charity? So I asked myself, What if I had a for-profit business whose charter stated that for every pair of shoes the company sold, it would give one pair to a child in need? The name TOMS comes from *tomorrow*—the idea is that you buy one today, we give one to a child tomorrow.

After you put together the concept, what was the next step in creating the line?

The next step was to make a prototype. That would be my advice to anyone starting a fashion line: Create a product. A business does not become real until you have something. Especially if you are trying to raise

ON THE SOUTH AFRICAN SHOE DROP, MYCOSKIE AND HIS TEAM OF VOLUNTEERS PERSONALLY FIT EACH CHILD WITH HIS OR HER NEW PAIR OF SLIP-ONS.

advice, we'd love to do it." I left the meeting, and three weeks later I got a call from David. He said, "I showed my dad your shoes and he wants to meet you." I'll never forget it: I went into the room and Ralph said, "Let's hear your story." We talked for almost two hours. A few weeks later, David called and said, "We're interested in exploring a collaboration with the Rugby brand." So I sent a bunch of shoes, and Ralph did some designs. It took several months to get to something that looked like their style yet still represented the TOMS brand. The Purple shoes hit stores in October 2008. A portion of the proceeds of each pair sold goes to the Match Rugby Fund, which provides grants to young activists around the world.

You describe yourself as an entrepreneur. Where did the idea for your first business originate?
Growing up, I was an athlete. I went to Southern Methodist University in Dallas on a tennis scholarship. But sophomore year I got a bad Achilles tendon injury and was on crutches. I couldn't carry my laundry, so it kept piling up in my room. One day I went to the yellow pages to look for someone to pick up the laundry, wash it, and deliver it back—and there wasn't such a place. So my friend and I started our own service, called EZ Laundry. All of a sudden we were doing hundreds of people's laundry. So we had to buy trucks and hire people, and that's when it became a business. In one year I had 40 employees and four offices around the country. It's still around today.

money, just having an idea isn't really worth anything; it's the execution that makes it valuable. So I stayed in Argentina for another month and immersed myself in the people who made alpargatas. I visited the factories and said, "I want to create an alpargata for the U.S. market, and I want it to have a rubber sole instead of a rope sole, and an arch support and leather." My first step was to learn how to make shoes. And I did that just by showing up and asking questions.

Was it more complicated than you had expected?
Yes, but when I brought over the first 250 pairs and my friends loved them, I knew it could work. The few people I knew in the fashion business loved them too. Within two months I got a call from Sally Singer at *Vogue* and I was featured in the magazine. I was very fortunate. It came at the right time. In 2006, flats were really hot. And I think the fact that I didn't know anything about the business made people trust me more.

Tell me a little about the collaboration with Ralph Lauren and Rugby. How did that come about?
I met David Lauren, Ralph's son, through a friend of a friend. David called me up one day and said, "Hey, come by the office; I've seen several people wearing your shoes and I think they're cool." So I went in with some shoes, thinking, Maybe we could sell them in their stores. But David made it clear: "We've been doing this for 40 years and have never done a collaboration. But we love what you're doing, and if we could give you any

With your first company, did you face issues where you had to creatively think around problems?
The hardest thing for us to come to terms with was that no matter how good of a service we ran, dealing with clothes was an imperfect process: No matter what, a certain percentage of the clothes would get ruined or lost. I'm a perfectionist, so it was hard to accept that even if we had less than 1 percent error, there were still people who'd get upset. Being criticized and not taking it personally was a big lesson I had to learn.

In the two years since you started TOMS, have you noticed a trend toward fashion philanthropy?
I think we're seeing more of it. If you can find a way to use some of your profit margin to do good, your customers will really appreciate that.

What are your inspirations?
One of my inspirations has always been great entrepreneurs who defy the odds, like Richard Branson, Ted Turner, and Sam Walton. The other people who inspire me are the kids I've met in Argentina. They have so little, yet they are so happy. I spend five to eight weeks a year in either Africa or Argentina—with no cell phone, no connection to the world—so that allows me to put all of this aside and focus on what life, I think, is really all about. ★

*teen*VOGUE TIP / Be tenacious. "One thing that has allowed me to have some level of success is that I am fine with cold-calling people. It doesn't scare me to call someone who has no idea who I am and say, 'I'd love to take you to lunch.'" —BLAKE MYCOSKIE

MYCOSKIE'S MISSION

A look at how the designer is using fashion to make a difference.

ALTHOUGH THE BASIC SHAPE REMAINS CONSTANT, TOMS COME IN A VARIETY OF PATTERNS, INCLUDING CAMOUFLAGE, POLKA DOT, PAINT SPLATTER, AND GLITTER.

FOR MYCOSKIE'S FIRST-EVER SHOE DROP, IN 2006, HE RETURNED TO ARGENTINA, THE SITE OF HIS INSPIRATION FOR THE BUSINESS. DURING THAT TRIP, TOMS DONATED 10,000 PAIRS OF SHOES. TO DATE, THE COMPANY HAS BROUGHT THAT TOTAL UP TO MORE THAN 130,000.

A MODEL WEARS A PAIR OF TOMS IN A 2009 ISSUE OF *TEEN VOGUE*. THE SHOES HAVE WON FASHION AND CELEBRITY FANS SUCH AS SCARLETT JOHANSSON, LIV TYLER, AND KRISTEN STEWART.

The Legend
Karl Lagerfeld

THE LARGER-THAN-LIFE DESIGNER FOR THE ICONIC HOUSE OF CHANEL IS THE ACKNOWLEDGED MASTER OF BOTH BUILDING A FASHION POWERHOUSE AND CREATING HIS OWN CELEBRITY PERSONA.

It's difficult to imagine a time when the name Chanel stood for anything other than boundary-breaking fashion. Yet in the wake of founder Coco Chanel's death, in 1971, the storied house began to languish. Enter Karl Lagerfeld in 1983, a headstrong German native who, since first winning an international coat-design competition in 1955, had been jumping restlessly between design posts at heavyweight houses like Balmain and Chloé, at one point growing so disillusioned with fashion that he fled to Italy to study fine art. At Chanel the designer finally met his match. Not only did Lagerfeld rapidly revitalize the French brand, restoring it to the vitality of its glory years, he also launched it into the twenty-first century by reinventing its signature motifs—which include quilted chain-link bags, tweed jackets, two-toned pumps, and camellias—with his own personal twists.

To this day, Lagerfeld has kept his wandering eye in check by supplementing his work at Chanel with projects old and new, including continuing the design partnership he began with Italian house Fendi in 1967 and launching an eponymous collection in 1984. The renaissance man and voracious reader also packs his schedule with endeav-ors such as costume design, fashion photography—lensing both the Chanel and Fendi campaigns—book publishing, and lecturing as a professor at the University of Applied Arts Vienna, in Austria, where students can benefit from his famously witty, incisive bon mots.

What is your advice to young people who want to be designers or break in to the fashion industry?
Are you sure this world is for you? And are you sure you are the right person to survive in this world—the world of fashion—a world with no rules, no laws? Answer that question honestly for yourself. Are you ready to accept injustice? The idea of the fashion industry may look better from the outside. It can look like the world of dream jobs—for a very happy few.

What do you look for when hiring new assistants? Do you like having interns around the atelier?
Mostly they are people I know through their parents or through friends I can trust. I must admit I prefer more girls than boys. I like the idea of having interns around, but a fashion house is not a fashion school.

LAGERFELD HAS PROVED TO BE AN ACE AT CULTIVATING THE NEXT GENERATION OF CHANEL FANS. HERE HE PAUSES WITH EMMA WATSON AFTER THE SPRING 2009 SHOW.

CHANEL

LAGERFELD'S ELABORATE RUNWAY PRESENTATIONS, BASED ON CHANEL ICONOGRAPHY, HAVE INCLUDED A CAROUSEL FITTED WITH MOVING CAMELLIAS AND QUILTED BAGS, AS WELL AS A GIANT CHANEL JACKET FROM WHICH MODELS EMERGED ONTO THE CATWALK. HERE, HE RECONSTRUCTED A LIFE-SIZE FACADE OF 31 RUE CAMBON, COCO CHANEL'S STORIED WORKSHOP.

What can young people do to distinguish themselves at work? What are some mistakes you see?
Be polite, interested, and always in a good mood. Pretension is the worst. You also must be ready to help out in areas where you never expected to be involved.

Do you have a list of movies, books, artwork, or other inspirations you suggest young people look at?
Be informed, not only about fashion but also about art, history, and music. Bring the fresh air of the world of youth to a studio, but don't think only because you are "funny" that you will be a hit—know better. In the days of the Internet it's easy to be informed. Also, speak other languages. Show that you are interested in things, that you want to learn. And never look bored. It can be boring sometimes in the world of fashion.

How has the job of being a fashion designer changed in recent times, and how can young people best prepare for new challenges in that role?
It's a different world now, and the economic crisis will not help make it easier to enter that world and be a success in it. It's difficult to say how to prepare for a role in the world of fashion. Take every opportunity and use it the best way you can. Flexibility is important. If you are gifted, it will only impress people later, once you've started a job. Accept any job offer in fashion if you want to be in that world.

What makes a person successful—or not—in the fashion industry?
Ideas—good ideas—and enthusiasm, loving the job, working hard, and never giving up. Talent is like a muscle: It has to be worked on and be adaptable and flexible. Personal charisma comes a little later, and it helps, too—but it must be handled carefully. Don't play the star before you are one. That is a great danger for young designers. Let other people tell you that you are a star. It's not for you to tell them. They would already have noticed. ★

*teen*VOGUE TIP   Don't let your ego get ahead of your fame. No matter how talented you are, Lagerfeld warns, overconfidence can turn people off to your designs before they even really have the chance to see them.

LAGERFELD HAS KEPT CHANEL AT THE FOREFRONT OF FASHION WHILE RESPECTING THE HOUSE'S LEGACY BY BLENDING ITS CLASSIC PIECES WITH THE SEASON'S MOST COMPELLING TRENDS. FOR SPRING 2007, CHANEL'S TIMELESS TWEED BLAZER WAS BROUGHT INTO THE PRESENT WITH A SPARKLY BORDER, SEQUINED HOT PANTS, AND LUCITE PLATFORMS.

DESIGNER TOOL KIT
essential items of the pros

SEWING MACHINE
A must-have to hone the craft.

WOMEN'S WEAR DAILY
This newspaper is crucial for keeping up with both the creative and business sides of the industry.

DESIGNER BIOGRAPHIES
Career inspiration from fashion's greats.

PATTERN NOTCHER
Punches patterns with tiny matching slits so that seamstresses know where to line them up.

COLORED PENCILS
For illustrating fashion sketches and story boards.

ART MARKERS
Create vibrant, detailed illustrations.

MUSLIN AND PATTERN
A rough model of the final outfit, sewn from a basic, inexpensive material.

BIAS TAPE
A fabric trim that covers up exposed seams to prevent raw edges from fraying.

PANTONE COLOR GUIDE
A standardized color system that ensures designers always get the exact shade they're looking for.

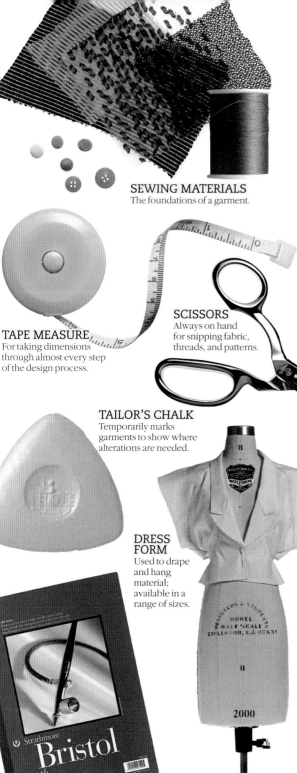

SEWING MATERIALS
The foundations of a garment.

TAPE MEASURE
For taking dimensions through almost every step of the design process.

SCISSORS
Always on hand for snipping fabric, threads, and patterns.

TAILOR'S CHALK
Temporarily marks garments to show where alterations are needed.

DRESS FORM
Used to drape and hang material; available in a range of sizes.

SKETCH PAD
Where great ideas first take shape.

Break in to the industry with these tips.

★ DESIGN SCHOOL CAN SHARPEN SKILLS AND CREATE INDUSTRY CONNECTIONS, BUT IT'S BY NO MEANS ESSENTIAL. TRADITIONAL EDUCATION HAS ITS MERITS TOO, LIKE INFORMING YOUR CREATIVITY OR BOOSTING YOUR BUSINESS PROWESS.

★ GET A JOB IN RETAIL. YOU'LL LEARN WHAT MAKES SHOPPERS TICK AND BE ABLE TO NETWORK WITH PEOPLE WHO CAN HELP YOU DOWN THE ROAD BY OFFERING FEEDBACK ON YOUR LINE OR POINTING YOU TOWARD INTERNSHIPS WITH DESIGNERS.

★ FIND WAYS TO INCORPORATE YOUR PASSION—WHETHER IT'S FOR THE ENVIRONMENT, A CHARITY, OR THE ARTS—INTO YOUR WORK. IT WILL ONLY ADD TO YOUR VISION.

★ INTERN! IT'S WORTH MAKING SACRIFICES TO ENSURE SUCCESS. REAL-WORLD EXPERIENCE CAN TEACH YOU THINGS YOU CAN'T LEARN IN SCHOOL, ESPECIALLY AT A SMALLER LABEL, WHERE YOU'LL BE EXPOSED TO SEVERAL LEVELS OF THE COMPANY.

★ KNOW YOUR CUSTOMER. CREATE AN INSPIRATION BOOK OR BOARD WITH VISUAL CUES.

★ IF YOU HAVE NO BUSINESS BACKGROUND, CONSIDER TAKING A FEW SUMMER COURSES OR CHECKING OUT BOOKS ABOUT THE TOPIC. BEING A DESIGNER INVOLVES MUCH MORE THAN JUST SEWING AND SKETCHING.

★ PAY ATTENTION TO INDUSTRY NEWS SO THAT YOU CAN SPOT THE TRENDS BUT REMAIN TRUE TO YOUR VISION. PLENTY OF LABELS FOUND SUCCESS BY GOING AGAINST THE PREVAILING STYLES OF THE MOMENT.

Question:

I love fashion maga

I get my foot in the

Answer:

Teen Vogue's editors

journalists give you

to land your dream

zines! How can
door?

and other top
the scoop on how
job.

The Teen Queen
Amy Astley

THE FOUNDING EDITOR OF *TEEN VOGUE* HAS REINVENTED THE YOUTH CATEGORY WITH AN ULTRASTYLISH MIX OF FASHION AND ADVICE THAT INSPIRES TEENS AND INDUSTRY INSIDERS ALIKE.

Before Amy Astley became the editor in chief of *Teen Vogue,* she spent her teenage years training to be a professional ballerina, an experience that she says proved to be surprisingly apt preparation for her eventual career in publishing. "Ballet taught me a lot about line and proportion," she says, "and it's a rigorous, insidery subculture, just as fashion can be." But the greatest commonality between fashion and dance, according to Astley, is the way they both conceal the copious effort involved, preferring instead to present only the elegant finished product. "Blood, sweat, and tears go on behind the scenes, and all that people ever see is the beautiful, seemingly effortless end result," she explains. Here, Astley breaks down her own process by sharing the details of her professional evolution and the lessons she has learned along the way.

When did you first become interested in fashion?
Ballet dancers are really specific about their look and their lines—the bun, the cut of the leotard, the slenderness of the body—everything is a bit fetishized. I grew up in that intensely visual world. My father was a painter and an art professor, so he used to take me to lots of museums and galleries. And I was always surrounded by artists and creative people who

placed value on being individual or unconventional. I think that I fixated on magazines because, like ballet, they were a fantasy world, an escape from reality—a beautiful creation. I was attracted to that, and furthermore, magazines seemed like a place where I could unite my interests in visuals and words—I had always loved reading and writing as well. I was a major bookworm from childhood on. My interest in clothes came later.

How did you go about securing your first magazine job, assisting the editor in chief of House & Garden?
After I graduated from college with a degree in English literature, I moved to New York City. That may seem an obvious first step, but not everyone sees it that way, and I think it's important to remember. You can't just sit around in Omaha, or wherever you're from, wishing that you could work in the fashion business. You need to move. Go to where the opportunities are! I wanted to work at Condé Nast because my family had always subscribed to the company's magazines—*House & Garden, Vogue*—and fortunately I found that I had an in: One of my mother's friends had gone to college with a woman who worked in HR. That's a tip:

ASTLEY IN HER NEW YORK CITY OFFICE, WHERE SHE EDITS STORIES, TAKES MEETINGS, AND OVERSEES LAYOUT DESIGN.

From in-store appearances to glamorous charity galas, Astley's duties extend far beyond working nine to five.

SIGNING AUTOGRAPHS FOR HUNDREDS OF EAGER FANS.

WITH BURBERRY CREATIVE DIRECTOR CHRISTOPHER BAILEY.

IN OSCAR DE LA RENTA AT THE CFDA FASHION AWARDS.

WITH ANNA WINTOUR AT A TOMMY HILFIGER SHOW.

OVERSEEING A STAFF MEETING WITH WHITNEY PORT FOR THE MTV SHOW *THE HILLS*.

"KEEP AN *open mind* AND BE *curious* ABOUT *everything.* THE BEAUTY OF *magazines* IS THAT THERE ARE SO *many different* PATHS *forward.* MINE WASN'T *direct,* BUT IT MADE ME A BETTER *editor.*"

—AMY ASTLEY

Network like crazy, because even if *you* don't know anyone in the industry, someone in your life might know of someone who can help.

Having a connection in HR is helpful, but it only gets your foot in the door. Once you got that first job, what did you do to make yourself stand out?
I worked hard! I am a very can-do person. Anything that my boss wanted done—even things that she hadn't thought of—I would do as well as I could. I remember one instance in which I had to write a very delicately worded letter to a reader, and I really labored over it. Then my boss came to see me with that letter in her hand, and she said, "You are a good writer, and I can see that you love it. We've got to get you writing more." And she did—I started getting small assignments, stories about dessert plates or wastebaskets, and I took them seriously.

Early in your career you may be asked to do things that you don't feel are worthy of your education or that don't seem explicitly related to your career goals—but if you do them well, they can inspire people to put their faith in you and give you the work you *do* want. Especially when you're at the intern or assistant level, your job is really just to make other people's jobs easier. So if you soak it all up, pay attention to everything, and do things that nobody else thought of, then you're more likely to get promoted. That's who I want to promote: people who solve problems and are enthusiastic and eager to take on more work, more responsibility.

What else can an intern or assistant do to increase her chances of moving ahead?
Remember to keep your interactions professional. You're

at work, and it's not always glamorous—it's not *The Hills,* and you're not making thousands of dollars an episode. Be prepared to arrive at work before your boss does and to stay until after she leaves, so that you're always there. Don't ask for favors or feel entitled; stay focused on what you have to offer the company. I have seen so many promising employees derail themselves by becoming too caught up in the social aspect of the office and the industry. Remember that you are there to work and to produce. Also, don't just think about how to make *yourself* stand out. Study the people you admire. From their editing style to small details like phone manners or thank-you notes, what makes them successful? Many women have been mentors to me, including dance teachers, *House & Garden* editors, and Anna Wintour.

As the editor in chief, you don't have too much day-to-day interaction with interns and assistants other than your own. Is there anything aside from hard work that a girl can do to impress you?
Every so often an intern will introduce herself to me, and I actually find that quite charming. As long as it's a quick, professional interaction and it happens at a well-chosen moment, then it's great and it really does make an intern more memorable. But don't fixate on the head of the company or the editor in chief—the smarter move is to impress the person you've been hired to help. Then that person will sing your praises to her boss. *Teen Vogue* has hired many interns in this way.

Let's get back to your early career. How long did you stay at H&G, and how did you get from there to* Vogue*?
I stayed there for four years, starting as the assistant to the editor in chief, becoming an assistant editor, and then an associate

"I always have reference books around. This book on Stephen Sprouse is a must-read for anyone aspiring to work in fashion."

"It's always lovely when designers send bouquets as thank-yous. It's nice to have a little nature in the office—we work on the ninth floor of a high-rise!"

"This intricate origami star was made for me by a reader when the magazine first started. I've had it on my desk for years—it's beautiful!"

"I stick Post-it notes on everything! They help me communicate with my staff—I flag layouts that need changes and jot notes to editors about interesting newspaper articles I find."

"This dummy book is a mock-up of the entire issue. It helps with the flow of the magazine. I can see what's missing from the pages—it might be a great food still life or more celebrity coverage."

"My assistant keeps track of my schedule in this planner. Each day is packed with staff meetings, showroom appointments, and a million other engagements."

"I met British designer Henry Holland through model Agyness Deyn. They were guests at several *Teen Vogue* events and at the Costume Institute benefit. This card was Henry's fun, personal way to say thank you."

"This is a stack of about a year's worth of back issues. I refer to them to see what worked in the past, from cover lines to layouts."

"I'm a newspaper hound and typically read my papers before work. They're a constant source of inspiration for stories!"

"This picture of my desk was taken during New York Fashion Week. My assistant puts together a tight schedule of shows, presentations, and parties that I attend. This envelope contains all the invitations."

AT THE NEW YORKERS FOR CHILDREN GALA WITH ACTRESS SCARLETT JOHANSSON.

WITH MODEL AGYNESS DEYN AND DESIGNER HENRY HOLLAND AT A *TEEN VOGUE* EVENT.

WITH ACTOR ROBERT PATTINSON AT *TEEN VOGUE*'S ANNUAL YOUNG HOLLYWOOD PARTY.

editor in the decorating department. And when the magazine first closed, a writer who had left for *Vogue* the year before recommended me to Anna Wintour. If it weren't for him, I don't think I would have ever gone to *Vogue,* which really illustrates the importance of networking and remaining open to new opportunities. You never know where you'll end up. There was a job available in the beauty department, and the managing editor asked me why I thought I could write about beauty when I had no experience in the field. I've always thought of myself as a journalist, first and foremost, with a deep passion for style—fashion, beauty, decorating. I could write about anything or anyone style-related. So I told her that, and it was the right answer. It should never just be "I love makeup" or "I live for fashion." At magazines, we look for curious, educated people who can place trends into a context and give banal things—like lipstick and shoes—journalistic credence.

How did working at Vogue *influence you?*

I learned so much during my years at *Vogue*—how to assign stories to writers, how to line-edit copy. And I was able to soak up the culture, hone my eye and my taste, and observe the massively talented stylists, photographers, and writers—and, of course, Anna—all doing their work. I became the beauty director soon after joining the magazine, but even then I was fascinated by the magazine's bigger picture. One thing I did that encouraged people to see me in a new way was to ask if I could edit the Index fashion section after the editor who was doing it left. I wasn't the obvious choice, but I knew it would be a good way for me to round out my skills, and I flung myself into it. There was a learning curve, but it made me a better candidate for my current position.

You oversaw the test issues and, in 2003, the launch of Teen Vogue. *What does your job consist of now?*

It's about assembling a great team of editors, stylists, writers, and photographers and getting the best out of them. I don't style clothes, and I don't go on shoots—I find people with the right vision, point of view, and taste for the magazine. I guide the team, but I also want them to surprise me and push me outside my own comfort zone. That keeps the magazine fresh and, in turn, encourages their own creativity. And I build the brand, which includes television shows, this book, the annual *Teen Vogue* Fashion University, our Web site, and our CFDA scholarship, which supports young design talent. *Teen Vogue* is much more than just the magazine—our readers want to experience our world in other mediums than just print.

teenVOGUE TIP "The truth is, when you're an intern or assistant, your job is to make editors' lives easier. If you prove yourself by doing a good job of that, it can inspire them to put their faith in you and give you more responsibility." —AMY ASTLEY

ASTLEY'S DAILY SCHEDULE

★ *Morning:* At 6:00 A.M., I begin the day by reading the *New York Post*, *The New York Times*, *The Wall Street Journal,* and *Women's Wear Daily.* I arrive at the office by 9:00 and meet with photographers, editors, and stylists to discuss upcoming photo shoots and look at possible shoot locations. I have run-throughs to look at the clothing and accessories we're planning to photograph. I also spend a lot of time brainstorming article ideas with editors; there are often meetings about the budget or events, like our annual Young Hollywood party.

★ *Afternoon:* Lunch could be with a fashion-industry executive or a designer, and then my afternoons are occupied in much the same manner as my mornings—sometimes I'll go out to the market to look at clothes in showrooms, and I also read and edit copy, look at film and page layouts in the art department, and plan the overall flow of the magazine.

★ *Evening:* My evenings are often devoted to fashion-industry events like award ceremonies, product launches, and cocktail parties, but my favorite thing is going to an art opening, movie, or the theater.

Jackie Randell, ASTLEY'S ASSISTANT
AGE 24 COLLEGE THE UNIVERSITY OF NORTH CAROLINA AT CHAPEL HILL HOMETOWN WINTER PARK, FLORIDA

"I double-majored in English and journalism and mass communication at the University of North Carolina at Chapel Hill, and I worked at the newspaper there as a staff writer for the arts-and-entertainment section. I was also the entertainment editor for the student magazine *Blue & White*. When I graduated, I moved to New York to pursue a master's in English language and literature at New York University, hoping to work at a magazine eventually. I started as an intern at Seventeen.com (I got the position after seeing a listing on the Web site Ed2010), and they took me on as a part-time Web freelancer when my internship ended. Then a friend of mine who worked at *Men's Vogue* passed my résumé to HR just when Amy started looking for a new assistant; after a couple of interviews, I got the job. I had decided that the full-time position was worth putting my master's on hold, but on my first day, Amy encouraged me to continue my studies. So I've been attending evening classes at New York University once a week since I started working at *Teen Vogue.*

I can see myself working at magazines for a long time. I like working at *Teen Vogue* because I enjoy the combination of pop culture and fashion. My administrative tasks include answering Amy's phone calls, coordinating her schedule, setting up meetings, and handling contracts and payments. But having a front-row seat to the way the magazine runs has been invaluable. I see everything that comes across Amy's desk—exactly what her job entails—and I've learned a lot. Now I edit the V-Mail and Contributors pages and write articles for the People Are Talking About section. Ultimately, I'd like to write and edit even more as I work my way up the masthead."

Any parting words of advice?

People need to assess what their strengths are fairly soon after they start working, to face reality and see where they stand. I had to do this for myself at age eighteen, when I realized that I wasn't going to be able to dance on the level that I wanted. So perhaps it was natural for me to be brutally honest with myself—but I think it's an important thing for everyone to do. You may think that you want to be a stylist but then realize that you're actually more suited to being a market editor. Don't feel that you have to be a superstar—there are so few! Instead, try to be a part of the team and focus on the joint goals, not just individual glory. All magazines are a group effort and are only as good as the sum of their parts. If you find you're having a hard time with something, realize that it may not be the right fit—don't be afraid to try something new. That's the beauty of magazines: There isn't any one path in our business. It's not like being a doctor or a lawyer, where you go to a specific school and learn the trade. There are many different ways forward. Mine wasn't direct at all. ★

The Fashion Know-It-Alls

TEEN VOGUE'S MARKET EDITORS DIVIDE AND CONQUER THE FASHION WORLD TO BRING THE HOTTEST DESIGNERS, THE FRESHEST LINES, AND EACH SEASON'S MUST-HAVE ITEMS TO THE PAGES OF THE MAGAZINE.

FROM LEFT: MARKET EDITORS JOANNA HILLMAN, GLORIA BAUME, MARY KATE STEINMILLER, SARAH FRANCES KUHN, AND TAYLOR TOMASI HILL MEET OUTSIDE THE MARC BY MARC JACOBS SPRING 2009 SHOW AT THE 69TH REGIMENT ARMORY IN NEW YORK CITY.

"When I was in college, I thought I wanted to be a photographer, and I was lucky enough to get an internship in the studio of a major photographer named Jim Moore. It was a great education: I quickly learned what each and every person in the industry really does. Because I had a strong sense of style, people always assumed I was a fashion person. Often, if there was a styling-related task—steaming clothes, for example—they would ask me to do it, and it wasn't long before I realized that fashion *was* the best place for me.

After I graduated from New York University, I sent out résumés to 30 or 40 different stylists—people I had worked with in the studio and those whose work I had seen in magazines. Within a couple of weeks, seven or eight of them booked me to help them on shoots. It was great. Every two or three days I worked with a new group of people and learned so much more than I could have in any school. I was never shy—I spoke to people quite easily, and that helped. You don't want to be full of yourself, and you want to listen and absorb as much as you can, but if you have something to contribute, then you should. I applied for a job in the fashion department at *Vanity Fair,* and I think that I got it mainly because the editor was, like me, Italian, and she wanted someone to gossip with in her native language. That was where I learned about the fashion market, and from there I went on to market editor jobs at *Glamour* and *Vogue.*

Being in the market means going to appointments at showrooms with designers and seeing the clothes. I really enjoyed that. I loved speaking with designers and being able to see firsthand how trends change each season. And at *Vogue,* for the first time, I was asked to represent the magazine and impress upon the designers what the magazine's point of view was. Fashion suddenly seemed broader to me, and I started devouring books about the lives of Christian Dior and Coco Chanel, checking out exhibitions at the Museum of Modern Art, and even taking pattern-making classes at Parsons the New School for Design. I think that in order to be a good editor, you really have to study fashion—like a doctor studies biology—because you need to understand the history behind the trends.

I've been with *Teen Vogue* since the very beginning, and it's a perfect fit with my sense of style. It's fashion, yes, but the *Teen Vogue* girl also brings her own personality to what she wears, just as I do. I think that style is very innate—you become attracted to things and you develop a sense of what you're all about. For me, those things haven't really changed, and I think it's that way for a lot of people. I love wearing strong accessories and short skirts. I can always tell when an intern, for example, has her own unique perspective on fashion, and having that is really half the battle if you want to succeed in the industry."

Gloria Baume
Fashion Director

TEEN VOGUE TIP When applying for that first big job, don't be shy. Baume flooded stylists with her résumé, reaching out to everyone she knew—and everyone she didn't. You have to take a chance to see results.

BEHIND THE SHOOT

Baume walks us through one of her favorite Teen Vogue *stories.*

INSPIRATION BOARD

THE FINAL IMAGES

ISSUE: April 2009

THE INSPIRATION: "Some of the most challenging fashion stories are the ones we do year after year, like prom, because we have to figure out how to give them a different twist each time. This story began as a more traditional prom concept, based on the bright, voluminous dresses at the Lanvin Spring 2009 show, until the stylist, Jillian Davison, spotted an inspiration board in my office. (I had originally made it for another story that wasn't shot, featuring 1950s teddy boys in London.)"

THE CLOTHES: "Jillian decided to go in a rebel-punk direction, even though that doesn't really come across in party clothes. A shoot's inspiration can be expressed in many ways aside from the fashion. Here you see it in the hair and makeup, the accessories, the boy models, and the overall attitude."

THE SCOOP: "When you see an image that you love, rip it out and save it for reference. Magazine covers, pictures of paintings, advertisements, anything—collect them all. Whether you want to be a designer, a stylist, a fashion editor, a makeup artist, or a photographer, these images will serve as inspiration to you as your career progresses."

PHOTOGRAPHER: Jason Kibbler

Taylor Tomasi Hill
Accessories Director

TOMASI HILL IN PARIS
FOR THE SPRING 2009
SHOWS.

Sarah Frances Kuhn
Accessories Editor

KUHN DURING SPRING
2009 NEW YORK
FASHION WEEK.

"I moved from Dallas to New York to study fashion at Pratt Institute, but it didn't take me long to realize I hated sewing and wasn't cut out to be a designer. So I switched to industrial design. Then when I was a senior, I was looking for an internship, and a listing for *W* magazine popped up.

It was already two days past the cutoff date, but I applied anyway, then called, faxed, and e-mailed, and finally they told me to come in. I had no clue about the industry—I didn't know how to pronounce Alaïa or Lanvin—but Carmen Borgonovo, who became my mentor at *W*, believed in me and taught me the ropes. I also worked hard to impress the fashion director, Alex White, and as a result I got the opportunity to assist her on set. I interned at *W* for six months, and after I graduated from college I got a job in the fashion closet. I was there for a year, working until 2:00 A.M. almost every night. It was insanity, but it was also exciting to see the merchandise up close. It paid off when I became an accessories assistant and then a fashion market editor there. In 2006, I came to *Teen Vogue* as a senior fashion editor, and now I'm the accessories director.

Each spring and fall I go to shows in New York, Paris, and Milan, then report on the trends and make trend boards with pictures from the runways. I also spend a lot of time in the market, running to showrooms: Three days a week I book back-to-back appointments from 9:00 A.M. until 5:00 P.M., and I cover every brand from Payless to Prada.

The ironic thing is that I have all these high heels that don't get any use. The idea of strapping them on and running to 20 appointments ... There's just no way. In reality, when I'm at work, it's all about a comfy boot or a sneaker."

"Growing up, my grandmother subscribed to *W* magazine, and every time I went to her house I would grab a stack and make collages. So when I decided to spend a summer during college in New York City, I applied for an internship at *W*. I literally opened the magazine, looked at the masthead, and called the main number. I didn't have anything special on my résumé—I was majoring in Russian and Middle Eastern history at Boston University and I had worked at Pizzeria Uno—but I think the fact that I was really motivated came across, and I got the internship.

After that, I started working at a store called Louis Boston, and I convinced my school paper to let me write a fashion column. I graduated and moved to London, where I wrote to *W* to see if they needed any help at the branch there. They gave me a part-time job, and it was a tiny office, so I got to do everything: go to fashion shows, assist stylists, even write and photograph a street-style story for *WWD*. I also attended a yearlong graduate program in fashion history and theory at the London College of Fashion, and assisted stylists for magazines like *Dazed & Confused*. So when I moved to New York, I had plenty of connections. I kept assisting stylists and wrote for small magazines and Web sites until I was hired as associate accessories editor at *Teen Vogue*.

Now I'm the accessories editor. We shoot several fashion stories at a time, so I'm constantly requesting items, and I also keep up with fashion. If I see someone in a restaurant wearing a cool necklace, I'll ask where she got it. Tonight when I go home, I'm spray-painting padlocks for a preppy-punk story we're shooting. Basically, I do anything I can to make the items we feature as creative and special as possible."

Joanna Hillman
Senior Fashion Market Editor

HILLMAN COVERING THE FALL 2008 RUNWAY SHOWS IN MILAN.

Mary Kate Steinmiller
Associate Fashion Market Editor

STEINMILLER MANEUVERING A TRUNK OF CLOTHES FOR A *TEEN VOGUE* SHOOT.

"My mother was a model in her twenties, and when I was little I begged her to let me be one too: I had a short-lived career as a catalog model, which exposed me to parts of the industry I might otherwise not be aware of, like what stylists do.

After I graduated from the University of Western Ontario, in Canada, I started working in a multidesigner showroom in Toronto. Stylists from Canadian magazines would come in to pull clothes, and I liked that side of the business. I decided to move to New York City, and when I got here I cold-called stylists from the fashion industry directory *Le Book*. I left messages for a lot of people I had no business leaving messages for, but I got hired to assist on commercials and other odd jobs as a result.

I got my break when I started working for the stylist Lori Goldstein. We shot Angelina Jolie in Paris for the cover of *Vanity Fair,* styled editorials for international *Vogues,* and worked on campaigns with photographers like Richard Avedon. I stayed with Lori for two years, then took a job as fashion market editor at *Teen Vogue.* I like working with a group of people in a creative environment and having a team to bounce ideas off of. Now I'm the senior fashion market editor, and I cover the higher-end New York brands—like 3.1 Phillip Lim, DKNY, and Ralph Lauren—and designers in Milan. I spend 80 percent of my time in the market or visiting showrooms. After I see the runway shows, I'll go back and take pictures of the clothes—which is called a re-see—and I also pull clothing for our photo shoots. But for me, going to Fashion Week in Milan is my favorite part. That's when my job is closest to how I imagined it would be when I was a kid."

"I've always been creative: I love making jewelry and putting together outfits. So although I started out as a journalism major at Marquette University in Wisconsin, where I'm from, I decided to transfer to Parsons after my freshman year.

My friend got an internship at *Teen Vogue,* but she had to give it up and she recommended that I take her place. I loved working here because every day I did something different like returning clothing to showrooms or making inspiration boards. I ended up interning here all through college. I have friends who switched internships every semester, and they made more contacts. But because I stayed in one place, the relationships I formed were strong. When a fashion assistant job opened up before I graduated, I was offered the job.

In that position, I was glued to the phone and the computer, sending requests, writing credits, and doing administrative work. After six months, I was promoted to associate fashion market editor. Because everyone knew me from my internship, they were confident I could handle it. Now I spend half my day on market appointments, meeting with fashion publicists and visiting showrooms. I cover denim, swimwear, surf and skate brands, and lower-priced chains like Old Navy and Gap. Back at the office, I meet with editors and stylists to see what they need, request items from showrooms, and distribute clothing that comes in onto racks.

I also volunteer to help with things that aren't technically my job. Once we were trying to get bracelets in for a shoot, and I realized I could create something similar. So I got materials and made them myself. (Charlotte Ronson saw them in the magazine and now sells them in her store!) I like being involved with every side of *Teen Vogue.*" ★

The Runway Insider

Jane Keltner

SITTING FRONT ROW AT FASHION SHOWS AND DISCOVERING BUDDING YOUNG DESIGNERS ARE ALL IN A DAY'S WORK FOR *TEEN VOGUE'S* FASHION NEWS DIRECTOR.

"I have always loved fashion, for as long as I can remember. When I was little, I used to go into my mother's closet before parent-teacher nights at school and edit what she was going to wear. And I still have piles and piles of old magazines at my parents' apartment—they're always begging me to clean them out, but I tell them that those are my archives! It wasn't until college that I put two and two together and realized that fashion could be a career.

My first chance to work in the industry came when a friend of a friend who had an internship at *Mademoiselle* asked me to cover a Daryl K fashion show for her because she was sick. I jumped at the opportunity, of course. I had taken some photography classes in school, so I brought my camera, stationed myself right next to the photographers' pit, and shot every single look that came down the runway. In hindsight, I probably took it a little too seriously, but when I presented her with the photos, she was definitely impressed. And when that same person helped me to get an interview at *W* magazine, the *Mademoiselle* project was something I included on my résumé. I had no real fashion experience at the time, so I put down anything I thought showed my interest. I remember the editor who scanned my résumé immediately picked up on that as something cool and different, and I got the internship. It started the summer after my freshman year, and I realized then that this was what I wanted to do.

Since I went to Barnard College in New York City, I was able to intern all through school and work as much as I could. The unique thing about *W* at the time was that it was linked with *Women's Wear Daily,* and the editor I assisted worked on both, so I was exposed to the format of a daily paper as well. Eventually, that editor moved to *Elle* and asked me to come with her; by graduation, I had already worked for the same person for three years, which made it easier to get a job when the right one opened up.

I was hired and started working as an associate in *Elle's* fashion news department immediately after graduation. That position was perfect for me because it blended the visual and the verbal. I had majored in English literature at school, and for my new job I began writing right off the bat, researching articles, and, after a few months, traveling to London to cover the collections. I came to *Teen Vogue* five years ago. I'm now the fashion news director. I oversee all the fashion features in the magazine and edit the Index and the View sections,

KELTNER EXITS THE TUILERIES GARDENS AFTER CATCHING A RUNWAY SHOW AT PARIS FASHION WEEK IN OCTOBER 2008.

Keltner's job takes her from attending runway shows in New York City and Paris to interviewing subjects in L.A. and beyond.

CONDUCTING AN INTERVIEW WITH MODEL CHANEL IMAN WHILE ATOP A FERRIS WHEEL IN PARIS.

SNAPPED BY PAPARAZZI WHILE INTERVIEWING ACTRESS RACHEL BILSON IN LOS ANGELES.

WITH DESIGNER JASON WU AT THE WHITNEY MUSEUM OF AMERICAN ART'S 2008 GALA IN NEW YORK CITY.

LEAVING THE BRYANT PARK TENTS WITH STYLIST TINA CHAI DURING NEW YORK FASHION WEEK.

which contain all the fashion news stories, including profiles of new designers and the biannual A to Z—something I started.

Much of my inspiration comes from the shows, which I attend twice a year, but I also look to street style, young celebrities, and pop culture. I jot down my ideas in a notebook and frequently visit designers' studios because I like to know what's on the horizon. I've styled some of our smaller fashion shoots and have even gotten to write the two *Teen Vogue* cover stories featuring models, which was amazing because when I was growing up, models—not celebrities— were on the covers of magazines, and they were part of what made fashion so exciting to me. The best thing about my job is the chance it gives me to be involved in every stage of the editorial process." ★

Evanne Gambrell, FASHION WRITER
AGE 28 COLLEGE **VASSAR COLLEGE**
HOMETOWN **EAST SETAUKET, NEW YORK**

"Growing up, magazines made my world go around. In junior high, my friends and I used to sneak off to the library during lunch to read magazines. Later on in college, I knew that eventually I wanted to write for one. At Vassar, I majored in English and did one internship, at a fashion publication called *ITS,* which is now defunct. I graduated with very little editorial experience, so I worked my alumni connections in an effort to find a job, calling and writing anyone who worked at a magazine. Someone gave me the idea to write to the executive editor of every publication I liked, so I went to Barnes & Noble, looked at the mastheads of a bunch of magazines, found the editors' names, and sent them letters. I also visited the career Web site Ed2010 constantly to check for available positions. I woke up at the same time every day and made it my job to send out résumés and read up on what was happening in the industry. Then I saw a listing for a freelance Web position at *Teen Vogue.* I interviewed for it and was hired. A year later, a job in the fashion news department opened up, and I got it!

I spend most of my time at my desk, writing and researching stories. I particularly like interviewing people, especially designers. At the beginning, doing interviews was nerve-racking, but since I always overprepare, I was fine. Although you need to be flexible while interviewing someone, you should always have an outline of the questions you'd like to ask.

I've learned that you need patience when looking for a job. I briefly temped at several law firms after college, but I never gave up on my dream to work in magazines. And in a sense, I believe that the right job will find you."

Lauren McGrath, FASHION NEWS ASSISTANT
AGE 24 COLLEGE **BOWDOIN COLLEGE**
HOMETOWN **BROOKLYN, NEW YORK**

"I've loved fashion my whole life. When I was a little girl, I was always reading my mom's issues of *Vogue.* Style was important to her, and it rubbed off on me!

I studied art history in college, but I wanted to work in media—I just didn't know exactly in what capacity. The summer after sophomore year, I got my first internship, in the features department at *Seventeen* magazine. I didn't do any fashion-related work there, but I got more exposure to the industry by working at a clothing boutique. I also did internships at a public relations firm and at Martha Stewart Living Television, where my mom worked as a producer. All these jobs were valuable experiences, and they helped me figure out what I did and didn't want to do. Then, after graduation, I found out that Amy Astley—the editor in chief of *Teen Vogue*—was looking for a new assistant, and I got the job.

Being the editor in chief's assistant allowed me to see in-depth how a magazine works, meet lots of people in the industry, and gain visibility within the company. I also got to listen in on editorial meetings, which taught me a lot about what makes a great story. Now I work in the fashion news department, and my job involves writing copy and interviewing girls who may be featured in the magazine. I even helped produce a room-makeover story with designer Lela Rose, which was fun!

Experience is important in landing that first job, though I didn't have any fashion editorial internships under my belt before I was hired at *Teen Vogue.* More than anything, you have to show people that you are a hard worker and passionate about what you do."

The Beauty & Health Expert

Eva Chen

TEEN VOGUE'S BEAUTY AND HEALTH DIRECTOR PASSED ON MEDICAL SCHOOL TO WORK IN THE MAGAZINE WORLD AFTER LEARNING THAT IT'S ALWAYS BEST TO PURSUE YOUR PASSION.

On her first day as an editorial intern at *Harper's Bazaar,* Eva Chen was asked to organize the beauty closet, a cupboard stuffed with full-size samples of everything from hair-thickening spray to nail polish—or what's known to those in the glamour industry simply as "product." Similar (and similarly stocked) pantries can be found on the premises of every major fashion magazine in the world. And Chen had never seen anything like it.

"Really, it ruined every other department of the magazine for me," she admits with a laugh. "I was the kind of girl who loved to go to Sephora. I could spend three hours in the hair-care aisle at Duane Reade, agonizing over which shampoo to buy. An editor took me into the beauty closet and told me that all the products were from the previous season and that I needed to, as she put it, get rid of everything. I asked her, 'What do you mean? Do you want me to throw it all out?' She said, 'I guess if you want to take some stuff home, you can.' So on my first day, I lugged about eighteen bags of products home, and I was like, 'This is the best job ever.'"

Then 20 years old, Chen had spent every summer from age fourteen taking college-level science classes: "Pretty much my whole life I thought I was going to be a doctor," she recalls. Chen was enrolled (and excelling) in a competitive premed program at the prestigious Johns Hopkins University and preparing to take medical-school entrance exams when she realized she had better address a nagging suspicion that she wasn't on the right path. "I needed to do something totally random, to give myself some time off to see if medical school was really right for me," she says.

So, in her typical methodical fashion, she applied for summer internships in a range of industries including advertising, publishing, television, and public relations—"I must have sent out a hundred résumés," she says—and subsequently received numerous offers. The magazine job, she decided, "sounded like the most fun"; she had always been a voracious reader. By the end of her second day at *Bazaar,* Chen was certain that she didn't want to be a doctor after all.

And it wasn't just the swag: That summer, she got her first shot at writing copy by penning a short beauty note—"literally, just a line about a product that corresponded to a fashion image"—and she found the sensation of seeing her own sentence in print so exciting that she bought 20 copies of the issue in which it appeared.

THIS IMAGE OF A MODEL'S FACE DUSTED WITH BRONZING POWDER WAS SHOT BY PHOTOGRAPHER RAYMOND MEIER FOR THE MARCH 2003 ISSUE OF *TEEN VOGUE*. AS BEAUTY DIRECTOR, CHEN'S JOB INVOLVES DREAMING UP ARRESTING VISUALS FOR STORIES IN THE MAGAZINE.

HEALTH UPDATE: SUPERBUGS

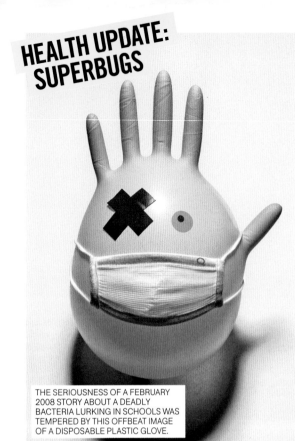

THE SERIOUSNESS OF A FEBRUARY 2008 STORY ABOUT A DEADLY BACTERIA LURKING IN SCHOOLS WAS TEMPERED BY THIS OFFBEAT IMAGE OF A DISPOSABLE PLASTIC GLOVE.

or comments, and that's inspiration enough for a story. Other times I'll see something in my everyday life, and that's the impetus—one example is a story we did on copy-cat friends, which I came up with after seeing a group of ten girls, all dressed very similarly, standing together on the street. I read at least eight newspapers daily, and I get so many different beauty products—up to 300 items a day—that I can clearly see trends."

Furthermore, Chen loves the built-in variety of her position. "The best part of my job is that there's no such thing as a typical day," she says. "This morning I went to the launch of a gourmet fragrance inspired by Thailand and Vietnam—chef Jean-Georges Vongerichten had prepared a breakfast that featured all the fragrance's notes—and I'll spend the rest of the day editing copy. Two weeks ago I was in Paris, doing a photo shoot with designer Jean Paul Gaultier for his fragrance launch; next week I'll be on the phone, interviewing doctors about the dangers of smoking. Being able to do so many different things is fulfilling."

So far in her career, Chen says the biggest lesson she has learned is always to listen to your instincts. "I had a feeling, in my stomach, that medical school wasn't right for me, and I'm glad I didn't ignore my intuition," she says. "You need to do something that you feel passionately about, and if you're not sure what that is, then try different things until you find it." ★

"The experience was really eye-opening for me," she explains. "I was somebody who loved beauty products, who loved magazines, who loved words, and I didn't realize that those things could come together and coagulate into a real job. While I was interning, they could have asked me to do anything—organize paper clips by size, for example—and I would have been excited to do it because it was all so different from anything I had ever done before. I think it's important for people to know that no matter what your background is, no matter how much schooling you've had, in beauty journalism you have to start out by messengering products and picking up the phone. You need to be willing to do anything. I once had an intern ask me if she could write the next cover story: That's not going to happen. Instead, focus on soaking up everything around you. It's a learning experience, and it's how you start to make contacts."

Indeed, the contacts that Chen made at *Bazaar* led to her first postcollege jobs in publishing. Six months after she graduated, a former *Bazaar* editor pointed her toward a freelance fashion gig at *Lucky,* and a few months later Chen was hired to assist another former boss who'd moved to *Elle.* Now Chen heads her own department and edits her own section. "It's thrilling to be able to realize my vision," she says.

Story ideas can spring up in different ways, she explains: "A lot of the time, readers will e-mail me with questions

NUTRITION FEATURE: TEEN DIABETES

FOR AN AUGUST 2006 ARTICLE ABOUT DIABETES, AN APPETIZING TOWER OF SUGARY FOODS THAT CAN CONTRIBUTE TO THE DISEASE ILLUSTRATED THE STORY.

BEAUTY CHECKLIST

FOLLOW CHEN'S SIMPLE TIPS TO LOOK AND FEEL YOUR BEST.

1. PREPARE FOR AN *important interview* BY EATING A *brain-boosting meal* BEFOREHAND. EGG WHITES, FISH, AND OTHER *protein-packed foods* HELP KEEP YOU FEELING ALERT.

2. TAKE A LOOK AT YOUR DAILY DIET AND THINK ABOUT WHAT *you're not eating.* ARE YOU GETTING ENOUGH *omega-3 fatty acids* FROM FOODS LIKE FLAX SEEDS, WALNUTS, AND FISH, WHICH ARE IMPORTANT FOR *healthy skin?* ARE YOU EATING LOTS OF *nutrient-rich vegetables?*

3. *Treat* YOUR SKIN GENTLY. *Too much exfoliation causes irritation,* AND OVERUSING *acne products* WILL DRY SKIN OUT. AS WITH ALL THINGS, *moderation is best.*

CHEN PHOTOGRAPHED AT A BENEFIT IN NEW YORK CITY.

"IF YOU ABUSE YOUR BODY BY SMOKING, YOU CAN'T EXPECT TO HAVE GORGEOUS GLOWING SKIN, SHINY HAIR, OR HEALTHY LUNGS," SAYS CHEN, WHO WROTE ABOUT THE DANGERS OF CIGARETTES IN THE OCTOBER 2005 ISSUE.

TEEN VOGUE TIP "No matter how much schooling you've had, in beauty journalism you have to start out by messengering products and picking up the phone. You need to be willing to do anything." —EVA CHEN

The Creative Force
Aoife Wasser

THROUGH HER KEEN LOVE OF ART, *TEEN VOGUE'S* CREATIVE DIRECTOR HAS MADE HER MAGAZINE DREAMS A REALITY.

"When I was growing up in Dublin, Ireland, my friend and I used to make 'magazines' for each other by chopping up real magazines and reassembling them. We would cut out pictures from one magazine and use the letters from another to create our own layouts. That's how I fell in love with the medium.

I went to the Dublin Institute of Technology to study visual communications: photography, illustration, and design. I did a summer abroad in New York and fell in love with the city. When I finished school, I decided to move there—I left home right after my graduation, even though I didn't have a job yet. At one point or another, pretty much everyone who studies design has read about a graphic designer named David Carson—I did while at school in Dublin—so I decided to try and intern for him. I couldn't believe I could just pick up a phone and ask for an internship, but I did, and he said, 'Sure.' When I found a copy of *Visionaire* magazine on the street, I thought it was the coolest thing, so I called and asked if I could intern for them also, and they said yes too!

I worked at both places at the same time for about

"PICKING THE PERFECT IMAGES FOR A LAYOUT IS EXTREMELY TIME-CONSUMING," WASSER SAYS. "WE SHOT MORE THAN 500 PICTURES FOR THE STORY ILLUSTRATED ON THIS CONTACT SHEET."

"HAVING A BEAUTY SHOT [LEFT] IN THIS DENIM FASHION STORY ADDED TO THE RHYTHM OF THE LAYOUT—IT GIVES THE READER A NICE BREAK," WASSER SAYS.

THIS SUMMERY STORY WAS SHOT IN CHILLY MID-NOVEMBER. BETWEEN SHOTS, WASSER (RIGHT) KEPT THE MODEL WARM WITH BLANKETS.

six months, and then *Visionaire* offered me a full-time position as a junior designer, which I accepted. Over the years, I made my way up to senior designer, then to associate art director, and finally to art director. In that position, I went on shoots with the editor in chief, Stephen Gan. That was when I got a real taste of doing photo shoots, meeting with photographers, and seeing that whole side of the world. Up to that point, I had only been behind a computer. That experience ended up proving instrumental as preparation for my current job.

As *Teen Vogue*'s creative director, I'm responsible for the overall look and feel of the magazine. I work with the photographers to come up with great locations and cool concepts—basically picking the right team for each story idea. Then I work with the designers to tie together the pages to make sure that the magazine flows well. I always design a few of the stories myself, but I don't have an ego about it—if it's not working, I'll pass it onto another member of my team. The reader shouldn't look at the magazine and say, 'This is Aoife's page.' They need to look at the page and think, This is so *Teen Vogue*. For the result to be as good as possible, the entire department needs to be involved." ★

"BE BRAVE *and* ASK FOR *internships anywhere* YOU'VE *dreamed* OF *working.* YOU NEVER *know who* WILL SAY *yes.*"

—AOIFE WASSER

THE LORD OF THE FLIES INFLUENCED THIS MAY 2009 SURFER-CHIC FASHION STORY.

Zan Goodman, ART ASSISTANT
AGE 22 COLLEGE PARSONS THE NEW SCHOOL FOR DESIGN HOMETOWN NEW YORK, NEW YORK

"The fact that both my parents are graphic designers definitely sparked my interest in design. My mom designs books, and my dad was an art director for medical magazines. When I was a teenager, I wanted to be a fashion designer, so I decided to go to Parsons to pursue that dream. They require each student take core classes in subjects including drawing, painting, and construction. By the end of it all, I realized I wasnt suited to be a fashion designer—I was better working two-dimensionally, versus in the three dimensions that clothing requires. I ended up majoring in communication design (a mix of technology-based media and traditional graphic design).

While at school, I attended a job fair and got an internship in the marketing department at *Spin*. My junior year, I asked a photographer friend who worked for *Nylon* if he knew anyone I could talk to at the magazine. He helped me get an internship in marketing there. But because *Nylon* is so small, I got the chance to do some editorial layouts, too. Liz Higgins [a designer in *Teen Vogue*'s art department] worked there at the time, and after she went to *Teen Vogue*, she called to let me know about an opening. I met with her and Aoife, and it was a perfect fit! My job now consists of so many different things. I'm Aoife's assistant, so I handle her flights and expenses—basically, anything she needs. I also design layouts, research typefaces, and coordinate all our interns' schedules.

All in all, my top advice is to follow your passion, but don't pigeonhole yourself. There are a lot of obvious jobs out there that everyone's heard of, but there are also cool careers that you may not know about yet. Marketing wasn't what I wanted to do, but it led me to where I am now."

vamped up

Dark beauty Kristen Stewart **sinks her teeth into a lead role as the unlikely heroine of megahit book turned film** *Twilight.* **Photographed by Alasdair McLellan.**

The first time that Kristen Stewart graced the cover of this magazine, a little more than a year and a half ago, the accompanying article spent a good deal of space detailing how she differed from the typical too-polished sixteen-year-old aspiring starlet. The down-to-earth actress's evident unease with the posh, precious restaurant selected by her publicist to serve as the interview setting—"Oh, it's fancy food," she said lightly, looking utterly out of place amid the ladies who lunched—was presented as being all but emblematic.

So it seems relevant to note that today, when Kristen arrives for a chat at Hollywood's celeb haven Chateau Marmont, she is perturbed only by her own unwilling tardiness. ("Mother of God, I'm less than a mile away and creeping to you," she texted by way of a traffic update.) Dressed in dark, skinny jeans and a T-shirt bearing the black-and-red icon of an indie record label, her thin fingers festooned with rings and her auburn hair shot through with thick streaks of ebony. But this time around, the differences don't seem to translate, for Kristen, to discomfort. At eighteen, she appears completely at ease.

That confidence couldn't come at a better time for the actress: After almost a decade in the business—she was "discovered" at one of her elementary school plays—she has, with this month's *Twilight,* a project that might just prove to be her first bona fide blockbuster. (Her second film, 2002's *Panic Room,* was big, but Jodie Foster's face was on the posters, not Kristen's.) *Twilight* is the hotly anticipated adaptation of author Stephenie Meyer's smash-hit debut novel—all four titles in the now-complete series continue to be best-sellers—but before Kristen got the script, she had never even heard of the books. "I guess I was just living under rocks and mountains," she says cheerfully. "And though we were warned, I figured it would be a pretty exclusive fan base. I thought we were making a cult movie; I had no idea it was going to be this, like, phenomenon."

Then again, perhaps no one accustomed to starring in such independent fare as 2007's *Into the Wild* and *In the Land of Women* can really be prepared to have her merits debated on Internet message boards before she's even shot a frame of film. There was a small contingent of online doubters, but the fact is, Kristen is actually almost improbably perfect to play the part of Bella, a   continued ➤ 172

EASY RIDING
KRISTEN WEARS A RODARTE HAND-KNIT CARDIGAN. RAIN LABEL POCKET T-SHIRT, ABOUT $88. SEQUIN NECKLACE, $85. FOR DETAILS, SEE IN THIS ISSUE.
FASHION EDITOR: HAVANA LAFFITTE.

TEENVOGUE.COM

180 DECEMBER/JANUARY 2009

> "This was my first *Teen Vogue* shoot, as well as the first *Teen Vogue* assignment for photographer Alasdair McLellan. Kristen Stewart was just about to become a superstar in *Twilight*. It was a brave new world for all of us!"

> "Kristen is beautiful, but she's also such a cool, down-to-earth girl. We were originally going to do the shoot on the beach in Malibu, but she seemed right at home in this garden location we found. I think the bike and the fashion styling—including the Rodarte sweater she has on—really reflect her personality."

> "Shooting products—called still life—is a totally different experience than taking pictures of people. In still-life shoots, it's totally up to you (and the photographer and the prop stylist) to make the item look good—you can't direct them as you would a model or a celebrity."

> "For this accessories story shot by photographer Dan Forbes, we wanted each bag to have its own personality with the contents spilling out. With this one, we took ordinary items and made them extraordinary and superhero-esque. We painted the eggs blue and the bananas green—it was like something out of a fantasy. The idea ended up working really well and reflected the bold colors of the bag."

THE MAKING OF A LAYOUT

WASSER BREAKS DOWN HER CREATIVE PROCESS.

★ **CONCEPT:** The idea for a story comes from the fashion and styling. Are we shooting it on location or in a studio? Are the clothes influenced by a certain era? Do we need sunshine and beaches for a summer story, or snow-capped mountains for winter trends?

★ **ASSEMBLING THE TEAM:** Once we decide where we're shooting—such as in a studio or on location—we determine the photographer and stylist. Hair and makeup are next. It's crucial to have a team that will work well together.

★ **EDIT:** After the shoot, we get back all the images—sometimes hundreds of photos at once. The hardest part is trying to narrow down choices.

★ **RETOUCHING:** After we make the edit, the images are sent out to be retouched. We'll remove things like fallen hems, tags, and even passersby in the background. This typically takes about two weeks.

★ **LAYOUT:** While images are being retouched, we play with layouts—borders versus full-bleed (when a photo takes up the entire page), where captions should be placed, what color font to use, what typeface for the title (every story has a unique title). Then we input all the editors' text into the layout.

★ **PREPRESS AND COLOR PROOFING:** After the images are retouched, we have to check that the colors are exactly as the photographer wants them to be.

★ **SEND TO PRINTER:** The last step!

The Closet Keepers
Truc Nguyen & Blake English

TO MAKE IT ONTO A MAGAZINE PAGE, CLOTHES TAKE AN EPIC JOURNEY, FROM PR OFFICES TO FASHION SHOOTS AROUND THE GLOBE. OUR CLOSET ASSISTANTS TRACK THE GARMENTS EVERY STEP OF THE WAY.

The title *fashion assistant* sounds deceptively simple to *Teen Vogue's* Blake English, who works alongside Truc Nguyen in the sought-after position. "We really should have at least a couple more titles added to that," English suggests. Around the office though, the two are most often simply referred to as "the closet girls," because the 500-square-foot fashion closet is both their regular location—their desks are tucked inside amid countless shoes, handbags, and overstuffed clothing racks—and their domain. English and Nguyen (with the help of their small army of interns) are responsible for every single piece of merchandise that comes through the office.

The duo manages this flow of product with an intimidatingly intricate system that they have down to a science. "After each fashion week, we print out all the pictures from the runway shows for the stylists and market editors," English says. "Once they have a concept for a shoot, they look through the printouts to pick out the items they would like to use in the story." Nguyen continues: "Then the stylists e-mail me images of the looks they want, and I have my interns print out pictures and make boards of everything. I use the boards to request the merchandise from PR companies and designers. This can be a balancing act, because you're sharing a limited number of samples with every magazine in the world, not to mention salespeople for the designer, advertising and retail shoots, and trunk shows in stores. And whether you get what you want depends on your relationships with the PR people and whomever you're competing against. We're lucky that our market editors have really good relationships and that our stylists are well known."

And all this is before any of the merchandise even arrives at the office. "When the clothing comes in, we make sure it has labels so that we can identify it later," English says. "I write detailed records of what's what. And because we're responsible for making sure that everything that goes out to shoots comes back, we take pictures, both to identify the pieces and to document their condition. When the clothing comes back, I have to return it to the designers. On shoots abroad, things get even more complicated. There are days when I feel like I work for FedEx!"

Although English and Nguyen are clearly on top of their game, they couldn't do it without their trusty team of interns. So how exactly does one get his or her foot in the fashion-closet door? English says what stands out to her when looking for candidates is a true passion for fashion—retail experience is a plus—and most of all, "We're not impressed by attitude. When people come in here and get ahead of themselves, we tell them to take it down a notch. It's important to be humble and always willing to help." ★

NGUYEN (LEFT) AND ENGLISH, IN *TEEN VOGUE*'S FASHION CLOSET, HAVE A HAND ON ALL OF THE MERCHANDISE THAT COMES THROUGH THE OFFICE FOR SHOOTS.

NGUYEN LOOKS OVER A REQUEST BOARD THAT SHE AND HER INTERNS CREATED WITH PICTURES OF SHOES THEY WILL CALL IN FOR SHOOTS.

8:00 a.m.

TRUC NGUYEN While eating my breakfast at home, I respond to e-mails from press contacts in Europe that came in overnight (they're six hours ahead).

9:00 a.m.

BLAKE ENGLISH I arrive at work and let the interns into the fashion closet. We have up to eight or nine at any given time. As I check the 50 or so new e-mails in my in-box and listen to my voice-mail messages, the interns move the clothing racks from editors' offices (where they're stored at night) into the halls. They label each rack with the name of the fashion story it's for.

TN As soon as I get in the office, I start requesting clothing samples from press offices and designers for photo shoots and following up on outstanding requests.

10:00 a.m.

BE The market editors call me at my desk to check in. Since most of them are out on appointments all day, I'm the point person inside the office, and I more or less have to stay planted at my desk to field incoming e-mails about sample pick-ups, returns, meetings with stylists, and any other instructions from the market team. Good thing I have my interns, so I can delegate.

11:00 a.m.

BE It's time to get going on checking samples into our system and returning old ones back to vendors. This is how my interns and I spend the majority of our day—which sometimes means sending them on investigative searches to track down missing merchandise.

TN I look at layouts in the art department for an upcoming issue of *Teen Vogue,* to see which products made it into the magazine. Then I e-mail the companies that loaned them to us, to request credit information, so that when the issue comes out, our readers will know where to buy everything and how much it costs.

1:30 p.m.

TN I meet with a stylist and her assistant to review her requests for an upcoming fashion story, making note of what she still needs. Next, I check with publicists and editors at other magazines to see if we'll be able to get those items in time for the shoot. Designers often make only one sample of each piece in a collection, so everyone in the industry has to share.

2:30 p.m.

TN The accessories director gives me her request boards—visual aids with printouts of the items she wants for stories she's working on—and I start calling them in.

4:00 p.m.

TN As part of my job, I cover the market for gadgets, T-shirts, and athleticwear. In the afternoons, I conduct "deskside" meetings to see new products, then pitch what I like to a few of the fashion editors for their pages.

5:00 p.m.

BE Things start to slow down as the editors get ready to leave, so I finally have a chance to catch up on filling in PR people on the status of their sample returns, arranging pick-ups for tomorrow through our messenger service, and following up with the interns to make sure they've completed the tasks I've given them.

6:30 p.m.

BE We rush to get the last of our returns down to the messenger center, because they close at 7:00 P.M. sharp! After that, we straighten up the closet—by the end of the day it usually looks like a tornado has hit.

TN Now is a good time to call and e-mail my press contacts in L.A. for updates on sample requests, since they're three hours behind New York and will still be at work.

7:30 p.m.

BE We finish tidying up, filing all the paperwork from everything we've messengered and shipped to showrooms and shoot locations today, then put the clothing racks back in the offices and lock them up for the night.

FLORALS

AN INSPIRATION BOARD A STYLIST MADE TO COMMUNICATE HER VISION FOR A STORY ON FLORALS.

ENGLISH AND AN INTERN TRY ON HEADBANDS WHILE ORGANIZING THE FASHION CLOSET. LEFT: NGUYEN ROUNDS UP T-SHIRTS FOR A SHOOT.

teenVOGUE TIP Keep the attitude to a minimum. It's important to be humble and always willing to help. With English, Nguyen, interns, racks, and accessories all packed into the fashion closet, there's no room for egos!

INTERN TOOL KIT
essential items for interns

BACK ISSUES
Read up! Past issues help you prep for an interview.

INTERVIEW TIPS

★ PREPARE A LIST OF YOUR FAVORITE DESIGNERS, PHOTOGRAPHERS, AND STYLISTS. A COMPREHENSIVE KNOWLEDGE OF THE FIELD DEMONSTRATES YOUR PASSION AND SHOWS THAT YOU'VE DONE RESEARCH.

★ ARRIVE ON TIME AND DRESS TO IMPRESS. YOUR ENSEMBLE SHOULD REFLECT YOUR PERSONAL STYLE AS WELL AS THE POSITION YOU'RE APPLYING FOR.

★ REMEMBER TO ASK SOME QUESTIONS OF YOUR OWN. INQUIRING ABOUT THE DETAILS OF THE JOB INDICATES ENTHUSIASM.

★ SEND A HANDWRITTEN THANK-YOU NOTE—NOT AN E-MAIL—AFTER THE INTERVIEW. IT'S A THOUGHTFUL GESTURE.

MINTS
Pop one before an interview to make the best impression.

METROCARD
The subway is the fastest way to get from point A to point B in New York City.

INTERNSHIP SEARCH TIPS

★ SUSS OUT ANY CONNECTIONS YOU MIGHT HAVE. DO ANY OF YOUR EXTENDED FAMILY MEMBERS OR FRIENDS WORK IN THE BUSINESS? IF SO, THEY MAY BE ABLE TO PASS ALONG YOUR RÉSUMÉ TO SOMEONE WHO NEEDS AN INTERN.

★ WEB SITES LIKE ED2010 AND MEDIABISTRO ARE GOOD RESOURCES WHEN HUNTING FOR AN INTERNSHIP— SCOUR THEM OFTEN FOR UPDATES AND CAREER ADVICE.

★ CONTACT YOUR COLLEGE ALUMNI ORGANIZATION. MANY PEOPLE RECRUIT INTERNS FROM THEIR ALMA MATER, SO ASK AROUND OR BROWSE YOUR UNIVERSITY'S ALUMNI WEB SITE FOR TIPS.

MAP
Navigate unknown streets efficiently.

DATE BOOK
Keep your schedule and all your contacts organized.

FLATS
Pack a pair for midday errands and subway rides.

JANE DOE
95 Jane St., Apt. X
New York, NY 10014
JaneDoe@gmail.com
(555) 555 5555

EDUCATION

The University of North Carolina at Chapel Hill
School of Journalism and Mass Communication
B.A., Journalism/News Editorial sequence, May 2009
Second major, English

Honors Study Abroad: St. Edmund Hall, Oxford, Sum

HONORS

Graduated with honors and highest distinction
Dean's List (all semesters)
National Society of Collegiate Scholars
Dow Jones Newspaper Fund Top Prospect 2007

EXPERIENCE

Blue & White M
EDITOR OF ART
- Conceived i
- Planned iss
  with distrib
- Copy edite

Orlando Sty
INTERN, May
- Wrote pr
- Copy ed
- Maintai
- Conceiv
- Set up

The Daily
STAFF WR
- Wrote
- Wrot
- Inter
- Aide

Blue &
EDITO
- C
- P
  w
- C
STA

December 15, 200X

Jane Doe
95 Jane St., Apt. X
New York, NY 10014
(555) 555-5555

John Smith
Web Editor
Teen Vogue Magazine
4 Times Square, 9th floor
New York, NY 10036

Dear Mr. Smith

I recently heard about the open Web internship thi
Vogue and would like to be considered.

As my resume indicates, I just wrapped up a four-m
internship at Seventeen.com. I wrote content for the
daily updates and assisted with weekly and monthly
versed in HTML and am completely comfortable w
management system.

Given my experience, I would love the opportunity to
your website. I am available to interview at your earl
and look forward to hearing back from you.

Sincerely,

Jane Doe

Elana Fishman, FASHION NEWS INTERN
**AGE 22 COLLEGE NEW YORK UNIVERSITY
HOMETOWN MIAMI BEACH, FLORIDA**

★ **9:00 a.m.** Trip to Starbucks to pick up lattes for my bosses and myself. Working at *Teen Vogue* requires long hours and hard work, so caffeine is a necessity.

★ **10:00 a.m.** At my desk, I check e-mail and read fashion blogs to get the scoop on industry happenings.

★ **11:00 a.m.** I pore through this season's backstage binders—which hold photos of models—to find possible images for the opening page of the Index section. My editor will review the images and select one.

★ **noon** Lunch in the famous Condé Nast cafeteria!

★ **1:00 p.m.** We've begun planning an upcoming room-makeover story, and it's time to line up furniture options. Since the theme is Marie Antoinette, I find inspiration by pulling up online stills from the movie version starring Kirsten Dunst.

★ **2:00 p.m.** Do research in the Condé Nast library for a House of Style feature.

★ **3:00 p.m.** The art department informs me of a last-minute layout change for a Model Scout story I wrote—we're going with a different runway photo. So I submit new caption options to the editors.

★ **3:45 p.m.** I hop on the uptown train to meet a high school junior, a contender for the Room of My Own page.

★ **5:00 p.m.** Ideas for *Teen Vogue*'s biannual A to Z guide are due tomorrow, so I brainstorm at my desk.

★ **6:00 p.m.** Print out answers to interview questions from the British college student I'm profiling for the Snapshot page. Later this week, Jane Keltner and Amy Astley will edit my copy.

RÉSUMÉ AND COVER LETTER TIPS

★ MAKE YOUR RÉSUMÉ AND COVER LETTER SUCCINCT. ONE PAGE WILL SUFFICE FOR AN ENTRY-LEVEL RÉSUMÉ; THREE PARAGRAPHS FOR A COVER LETTER.

★ STEER CLEAR OF SILLY STUNTS. SCENTED RÉSUMÉS MAY WORK IN MOVIES LIKE *LEGALLY BLONDE,* BUT IN THE REAL WORLD YOURS SHOULD BE CLEAN AND SIMPLE, TYPED IN A FONT BETWEEN TEN AND FOURTEEN POINTS, AND PRINTED ON PLAIN PAPER.

★ ADDRESS EACH COVER LETTER TO A SPECIFIC PERSON, NOT "TO WHOM IT MAY CONCERN." TO DO SO, CHECK THE MASTHEAD OF THE MAGAZINE OR CONDUCT SOME ONLINE RESEARCH.

The Washington Post

STYLE & ARTS

ROBIN GIVHAN

For American Designers, an Obama Endorsement W[...]

A Role That Nicely Suits the Next First Lady

Fashion Designers Hope to Stitch Up an Obama Win

Fashion

[...]don,
Your Slips
Are Showing

'Project Runway' Hopefuls Get a Wobbly
Foot in the Door, on an Unforgiving Stage

They're Going, [...]

As Industry Demands Thinner M[...]

By ROBIN GIVHAN
Washington Post Staff Writer

keeping dang[...]
haps [...]

If anyone ever needed [...]

[...]BIN GIVHAN
[...]on Post Staff Writer

[...]he Bravo television series "Project Runway"
[...]taped its finale Friday morning under the tents
of Bryant Park, the same place where
established designers such as Oscar de la
Renta, Carolina Herrera, Bill Blass's Michael
Vera Wang and "Project Runway" judge
[...]l Kors had debuted their spring 2007 collections
earlier in the week. While the other shows had attracted
celebrities on the order of Usher and Janet Jackson [...]
"Project Runway" audience was treat[...]
Austin Scarlett (from [...]

NEW YORK

Runway Romp

ith Bold Color and Vibrant Detail. Designers Put Spring in Their

SUN

most uninspired or unattractive ones — have something to say.

Indeed, the romper masquerading as a suit and the strapless tops with faux sleeves wrapping around the torso that were part of the Max Mara spring 2008 collection say something profoundly distressing about common sense and good taste.

The more impressive fe...

rare acc...
The colle...
Sander a...
r and se...

Be Fitting

from wildly
w. The designers Stefan
Domenico Dolce presented
collection Thursday afternoon and
how began hinted at what was
itors hanging just abo
could see

The Critical Eye

Robin Givhan

Viva la Difference

What Happens in Paris,
Stays in Paris.
What a Pity.

By ROBIN GIVHAN
Washington Post Staff Writer

PARIS, Oct. 3

t Tuesday morning's runway presentation by Balenciaga, the models balanced atop ...

Simply Pretty & Pretty Ugly

In Milan, Designers
Draw Fine Lines, or
Need an Eraser

By ROBIN GIVHAN
Washington Post Staff Writer

MILAN, Feb. 21

pital of Italian
n typically is cele-
d for its most flam-
t design houses,
ce, Gucci and Dol-
Gabbana, which
been lionized in
ranging from dis-
designers here un-
, it has been those
es of gray or who
hoods in the drape
offered the most to.

cessful was Raf Si-
his women's collec-
n Tuesday. The
e and mesmerizing
e presentation was
controlled, focused,
complexity that be
design and austere
and femininity. Si-
et of brush strokes
evoke luxury, confi-

ng . . . Gaunt

ls, Health Policy Rings Hollow

e send out a seem-
arrow navy trousers
ting ribbed sweater
g the beauty of it
ork so much more
trousers and sweater
a quarter of the
The difference
bric. Even a
heen and
details

ployes - nationwide campaign

FOR THIS FASHION WRITER, THE BEST STORIES ARE FOUND WHERE CLOTHES AND POP CULTURE MEET.

In high school, Robin Givhan says, her interest in fashion was pretty much limited to a typical Midwestern teenager's willingness to loiter at the local mall. "You know," she explains, "it was what you did." She didn't subscribe to fashion magazines and could be "completely content," even in college, with a dress purchased for her by her mother and received via the Princeton post office. "I wasn't picky. I wasn't too focused on personal style and all of that."

Today Givhan is paid to focus on "all of that" by *The Washington Post,* where she's a Pulitzer Prize–winning fashion critic (the first such writer ever to win the honor). But she still considers herself "a journalist who writes about fashion, as opposed to a 'fashion person.' I'm someone who gets to be in the room but is still kind of standing against the wall, watching. And I like that perspective," she says. "I think that if you're writing about the fashion industry for a newspaper, it's important to maintain a degree of skepticism."

Did you want to be a newspaper reporter from a young age?
When I was growing up, in Detroit, I had 5 million different things I wanted to do. In college I started out premed, taking English classes just to round out my schedule, but somewhere along the way I realized that I loved English a lot more than chemistry. Then I went through a whole series of ideas: Maybe I would open an art gallery or go into business. I applied to law school, but my mother suggested that I go to graduate school for English or journalism instead, and a lightbulb went off in my head: Oh, that's an interesting idea!

Had you worked on the school newspaper?
I did in high school but not in college. But I always loved writing. I used to compose short stories and enter essay contests. I was one of those kids who was glad if a test had essay questions, because I knew I would be able to ace it.

So where did you go to journalism school?
At the University of Michigan. I chose it because, at the time, you were essentially guaranteed that one year of the two-year program would be spent at internships—which, in newspapers, is crucial. When students ask me what they can do to improve their job prospects, I always tell them to write as much as they possibly can. Even if your heart's desire is to cover politics or fashion, but the only writing job you can get is covering the city council, then go cover the city council. The key is to improve your writing and reporting skills. I did internships at the *St. Petersburg Times,* in Florida, and at *The Detroit News;* both were on the city desk.

What kinds of stories were you writing at that point?
I remember going out on

a lot of cop calls. In Detroit, I was in one of the suburban bureaus for a while, and it was part of my job to call the police stations in all of these tiny communities every morning and ask, "Any interesting crimes happen overnight?" It was educational in the sense that I got to see the way a newspaper functioned, and I became comfortable with interviewing all kinds of people and asking difficult questions, but these were not major stories. They were the newspaper equivalent of having to spend the afternoon steaming clothes.

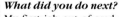
MICHELLE OBAMA AT AN INAUGURAL BALL.

What did you do next?
My first job out of grad school was a general assignment position for the entertainment section of the *Detroit Free Press.* I was thrilled because I wanted to be a features writer, and the *Free Press* was the newspaper that my parents read and that I had read growing up. I wrote a lot of second-tier film reviews there—ones that the main critic didn't want to do. After about a year, I started looking for a new beat, and it just so happened that the fashion editor became a features columnist, and I thought, Fashion. I wear clothes. I can do that. I applied for the job, and although they ended up hiring someone who had actual fashion experience, they did ask me to cover menswear. After three years of that, I got bored with Michigan and moved out to San Francisco to be a general features writer at the *Chronicle.* But nine months later I got a call from the fashion editor at the *Free Press.* She said they needed someone to take over her job and asked if I was interested. And I was. So I went back to Detroit. Three years later I came to the *Post.*

Did The Washington Post *call you? Or were you just once again sick of Michigan?*
I had heard that they were looking for a new fashion editor, but I thought they would want an insider, someone from, say, *Women's Wear Daily,* so I wasn't even going to apply. But a friend said, "You should. It will be a good exercise." And I thought, Okay, I could use a little exercise. So I called them. I sent off my résumé and clips and heard nothing for weeks, and then I finally got a call asking, essentially, for a game plan on how I would cover fashion if I had the job.

Was that game plan very different from the way you were then covering fashion in Detroit?

"JASON WU'S *dress* BARES *Obama's* ARMS AND SHOULDERS AND *brings the* FIRST LADY INTO *the modern* ERA, IN WHICH *glamour* IS *defined* BY HOLLYWOOD AND THE *red carpet* RATHER THAN PROTOCOL AND *tradition.*"
—ROBIN GIVHAN
(THE WASHINGTON POST, JANUARY 21, 2009)

Yes. Part of what was frustrating me in Detroit was that they mainly wanted consumer-driven, how-to-buy-a-sweater type of coverage. I wanted to write about fashion as part of popular culture and a vital industry. It's not just about the clothes.

When you started working at the Post, were you able to do that?
Well, my very first piece for the *Post* was about Batman paraphernalia, so not quite. My friend Teri Agins from *The Wall Street Journal* called and said, "Well, it's good just to get in the paper." My first story of any length was about a rash of sweatshop raids and how we're all culpable in creating that situation, which was more the kind of writing I had hoped to do.

How has your writing changed over the years?
Politics is an element that has increasingly fascinated me—the whole idea of that culture being so attuned to public presentation and, at the same time, denying an interest in fashion. I'm trying to get people to understand that you don't have to care at all about Gucci or Prada. Because every time you get up in the morning and decide what you're going to wear that day, that is, essentially, fashion. Everybody is affected by it.

Do you feel like that's very different from the way most fashion writers cover the industry?
I don't know that I go against the grain so much as that I've been given a greater degree of leeway to explore that. But I think most fashion writers do think deeply about their story ideas. It's very hard to write about a Marc

Jacobs show without referencing the visual arts; it's difficult to cover Prada without thinking about gender issues. It's really sad when people dismiss fashion as frivolous. I think some of that attitude stems from the way the industry presents itself, and some of it has to do with the way the industry is covered. A lot of times when budgets are tight, the only kind of fashion coverage you'll get in a newspaper is an article about what Penélope Cruz wore to the Oscars, and that's such a tiny part of it.

You won the Pulitzer Prize for Criticism in 2006, and you were the first fashion writer ever to do so. That must have been thrilling.
The most gratifying part of it all was getting notes from colleagues who write about fashion at other publications. They offered their congratulations and were incredibly supportive, and they also said that they felt as if their own roles had been elevated to a degree, because the award signified that fashion can be covered seriously.

Did winning a Pulitzer allow you to alter the subject matter or scope of your articles?
My column runs on Sundays now, and I can write about basically anything in the world of culture and arts, like political campaigns, race, and television, as well as fashion. Mostly it's been a recognition that any beat, honestly, is what you make of it. Many people disregard fashion as not being a priority, but I'd like to think that I've helped people see that everything—including fashion—is part of the broader world, and if you can make those connections, it can be relevant. ★

GIVHAN WITH COLUMBIA UNIVERSITY PRESIDENT, LEE C. BOLLINGER, WHO PRESENTED HER WITH THE 2006 PULITZER FOR CRITICISM.

teen VOGUE TIP "To improve your job prospects, write as much as you possibly can. Even if your heart's desire is to cover fashion, but the only writing job you can get is covering the city council, then go cover the city council." —ROBIN GIVHAN

The Cyber Pioneer
Natalie Massenet

THIS EDITOR BRIDGED HER LOVE OF TECHNOLOGY WITH A PASSION FOR FASHION TO CREATE NET-A-PORTER, THE ULTIMATE ONLINE LUXURY SHOPPING SITE.

In 2000, at the height of her career as a fashion editor (working for both American and British publications, from *W* and *Women's Wear Daily* to *Tatler* and *The Sunday Times* style section), Natalie Massenet risked everything to take a career leap into cyberspace. "I saw luxury online shopping as an amazing opportunity, but no one was listening," she explains. "So I did it myself. If no one else would do it, I would." Today Massenet remains the chairman and founder of the London-based luxury fashion retailer Net-a-Porter, an online store and magazine with global reach that has doubled its business each year since its launch.

When did you first become interested in fashion?
I lived in Paris until I was eleven because my mother was a model for Chanel. She used to dress me in extraordinary designer clothes made by her friends. All I wanted, though, was to fit in and wear the same shoes that my schoolmates wore! When I was eleven, I moved to Los Angeles with my dad. But I would visit my mother in Paris each summer and come back with cute clothes that were about a year ahead of what everybody was wearing in California. I realized that, as well as blending in, you could assert individuality through fashion. In college, I

liked the idea of starting trends that others would follow.

How vital has your education been to you throughout your career?
I studied English literature and Japanese at the University of California, Los Angeles, because I thought it would be very important to be able to communicate. Especially today, when the majority of communication in the professional world is through writing e-mail. There's nothing more off-putting than a piece of writing that is misspelled or grammatically incorrect.

What did you do before starting Net-a-Porter?
Living in Los Angeles, I fell in love with the movie business. After college, I got my first job in the film industry, but I still loved fashion. I was always the one in my group who would be asked, "What are they wearing in Paris? What are the trends?" A friend of mine opened the L.A. bureau for an Italian magazine called *Moda,* to do celebrity shoots, and she hired me because she knew I loved films *and* fashion. I couldn't believe that I was getting paid to do something that was so fun. I worked there for about three years and did

MASSENET, PHOTOGRAPHED IN MANHATTAN, CONSIDERS AUDREY HEPBURN, LAUREN HUTTON, AND KATE MOSS TO BE HER STYLE ICONS.

"WE'RE ALWAYS ON THE LOOKOUT FOR THE NEXT BIG THING. HERE, I'M BACKSTAGE AT THE 2007 FASHION FRINGE [A DESIGN COMPETITION IN THE U.K.] WITH AMINAKA WILMONT, THE DESIGN DUO THAT WENT ON TO WIN THE COMPETITION THAT YEAR!"

everything from styling shoots to scouting locations. Then I answered a want ad to be the West Coast fashion editor of WWD, and I got the job. I covered local L.A. fashion and did all the writing, styling, and celebrity shoots for W magazine [WWD's sister publication]. After WWD, I moved to London and worked at Tatler, in both the features and the fashion departments as a senior editor, doing front-of-book editorial and producing and styling shoots.

What was your first experience with the Internet?

At Tatler, we had one computer for the entire editorial department, and nobody really knew what to do with it. When it came to the Internet, people would be like, "What is that?" I was working for the late Isabella Blow at the time. We were discussing Edwardian fashion and I didn't know what she was talking about. My husband brought home his laptop that night and I typed "Edwardian" into Yahoo.com. All of a sudden, from my sofa in London, I was seeing these Web sites from all over the world about fashion and the arts-and-crafts movement. For the next four months, I was on that laptop every single day from 8:00 A.M. to 10:00 P.M. I could not believe what was going on! And I realized that there was an opportunity there.

How did you create Net-a-Porter?

I've always believed that the Internet was going to be the place to shop. I thought, If I want to shop for desirable clothing online, there must be other women who want to do it too. I wanted to form an Internet fashion magazine that took my love of visuals, telling stories, and breaking fashion news and combine it with the amazing ability to click and buy something.

Do you have any role models in your business and personal life?

I've always looked toward women leaders in the business. Anna Wintour has always stuck out to me for representing fashion in Vogue as both a dream and yet understanding that women need to be able to actually wear the clothes. She balances creativity and commercialism very well. I was also very influenced by Rose Marie Bravo, who was the CEO of Burberry until 2005. She really showed that you can run a business and still be soft-spoken and thoughtful about your approach. And finally, on a personal level, my father taught me never to be afraid of what's on the other side of the mountain and that nothing is a risk, everything is possible, and to believe in magic. ★

NET-A-PORTER.COM

Massenet's site fuses fashion show coverage with click-to-buy convenience.

"SOMETIMES IN YOUR *career,* YOU JUST HAVE TO *jump in.* YOU'LL LEARN TO *swim!*"
—NATALIE MASSENET

"NET-A-PORTER IS A MAGAZINE FOR THE TWENTY-FIRST CENTURY," SAYS MASSENET, WHO OVERSEES THE EDITORIAL CONTENT ON THE SITE.

TEENVOGUE TIP "With each job you have, you'll learn a skill to use for your next job. Every experience in your life goes on to shape who you are. Nothing is wasted." —NATALIE MASSENET

The Rebel Editor
Claudia Wu

PAVING HER OWN WAY IN THE MEDIA WORLD, THIS GRAPHIC DESIGNER CREATED A MAGAZINE THAT EXPLORES THE PRIVATE WORLDS OF ARTISTS, MUSICIANS, AND DESIGNERS UP CLOSE AND PERSONAL.

"When I graduated from the Rhode Island School of Design in Providence, the only type of career I *didn't* want was one in the magazine industry. I thought it would be monotonous to do the same thing every month. But after working at a few magazines—including *Harper's Bazaar, V,* and *Visionaire*—I found that whenever I was freelancing at an ad agency or at the in-house art department of Prada Beauty, I actually missed the magazines—there's a sense of community and you're exposed to new ideas constantly. They open you up to the world.

I majored in graphic design, and I applied for my first job, at *Visionaire,* because a friend told me he had heard the magazine was hiring 'like, ten designers.' So I went for an interview. The process there was pretty much like any interview I've been on since. I walked the interviewer through my portfolio, which contained all the work I had done up to that point: just a few months at a small design studio in New York City, plus what I'd done in school, which was more conceptual. Then my interviewer described the work they do, the position they were looking to fill, what the responsibilities would be, and how they run their office. That was it! I went home after that

and waited for a call. I got the job the following week.

Visionaire's offices are completely open and the staff is small, so I got to see how magazines are put together. It was a great experience—that's where I learned how to run my own magazine. And, of course, fashion is very much a part of what *Visionaire* does, so that has stayed with me as well. In high school I was definitely interested in fashion. I grew up in a suburb of New York City, but I read *Vogue* and went to Manhattan to shop. I would wear baby-doll dresses with green tights and Doc Martens. Now I realize that fashion is an integral part of everyone's life: No matter what, you have to get dressed in the morning.

I started my own magazine, called *Me Magazine,* in 2004. I wanted to be the one making all the decisions, and the idea of not having to answer to anyone was very appealing. I find it so satisfying to be able to do something from start to finish and have it be mine. The concept for *Me* is that each issue focuses in-depth on the life of one person. I feel that other magazines' one- or two-page interviews allow you to get only a small sense of who a person is. What I do is interview my subjects, but I also interview, or have them interview, their friends and family as well. They're not

"THE HARDEST PART OF MY JOB," WU SAYS, HERE IN HER NEW YORK CITY OFFICE, "IS FINDING TIME TO DO IT ALL."

Me Magazine #2 Winter 2004

Meet
Miho Aoki

and her friends
Rusty Santos
Justine D.
Sidney Prawatyotin
Vito Acconci
Mira Billotte
assume vivid astro focus
Ju Kim
Susan Cianciolo
Benjamin Liu
Rosalie Knox
Dave Portner
Tracy Nakayama
John Minh Nguyen
on Birch

CAN $6.50

Me Magazine #9 Autumn 2006

H
Nel

Me MAGAZINE #5 AUTUMN 2005

Arts

Mirabelle Marden
Melissa Bent
and
Darren Bader
Mathew Cerletty
Daniel Colen
Philippa Craze
Max Fasego
John Emmerip
Jacob Hodes
Erick Johnson
Hanna Liden
Melissa Marden
Annabel Mehran
Peter Miles

ME MAGAZINE #14 SPRING 2008

AUTUMN DE WILDE
JOHNSON HARTIG
CECILIA DEAN
M GORDON
RANDA JULY
URLEY KURATA
O ROCHA
A LOVE
E MILLS
RISTINE SUPPES
ANOR FRIEDBERGER
VON TEESE
LÁS HENDERSON
ALL HASTINGS
Y LEWIS
KALIARDOS
ELSON
LEE BITTON
AGUILAR
THAN RICE

nako on

Hab
Nicole &

RODARTE

ME MAGAZINE #12 SUMMER 2007

FEATURING:
ALANNA HESS
PATTERSON BECKWITH
MICHAEL J. BULLOCK JR.
GLORIA MAXIMO
RESTON FREY
IM NAKOYAMA
TTY ROTTEN COTTON
OM BURGESE
EAN MCKINNON
ZA MUNTOYA
VALE
LIE KNOX

keren ann

hardi johannsson · sean gullette · francoise hardy
ishai cohen · nicole renard · tom merae
Melton · jason hart

ME MAGAZINE #7 SPRING 2006

WHO ARE THESE KIDS
AND WHY ARE THEY CALLING ME MOM ?

NICKY ARROW
SARAH CLEN
RON KULLER
JESSICA CRAIG S
CLAUDIA DOLOTTY
AVHA FOX-LE
DAN & GARY SH
KANA GOTOA
MATHEW HIGGS
HANNA LIDEN
BILL & CAROLYN L
MICHELE MACCAG
ADAM MCEWEN
DAVID RIMANELL
TARA SUBKOFF
BLAKE TAYLOR
NEVILLE WAK
AARON YOUNG

just subjects—they're the guest editors of the whole issue. I feature people I'm interested in personally, including designers Thakoon Panichgul and Kate and Laura Mulleavy of Rodarte, as well as artists, actors, and musicians like Keren Ann. Once I even featured a movie, *Half Nelson*. And every issue is different; sometimes the guest editors do it all on their own, and sometimes they want a lot of help.

For the first year and a half, the expense of making a magazine was huge. I didn't have investors; instead, I just worked a lot of freelance gigs. I basically didn't have a life! Nowadays I still work all the time, but it has gotten a lot easier. I realized that in order to grow, I needed help. Until very recently, it was just me who worked—or at least tried to—on everything, along with the issue's guest editor and photographer, who shoots the whole thing whenever possible. (Most magazines use a mix of photographers; I like that, at *Me,* one photographer gets to know the subject intimately.) In addition, I was also selling the ads in the magazine, but, to be honest, I'm a horrible salesperson. So a sponsorship and advertising director, John Scalise, joined me. And because we've grown so much, we now have an editor at large, a fashion editor, and a Web site director. My goal is not necessarily to make a profit but to at least have the magazine pay for itself.

As with any career, there are things about it I love and don't love. The least glamorous part of my job is probably standing in line at the post office—though it gets me out of the office and away from my computer! And the most glamorous part is when everything is finished and we celebrate the issue at launch parties. It's always nice to spend more time with the people featured. I so enjoy learning about these different personalities and finding out how they see themselves, how they got to where they are, and what they see themselves doing in the future. Good design is important in everyday life, and I love that I am able to make things beautiful and more appealing through design. My magazine incorporates design, but it also has a voice. And I like that what I'm creating is something that you can just pick up; you don't need any background knowledge to appreciate it. A magazine has its own life, and I hope *Me* will be around for years." ★

ME MAGAZINE GIVES ITS READERS AN INSIDER'S POINT OF VIEW, FROM DESIGNERS TO MUSIC.

WU'S DAILY SCHEDULE

★ **8:30 a.m.**
Wake up. Turn on the news.

★ **9:00 a.m.**
Power up my laptop, answer e-mails, check the weather, watch more news, and update my iPhone so that I can listen to podcasts on the way to work.

★ **10:30 a.m.**
Head to the office (sometimes I end up working from home, though), make a stop at the bank or the post office to mail out magazines, and listen to BBC and NPR in the car.

★ **11:30 a.m.**
Arrive at the office, meet with my partner at Orphan (my ad agency) about ongoing and upcoming projects, and then answer more e-mails.

★ **noon–3:00 p.m.**
Get to work! Also, attend meetings.

★ **3:00 p.m.**
Take a break and have a snack.

★ **3:30–8:00 p.m.**
Continue working and attend more meetings.

★ **9:00 p.m.**
Head home, or go to an art opening when I'm not too tired.

★ **10:00 p.m.**
Eat dinner at home or with friends.

★ **11:00 p.m.–midnight**
Finish up any leftover work from the day, watch TV, play with my cat (if she's in the mood), and relax.

★ **midnight–12:30 a.m.**
Get ready for bed.

★ **1:00 a.m.**
Bedtime!

*teen*VOGUE TIP "Make a magazine with your friends. And learn both sides of the business—financial and creative. The creative side was easy for me, but the business side was trial and error." —CLAUDIA WU

The Fashion Blogger

Natalie Hormilla

A FIERCE—AND FAST—EYE FOR FASHION HELPS THIS YOUNG BLOGGER KEEP HER WEB SITE UP-TO-THE-MINUTE.

EYE-CANDY COLLAGES THAT ARE
EQUAL PARTS INSIDER AND IRREVERENT,
JUST LIKE THE SITE'S EDITOR IN
CHIEF, ARE A HALLMARK OF THE
FASHIONISTA.COM AESTHETIC.

Fashion trivia

Which model played in band called Plastic Has Memory

???

Fashion

Which aptly named model wishes she were named Ashley

"...AND ACTION

Which model can call Gerard Depardi a co-star?

trivia

fashion trivia

P.S. we know the dress isn't

Lanvin blue - it's just too pretty!

WHO: Karlie

WHERE: Church &

WEARING: French + Riding

DRESSED LIST

TEENVOGUE TIP "If you want to be a fashion blogger, what's stopping you? You can start your own blog tomorrow! Post the things—clothing, culture, whatever—that you wish you could see on other sites." —NATALIE HORMILLA

Ask Natalie Hormilla, the 24-year-old editor of style site Fashionista.com, when exactly it became clear to her that she wanted to write about fashion for a living, and she'll answer cheerfully, "I never really knew. I guess I've always just kind of gone with the flow."

Which isn't to say that Hormilla doesn't absolutely love her job. She does. She has been interested in fashion since she was a little girl—she fondly recalls fighting with her mother about what to wear to kindergarten ("I had a white sweatshirt with red hearts on it that I wanted to wear all the time")—and she always liked reading magazines. "But it never struck me," she admits, "that there were people who actually *worked at* these magazines, who showed up every day to put them out." It wasn't until Hormilla attended an on-campus internship fair during her first year at the Eugene Lang College the New School for Liberal Arts in New York City that she met *Teen Vogue's* then–beauty assistant, Holly Siegel, and figured it all out. Hormilla decided then and there that she wanted an internship. "I was so lucky she was at the job fair," Hormilla says of Siegel. "Because that's where it all started."

Hormilla's internships included a summer in *Teen Vogue's* health and beauty department (where she asked so many questions about how things worked that her supervisors suggested she start e-mailing them) and another in beauty at *Vogue;* by the end of her third internship, in the beauty department of *Women's Wear Daily,* she knew, she says, "everything that you could ever want to know about every beauty product ever." After graduation, she temped for a while and then applied for—and landed—the assistant editor post at Fashionista. She was not necessarily looking for something in fashion—or something online—she explains, but she "really appreciated how smart and critical the site was. I took an edit test, had my interview, and a week later got the job."

Less than two months after Hormilla started, though, the site's top editor quit, which left Hormilla in charge of the whole operation and caused her to have what she calls a mini heart attack. "I thought, How am I going to run this site? Nobody knows me. No one is going to give me any tips." But at the same time, she says, she sensed that "it was a huge opportunity and I had to step up."

And today she unquestionably has. Not only has the site's traffic continued to grow during her tenure as editor in chief, but Hormilla genuinely adores the feeling she gets from helming a favorite Internet destination of the fashion set. "I love that we're first to put out a lot of information and that so many people read the site," she says. "There are times when I do a 'Buy, Buy, Baby' [a section recommending fashion items] about something I think is cool, and by the end of the day it's sold out. That's amazing." ★

Editor's note: As this book was going to press in April 2009, Natalie Hormilla left Fashionista.com to pursue a freelance career.

HORMILLA'S DAILY SCHEDULE

★ *Every morning I wake up at 7:00 a.m.,* and the first thing I do is check my e-mail and my story list, which usually has ideas for that day—for example, a tip I got at a party, or a sample sale already marked on my calendar. We try to post fourteen stories a day, and on some days—the hard ones—I start with nothing.

★ I go online and read *British Vogue,* Business Wire, Fashionologie, PR Newswire, *The New York Times,* and *Women's Wear Daily.* If I come across a really important piece of information, I'll stop everything and put it up right away. *But no matter what, I try to have the first post up by 9:00 a.m.*

★ I also do what I call a market roll, which is like a blog roll but with clothing sites. I go on about a zillion of them a day: Net-a-Porter, Banana Republic, Shopbop, J. Crew. I like to see what's new and what's on sale, and *I look for things I can tell our readers about.* I try to get a few more posts done, and then I walk to the office.

★ *Even though I don't get in until 11:00 a.m., by then I've already been working for hours.* If there's nothing going on, I'll send an intern out to shoot street fashion so that we have something to post, and that's how the day continues. I write, assign, and edit stories and build graphics in Photoshop. Plus, there are lots of miscellaneous tasks. For instance, if I'm trying to set up an interview with a designer or get tickets to a fashion show, there's a lot of e-mailing back and forth.

★ *The last post of the day usually goes up by 5:00 p.m.,* and then I go home. If there's a party, I change my clothes and head out. During fashion week, I take my laptop to shows and try to blog between them at Starbucks. Our target readers work in fashion, so we don't have to tell them what the clothes look like—they can see them on Style.com. Instead, we try to provide experiential coverage, to let readers know what it's like to be there.

The Ultimate Fashion Editor
Anna Wintour

VOGUE'S EDITOR IN CHIEF NOT ONLY RUNS AN INTERNATIONALLY INFLUENTIAL MAGAZINE, SHE ALSO SUPPORTS YOUNG DESIGNERS THROUGH A FASHION FUND AND RAISES MONEY FOR CHARITY.

Anna Wintour is so renowned in the world of fashion—and, for that matter, in the world at large—that she scarcely needs an introduction. In the 21 years that she has been the editor in chief of American *Vogue,* Wintour has kept the magazine firmly at the forefront of fashion, matched numerous young designers with venerable brands in need of fresh expertise, and engineered and overseen the launches of *Teen Vogue* and *Men's Vogue.* "Fashion reflects the times just as much as a headline in a newspaper does," she says. "If you look at the miniskirts of the sixties or the Chanel suits and jewelry of the eighties, you can see that. *Vogue* informs the reader about what's going on in the world, not only through fashion but also through politics, the arts, philanthropy, and sports. Fashion does not exist in a vacuum."

How did you first become interested in fashion?
My father was a newspaper editor, so I was surrounded by journalists my entire life. I think the fact that he was so well known may be why I chose to go into magazines and move to the States at a young age. Everywhere I went [in England], I was being asked if I was Charles Wintour's daughter. But

I wanted to make it on my own. I moved to New York in the late seventies, after having worked for five years on a magazine in London, which was fantastic training because the staffs are smaller and you learn all aspects of the business. By the time I came to the States, I really understood how a magazine works. I came to *Vogue* as creative director, and three years later I went back to London to be editor in chief of British *Vogue.* I returned to the U.S. to work, very briefly, as editor in chief at *House & Garden,* and then I came to *Vogue.*

Describe your typical day.
There is no typical day. Every day is different, and that's why it's fun. Many things are routine—deadlines, certain meetings—but you never really know what's going to happen.

How involved are you with the photos and articles that appear on each page of the magazine?
I'm very good at delegating—people work much better when they have a real sense of responsibility. But at the same time, I don't like surprises. I don't pore over every shoot, but I do like to be aware at all times of what's going on.

WINTOUR IN HER USUAL
FRONT-ROW PERCH—
HERE AT VERA WANG.

"Create YOUR OWN INDIVIDUAL *style*. I'M NOT *interested* IN *the girl* WHO WALKS INTO MY OFFICE IN A *head-to-toe label* LOOK THAT'S STRAIGHT OFF THE *runway*. I'M *interested* IN A GIRL WHO PUTS HERSELF *together* IN AN *original,* INDEPENDENT *way*."

—ANNA WINTOUR

From fashion shows to movie premieres, Wintour attends hundreds of events each year.

IN CHANEL, WITH KARL LAGERFELD, AT AN AWARDS CEREMONY.

WITH KATE BOSWORTH AT A THAKOON SHOW.

SPORTING HER SIGNATURE SUNGLASSES AT THE *VOGUE* OFFICES IN 1993.

WITH KEIRA KNIGHTLEY AT A SCREENING, LEFT. IN CHANEL HAUTE COUTURE AT THE COSTUME INSTITUTE GALA, A BENEFIT SHE HELMS, RIGHT.

IN 1988, WINTOUR PIONEERED THE NOW-COMMON HIGH-LOW MIX WITH THIS PETER LINDBERGH IMAGE OF MODEL MICHAELA IN A COUTURE CHRISTIAN LACROIX JACKET WITH JEANS.

VOGUE

NOVEMBER $3.00

the real cost of looking good

paris couture
haute but not haughty

men
the new bimbos?

fashion
color catches on

still fail. If you have the basic building blocks behind you, you're much more likely to do well.

When you're hiring someone for an entry-level position at* Vogue, *what do you look for?

I look for someone who has actually *read* the magazine. People will say, "Oh, I love *Vogue,*" but when I ask them to tell me something specific they liked, or a photographer whose work they enjoy, they look at me as if I'm crazy. Do your homework, go online, visit every museum, and intern. I like having young assistants in my office; they have energy, and I spend time with them to make sure they understand what we're doing. By investing in them, I'm investing in the magazine. All over *Vogue, Teen Vogue,* and *Men's Vogue,* there are people who have been through not only my office but also many other offices at *Vogue.*

Is there a "wrong" thing to wear to an interview with you?

A suit, I have to say. But who knows? Maybe next year I'll love suits. And I don't mind jeans. If there's a girl

What advice do you have for a young person who is interested in fashion design?

Don't go too fast. Because of reality television and all these celebrities thinking they can be designers, everyone imagines that they can just become a designer, photographer, or model, but that's not the way things work. People have to go to school, learn their craft, and build a brand—that's the right, healthy way to do things. If you're an overnight sensation, you can be yesterday's news in no time, whereas building something slowly and carefully that has value and quality, that's what's going to have legs. You'd be amazed at how many people come in here, and they make perfectly nice clothes, but they don't understand how to differentiate their brand from another, or they don't have a business plan, or they don't know where to produce things. Don't run before you can crawl. It's a very hard business, full of many, many extremely creative, talented people who work hard and

applying to work in the fashion department and she comes in here with a great pair of jeans pulled together with the right top, it's fine.

You've been very involved with the Costume Institute at the Metropolitan Museum of Art and with 7th on Sale, which benefits AIDS-related charities.

The Costume Institute event is an evening unlike any other. It's not just fashion or Hollywood, but people from society, politics, theater, and the museum coming together. We're proud of the money we've been able to raise for the museum and of the very diverse exhibitions that we've put on. They're really among the most popular exhibitions at the Met, and people come from all over the world to see them. In regard to 7th on Sale, our industry was hit hard by AIDS, and that's why we were the first to step up and take it on at a time when a lot of people were still very frightened. The

THE EDITOR, PHOTOGRAPHED AT HER *VOGUE* OFFICE.

WITH HER DAUGHTER, *TEEN VOGUE* CONTRIBUTOR BEE SHAFFER, AT A JOHN GALLIANO SHOW.

fashion community is very generous, and we were incredibly moved by the loss of so many of our members—both high-profile and less well-known—and that's why we all wanted to support the cause.

The CFDA/Vogue *Fashion Fund provides support to three up-and-coming designers each year. How did it come about?*
After September 11, 2001, when fashion week in New York was canceled and the designers lost their deposits on venues and a lot of their money, we decided to do something to support young American talent. We put on a show at Carolina Herrera's showroom and invited the ten young designers we thought were most promising. Through our discussions with them, we realized how hand-to-mouth their existences could be, and that's when we started the CFDA/*Vogue* Fashion Fund. The finalists all say that it's great exposure and it's helpful to get the money if they win, but what's really fantastic is that it

brings them into contact with so many people they wouldn't normally meet or have the opportunity to talk to. The mentorship is extremely important, and we make a point of keeping in touch with all our finalists to see how they're doing. We're very, very proud of the fund. It's something that the whole industry has gotten behind, and unlike many other initiatives—which I think are more about exploiting young talent—this is really about nurturing and developing it.

Is there anything else you've learned that you'd like to pass on?
You just need to have a love for what you're doing. It's not about thinking that it's the cool thing; it's about really believing in it. I was brought up to believe absolutely in the importance of journalism and communication and to have a real love for the printed word. I have so much respect for all the talented people I work with because they're the best in their field and they care about what they do. ★

teenVOGUE TIP "Do your homework, go online, visit every museum, and intern. You just need to have a love for what you're doing. It's not about thinking that it's the cool thing; it's about really believing in it." —ANNA WINTOUR

EDITOR TOOL KIT

essential items of the pros

RECORDER
Essential for interviewing celebrities and designers.

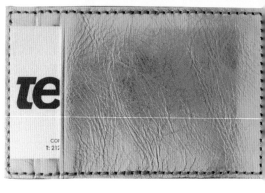

BUSINESS CARDS
Key for establishing contacts; editors don't leave home without them.

THE NEW YORK TIMES
The daily authority on current events.

PASSPORT
A must-have when jetting from shoot to shoot.

SUITCASE
A bright color makes for quick and easy spotting at baggage claim.

AIRBORNE
Stay healthy while juggling events and travel.

FACE POWDER
Helps to maintain a polished look throughout the day.

LAPTOP
Small and light does the trick for on-the-go editing.

DIGITAL CAMERA
A portable way to snap images of clothing samples.

PENS
Keep red ones handy for editing and a fountain pen for writing thank-you notes.

OVERSIZE BAG
Everything from newspapers to page layouts are easily stashed in a stylish carryall.

BOOKS
References—from the *Vogue* archives to contemporary art tomes—help to inspire unique layouts.

NOTEBOOK
To keep track of story ideas and to-do lists.

INSPIRATIONS AND IDEAS

HIGH HEELS
Give any outfit an instant boost with classically chic shoes.

350 Works from The Museum of Modern Art New York

MoMA Highlights

Break in to the industry with these tips.

★ **TAKE A CHANCE:** IF YOU ADMIRE A CERTAIN MAGAZINE EDITOR, E-MAIL THAT PERSON AND POLITELY REQUEST A FEW MINUTES OF TIME TO ASK QUESTIONS IN AN INFORMATIONAL INTERVIEW. IT COULD LEAD TO AN INTERNSHIP OR EVEN A LONG-TERM MENTORSHIP.

★ **MOVE TO A BIG CITY.** NEW YORK CITY IS THE FASHION AND PUBLISHING CAPITAL OF THE UNITED STATES. MOST WRITING AND EDITING JOBS ARE FOUND THERE.

★ **GO ABOVE AND BEYOND THE CALL OF DUTY.** PUBLISHING IS A COMPETITIVE INDUSTRY, AND ASSISTANTS NEED TO STAND OUT IN ORDER TO GET PROMOTED. ALWAYS DO MORE THAN YOU'RE ASKED, AND TRY TO ANTICIPATE WHAT'S NEEDED BEFORE IT'S EVEN REQUESTED. KEEP YOUR DESK TIDY AND MAINTAIN A PROFESSIONAL PHONE MANNER. NOT EVERY TASK WILL BE GLAMOROUS, BUT ATTENTION TO DETAIL CAN MAKE A BIG DIFFERENCE.

★ **STAY ABREAST OF CURRENT EVENTS,** NOT JUST THE LATEST FASHION TRENDS. READ THE NEWSPAPER EVERY DAY. FASHION DESIGNERS AND FASHION MAGAZINES ARE DIRECTLY INFLUENCED BY WHAT'S GOING ON ALL OVER THE WORLD.

★ **COLLECT IMAGES THAT INSPIRE YOU:** PICTURES FROM MAGAZINES, COLOR SWATCHES, DIFFERENT FONTS, AND EVEN ADVERTISEMENTS WILL HELP DEVELOP AND STRENGTHEN YOUR AESTHETIC.

★ **HONE YOUR PERSONAL STYLE**—DON'T WEAR ONE DESIGNER HEAD TO TOE. IF YOU'RE AN ASPIRING FASHION EDITOR, BEING ABLE TO MIX AND MATCH WILL SHOW ORIGINAL THINKING AND A STRONG EYE.

Question:

I'm obsessed with cl
I translate that into

Answer:

Stylists explain how
clothing into a job
stars for events and

othes. How do a career as a stylist?

to turn a love of that includes dressing models for shoots.

The Modern Romantic

Jillian Davison

THIS FORMER BALLERINA CHANNELED HER LOVE FOR COSTUME AND THEATER INTO A MULTIFACETED CAREER IN FASHION.

Jillian Davison's first foray into fashion came when she was a fifteen-year-old aspiring ballerina with an affinity for, she says, "the costumes, the theater, that whole side of things; we used to spend hours dressing up and doing our hair and makeup." Six years later, the Australian native swapped her slippers for stilettos and started working as an assistant in Chanel's public relations office in Sydney. "One of my main jobs, Davison recalls, "was to collect all the press clippings, so I would spend hours going through stacks of fashion magazines. That was when I realized that I wanted to be a part of the picture-making process."

She learned the ropes during a stint at Australian *Vogue,* where she worked first as an assistant and then as a sittings editor. "It's not a big staff there like at American *Vogue,*" she says. "We had to do everything! I would take all the clothes home with me the night before a shoot, carry them up three flights of stairs to my apartment, then put them back in the car the next morning and drive them to the location myself." A jump to *Harper's Bazaar* in the United States meant "kind of starting at the bottom again," but Davison soon rose to the position of fashion editor and parlayed that into a busy freelance career. "I felt like I had built up a small profile and enough connections to survive on my own," she says.

Today Davison styles many of *Teen Vogue*'s cover stories and fashion portfolios, works on ad campaigns, and often consults for labels such as Moschino Cheap and Chic.

"There's no such thing as a typical day," she says, "but that's what I love about my job. I go to the collections in Europe every season, of course, and that's part of how I formulate my ideas and my point of view for fashion sittings." Advertising work requires the same set of skills: "If I'm shooting a beauty campaign," she says, "I'll source all the clothing, the shoes, and the jewelry." But it's her consulting gigs with labels that require the most sustained commitment. "When I'm styling Moschino Cheap and Chic, I usually go to Milan about two months before the show to look at and edit samples, to give the collection focus," she says. "For example, I wouldn't want to have long skirts, miniskirts, A-line skirts, and pencil skirts all in the same show, so I pick what looks the strongest or the newest based on what I feel is going on in fashion at that time. Then I go back a few days before fashion week to help cast the models, do fittings and hair and makeup tests, and style the looks. The day of a show, I'm there with my lint brush and scissors, tucking in everything and tying bows." Just as with Davison's first love, dancing, she's found that fashion is 90 percent preparation, 10 percent presentation. ★

DAVISON WORKS
HER SIGNATURE HIGH-
LOW MIX IN A YOHJI
YAMAMOTO DRESS AND
CONVERSE SNEAKERS
NEAR HER HOME
IN BROOKLYN.

who: ANNE HATHAWAY ON THE SET OF HER 2007 COVER SHOOT
what: THE STYLE CONCEPT WAS OLD-HOLLYWOOD GLAM
where: MALIBU, CALIFORNIA

teen VOGUE

SEPTEMBER

APPLY YOURSELF
find the perfect-fit college

beauty breakthrough
THE SURPRISING SECRET TO CLEAR SKIN

THE PRESSURE TO BE SEXY

FALL FASHION SPECIAL
PREP-SCHOOL COOL RETURNS
• chic little blazers
• all-new capris & khakis
• superbright sweaters
• 16 must-have hats

ANNE HATHAWAY
hollywood glamour girl

"The idea on this shoot, photographed by Patrick Demarchelier, was twenties glam toned down with cozier pieces. I added this gray, long-sleeved tee under most of the looks that day because it was chilly at the beach and Anne had a cold."

"I often like to use the same shoe throughout a story, like I did with these Luella motorcycle boots, because they help create a strong character over a number of pages. Shoes can also give an outfit a surprising twist. You wouldn't expect to see chunky boots and bare legs with sequins and feathers!"

"Marc Jacobs did fabulous hats that season, so I topped many of the looks with big berets. I also layered on dirty faux diamonds. I love piling on jewelry to make a bold statement."

"I had seen Anne wear a lot of structured party dresses on the red carpet, so I wanted to put her in something cooler and more relaxed. She really loved the clothes and had fun with them, wrapping sweaters around her body and hiking up the skirts. She brought the clothes to life."

DAVISON AT WORK IN GOA, INDIA, WITH MODEL NATALIA VODIANOVA, WHO WAS JUST BREAKING IN TO THE SPOTLIGHT AT THE TIME. "WE WERE GOING FOR A ROMANTIC, SHIPWRECKED FEEL, AND NATALIA WAS SO NATURALLY RADIANT THAT WE BARELY USED ANY MAKEUP," RECALLS THE STYLIST.

teenVOGUE **TIP** Leave a lasting impression when applying for fashion jobs: "Before I interviewed at *Harper's Bazaar,* I blew a lot of money on a fabulous pair of fuchsia shoes, and to this day I'm remembered for them." —JILLIAN DAVISON

ON THE JOB

Davison walks us through a few of her favorite Teen Vogue *shoots.*

ISSUE: September 2008
THE INSPIRATION: "Natalie Wood's character in the Western movie *The Searchers,* about a prairie girl who's kidnapped by American Indians. The look was a fusion of those two cultures."
THE CLOTHES: "Fringed suede and ruffled frontier dresses."
THE SCOOP: "For one of the shots, the model, Jac, had to pose while sitting on a horse. Before you knew it, she was galloping across the Mojave Desert. She had no fear!"
PHOTOGRAPHER: Arthur Elgort

ISSUE: February 2009
THE INSPIRATION: "Tomboy denim from Current/Elliott, a cool L.A. label worn by celebs like Reese Witherspoon."
THE CLOTHES: "Pale blue jeans in oversize shapes, unisex cotton tanks, canvas sneakers, and shredded wristbands."
THE SCOOP: "To create the crushed look of the clothes, as if they had been placed in the dryer wet and forgotten, we sprayed everything with water and then twisted it up with rubber bands to dry."
PHOTOGRAPHER: Jason Kibbler

ISSUE: May 2005
THE INSPIRATION: "Tropical styles on the runway that season, like big Hawaiian prints at D&G."
THE CLOTHES: "Colorful jewelry and strappy palm frond–print wedges. I like to mix high and low, such as a visor from a surf shop with a Dior earring [left]."
THE SCOOP: "For accessories stories like this you need pieces with impact, because they take up the whole page. They have to be a strong representation of the trend."
PHOTOGRAPHER: Raymond Meier

The Image Maker

Andrea Lieberman

GWEN STEFANI'S STYLING PARTNER HELPS MULTIPLATINUM POP STARS MAKE A FIERCE FASHION STATEMENT.

"I was only thirteen years old when I decided I was going to work in fashion. I used to walk up Madison Avenue on my way to school on the Upper East Side of Manhattan, looking in all the store windows. At the library, I checked out old copies of *Vogue*. I even had a friend who was a photographer, and we would find a model, pull some clothes, and stage our own all-night fashion shoots. While I was in high school, I started taking classes at Parsons the New School for Design during summers and weekends, and in eleventh grade I applied to the fashion-design program there. The person who admitted me, funnily enough, was Tim Gunn, who's now on *Project Runway*.

Because I was so determined to have a career in fashion, I did anything I could to expose myself to the industry, whether it was working at a store, being an intern, or helping out backstage at a runway show. I worked at the clothing store Matsuda and for designer Giorgio di Sant'Angelo, and I found that once you're inside that world, it's like a domino effect: I would meet one person, and he or she would open a door, which would then open another door. That's why interning is

WORKING WITH GWEN

A few of Lieberman's fashion collaborations with singer Gwen Stefani.

LIEBERMAN, WHO CONSULTS ON STEFANI'S L.A.M.B. LINE, HELPS GET THE COLLECTION RUNWAY-READY.

STEFANI PERFORMS IN THE TOKYO-INFLUENCED "HARAJUKU GIRL" LOOK THAT SHE AND LIEBERMAN CREATED.

STEFANI AND LIEBERMAN LEAVE A PARIS FASHION WEEK PARTY ARM IN ARM, ABOVE LEFT. STEFANI AT THE 2005 MTV VIDEO MUSIC AWARDS IN A L.A.M.B. DRESS LIEBERMAN CUSTOM-MADE FOR THE EVENT, ABOVE RIGHT.

great: It's not that hard to get an internship, since you're basically working for free, and if you prove yourself, people will take note. After I finished school, I got a job in the press office of Romeo Gigli. That was where I first witnessed the ins and outs of what a stylist does.

Even though I've always worked really hard to create opportunities for myself, I've also done what I like to call surfing the wave: jumping on an opportunity and riding it until I land somewhere else. You have to know what you want, but you also need to allow for a certain amount of spontaneity. In my early twenties, I went to Paris—I thought that all I wanted to do was work for a designer like Jean Paul Gaultier—but after I arrived, the place just didn't feel right. So I ended up traveling through Africa for almost two years. When I got back, I opened a store in Manhattan with a friend, where we sold tribal jewelry and clothes I made with fabrics I had bought in Africa. It was short-lived, but it was fun while it lasted.

I started styling next because it was something I enjoyed that I could do freelance to make money. A friend in the music-video business asked me to help out on a video for a hippie band called Rusted Root, which was perfect since I had just been to Africa and was going through a real hippie phase. After that, I never looked back. I worked on photo shoots too, but the music-video work just kept coming. One

teen VOGUE TIP Make things happen for yourself: "If you live in Idaho but dream of interning in New York, do your homework. Maybe you have a family member who has a friend whose son knows someone." —ANDREA LIEBERMAN

day, a photographer I had met on a job called and asked me to style a last-minute Sean Combs cover for *Vibe*. I remember it so clearly: I had only 24 hours to get it together, I was already shooting another job, and it was pouring rain. But I knew this was a once-in-a-lifetime opportunity, and I was not going to let it pass me by. I called all my friends, I called an ex-boyfriend, I called anyone who could help me make it happen, and it ended up being a great shoot. I started working with Sean regularly, and he introduced me to Jennifer Lopez, who became my client.

I've been styling Jennifer since she started her music career and have put together most of her memorable looks, including the green Versace gown she wore to the Grammys in 2000. I was shocked—almost scared, actually—by the reaction to that dress. I remember going down in the elevator of my hotel the next day, and the dress was all anyone talked about, which freaked me out. The fact that it was on the front page of newspapers worldwide showed me what a huge impact a celebrity could have. That was the moment when the red carpet, as a fashion force, became really big.

Getting Gwen Stefani as a client was another major coup. I had always wanted to work with her, and I was sure that we

JENNIFER LOPEZ IN THE INFAMOUS VERSACE GOWN THAT LIEBERMAN SELECTED FOR THE 2000 GRAMMY AWARDS.

"I WAS *shocked*— ALMOST SCARED, ACTUALLY— BY THE *reaction* TO JENNIFER LOPEZ'S *Versace dress.* I REMEMBER GOING DOWN IN *the elevator* OF MY HOTEL THE *next day,* AND IT WAS ALL ANYONE *talked about,* WHICH FREAKED ME OUT. THAT WAS THE MOMENT WHEN THE *red carpet* BECAME *really big.*"

—ANDREA LIEBERMAN

would love each other. Then, coincidentally, I was booked to style the video for Eve's "Let Me Blow Ya Mind," which Gwen sang on. She and I have worked together ever since. Our process is extremely collaborative. Creatively, we truly inspire each other, though I don't like to call what Gwen does high-concept, because that almost discredits the passion that's involved. Everything she does comes from a genuine place.

I've now started my own clothing line, A.L.C. (Andrea Lieberman Collection), but I've been designing all along: I consult for Gwen's line, L.A.M.B., and I make some of her red-carpet outfits. I also create tour costumes for her and Jennifer. Designing for a tour is completely different from designing a collection. Tour wardrobes are extremely focused on one person, and the performer becomes your muse; also, the clothes have to be worn a hundred times by someone who's jumping up and down and dancing. But if you're not singing and dancing onstage, then I don't think your outfit should look like a costume. I prefer to design things that are effortless, modern, chic, sophisticated, and classic, with maybe a touch of rock 'n' roll, a touch of street. My line is very much influenced by everything I've done." ★

STYLISTS

EVERYTHING FROM REFINED ART BOOKS TO RAW STREET STYLE INSPIRES THIS VERSATILE STYLIST'S WORK FOR HIGH-FASHION HOUSES AND TEEN MEGASTORES.

"Fashion has always been in my life. My father was a photographer (he shot a lot of album covers in the sixties), and both my mother and grandmother were models and stylists. I started collecting vintage clothing when I was only eleven years old, but I resisted pursuing fashion as a career at first because I was around it so much.

When I was fifteen, I graduated from high school and began to study acting. I needed a day job, and assisting stylists seemed like a natural choice. My career just took off from there. At 25, I became the fashion director at *Nylon* magazine, which was an eye-opening experience. Prior to that, I had worked with photographers who simply told me what they wanted. At *Nylon,* it was a collaboration. It wasn't just about the clothes: I helped come up with shoot ideas, locations, and models. I was involved with the big picture, and that was far more exciting than what I had been doing.

I stayed at *Nylon* for a year, then went to London for a year to work on the relaunch of a magazine called *Nova.* Now I'm freelance, and I work for *Teen Vogue,* Japanese *Vogue, i-D,* and an Italian publication called *Flair.* I spend lots of time in the library, looking at art books, and at home I have a huge collection of monographs, which are detailed nonfiction books—they're

such an important source of inspiration for me. To prep for a shoot, I go on Style.com to view the shows, and I paste pictures of the looks I want to use on boards so that my assistants and I know what to request from showrooms. We decide on the models, hair, makeup, and shoot concepts, then pack everything up and take it to a studio or on a plane to get to our location.

I've also consulted with different labels, including Peter Som, TSE, Rebecca Taylor, and American Eagle Outfitters. I help with research for their collections, pulling references to inspire their designers. Those references can come from anything—people on the street, kids at concerts, art books, old magazines. I love to look at issues of *Vogue* from the fifties, sixties, seventies, and eighties. Some designers will even ask you to go vintage shopping to find things that can be included—not copied, but translated—in the collection. You have to take the audience into consideration. When I worked for American Eagle, it was important that the clothes be accessible, affordable, and fun, so I studied youth culture, kept a pulse on what kids were wearing on the street, and paid attention to pop music, since musicians have a huge influence on how teenagers look. For Peter Som, I let my imagination run a bit wilder, because with high fashion there are fewer boundaries. High fashion is a more idealized version of reality." ★

LAFFITTE PREPS FOR A *TEEN VOGUE* COVER SHOOT WITH ACTRESS EMMA ROBERTS ON THE BEACH IN MALIBU, CALIFORNIA. ON SET, ACCESSORIES ARE LAID OUT IN TRAYS, SO THAT STYLISTS CAN EASILY VIEW ALL THEIR OPTIONS AT ONCE.

HOW I GOT THIS PICTURE

who: MISCHA BARTON,
POSING FOR HER 2006
TEEN VOGUE COVER STORY
what: THE STYLE MUSE WAS
SIXTIES FOLKSINGER
JONI MITCHELL
where: LONG ISLAND,
NEW YORK

"After we threw this flannel shirt over the dress, it looked a little shapeless, so I decided to add a belt. I had selected studded accessories to give the outfits a rock 'n' roll vibe and also to make them feel more modern."

" The inspiration for this shoot was Joni Mitchell and other sixties musicians, including a young Bob Dylan. We pulled images from the Internet, looked at old album covers, and watched documentaries about Woodstock to develop the look we wanted. The photographer, Bruce Weber, even played Joni's music on set to create a strong mood. Mischa was really excited about it. **"**

" This was the season that Marc Jacobs revived the grunge trend, and we tried to capture the moment with flannel shirts and thermal tees. To add that *Teen Vogue* finishing touch, we pulled everything together with bits of sparkle, like rhinestone jewels. **"**

" This look started out with the dress, which was a beautiful Peter Som gown. For me the spirit of grunge is about mixing something precious with something cool. Layering is one of my styling signatures; I love playing with combinations of textures and patterns. **"**

SEPTEMBER

Teen VOGUE

OUR BIGGEST ISSUE EVER!

370 PAGES OF

FALL FASHION

all the trends from

A to Z

"IT WAS LIKE H... SCHOO... MISCHA... ON LEAVING THE O.C...

E BEST DRESSES, MINIS, PLATFORMS, COZY SWEATERS &
TRICKS F...

THIS SWINGING SIXTIES LONDON–
INSPIRED FASHION STORY WAS SHOT
ON LOCATION IN THE U.K. TAKING
CUES FROM CULTURAL ICONS OF
THE TIME, LIKE MARIANNE FAITHFULL
AND THE ROLLING STONES, IT MIXED
TRADITIONAL TWEEDS, PSYCHEDELIC
PATTERNS, AND POPS OF FAUX FUR.
"WE WERE REALLY LUCKY THAT THE
WEATHER WAS SO AMAZING—IT'S
RARE TO HAVE SUCH BLUE SKIES IN
LONDON," LAFFITTE SAYS.

teen VOGUE TIP Research as much as possible so that you have plenty of visual reference points to draw from. "Two photography books I love are Joseph Szabo's *Teenage* and Bruce Davidson's *Brooklyn Gang*." —HAVANA LAFFITTE

Laffitte walks us through a few of her favorite Teen Vogue *shoots.*

ISSUE: June/July 2005
THE INSPIRATION: "Bathing beauties of the fifties updated with poppy colors. We looked at old *Vogue*s for reference."
THE CLOTHES: "One- and two-piece suits in full cuts and sweet prints, and cool cover-ups like graphic tees. We made jewelry from plastic buttons and bungee cords."
THE SCOOP: "We were on location in Miami, and for one of the shots, at the city's Seaquarium, all three girls got to swim with dolphins."
PHOTOGRAPHER: Nick Haymes

ISSUE: March 2006
THE INSPIRATION: "Classic little boys' clothes and their influence on the important trends of the season."
THE CLOTHES: "The trend here was punky skinny pants. Another was khaki, so we put the boys in Scout uniforms."
THE SCOOP: "The boys were around seven years old. To get that many kids dressed and posed for each picture was wild! I remember trying to keep soda away from them so that they wouldn't get too hyper."
PHOTOGRAPHER: Thomas Schenk

ISSUE: November 2008
THE INSPIRATION: "Shakespeare's *A Midsummer Night's Dream* with a punk twist."
THE CLOTHES: "Paillette tees, combat boots, studded jewelry, plus costume elements like the Elizabethan collar and the donkey head."
THE SCOOP: "We staged the shoot as if the models were putting on a guerrilla performance of the play. Everyone got a script and was assigned a character."
PHOTOGRAPHER: Bruce Weber

The Visionary
Camilla Nickerson

THIS BOUNDARY-PUSHING BRIT, ADMIRED FOR HER KEEN MIXING OF STREET AND CHIC, MASTERMINDS SOME OF FASHION'S MOST INFLUENTIAL IDEAS.

Was fashion always a part of your life?
When I was growing up, my grandmother had every issue of *Vogue* from the 1930s on in her attic. She left them to me when she passed away. It was a question of whether I could overcome my fear of bats to go up there and get them! But style was always around me. My mother was an antiques dealer, and I used to go to markets with her. While she was buying furniture, I bought clothes.

So you knew early on that you wanted to work with clothes in some capacity. What was your first job in fashion?
At age fourteen I was scouted and asked to be a model, and that's when I found out there was such thing as a fashion editor. At sixteen, I spent the summer working as an assistant at *Tatler* magazine in London. A year later they offered me a job, and from there I went on to British *Vogue,* where Anna Wintour was the creative director at the time. I assisted the fashion director and styled fashion for the beauty pages, so I was going on every shoot, which was amazing. It was a very exciting time in fashion. My first story was with Christy Turlington!

You started your career at such a young age. Did you ever have second thoughts about what you wanted to do?
I left British *Vogue* to take a year off to travel. I had never seen a picture of Tibet, so I thought I should go! But being there with all sorts of hippies made me realize how lucky I was to have a passion, so I went back to London. I was still only eighteen at that time. I assisted at *Harper's & Queen* for a while before going freelance. I did a lot of work on music videos and films, as well as British magazines like *The Face* and *i-D.*

How did you go about getting freelance work?
I spent my evenings with other young designers, photographers, and models, and we'd just fool around, coming up with story ideas and going off to shoot them. There was one, "Peace Warriors," where we went to a car-wrecking yard, got hubcaps, and welded them into armor. Then we took our friends to an apple orchard and photographed them under the blossoms. We did shoots whenever we had a spare minute. Everyone was up for experimenting. It didn't have to be a product; it was just a journey. Then we'd phone up magazines and say, "Would you like to publish a couple of pages?"

NICKERSON, WITH HER SONS, IN A 2008 GAP AD CAMPAIGN LAUDING HER STREET-CHIC PERSONAL STYLE.

"THE IDEA WAS TO BRING TOGETHER STREET STYLE AND FASHION," SAYS NICKERSON OF THIS SKATE-INSPIRED STORY FOR THE JUNE/JULY 2003 ISSUE OF *TEEN VOGUE*.

from a certain era or it might come from the street today, but I always imagine a woman and find photographs that define her—how she might wear her hair, what her fingernail length is, what kind of shoe she has on. Is she from a world in black and white, or should she be photographed in color? Is she in a landscape that's a narrative, or is she on a journey? Does she love her boyfriend's wardrobe, or is she a party girl who likes short, colorful dresses—and where should she be photographed wearing those? Maybe she's no longer at the party, and it's pictures of her on her way home. She has danced the night away, her makeup is streaming, and she's photographed on the street outside the door of the party.

How do you express all this to the crew on a shoot?

I always bring a scrapbook of images with me. It can help get everyone on a similar path, from hair, makeup, and the model's body language to the photography. You have a very short amount of time in which to explore your ideas, so it's good to have some reference points.

How would you describe the relationship between stylist and photographer?

It's a completely collaborative process. It demands a lot of trust because you're trying to say something new that you don't really know the answer to. It involves putting your

You eventually relocated to New York and spent twelve years at American Vogue. *How did that move come about?*

Anna [Wintour] called one day and said, "Would you like to come to America?" It was superexciting and challenging. It was a time when new photographers were being asked to do shoots and Kate Moss was just coming about.

The industry has changed a lot since then. Most notably, the shift from models to celebrities in fashion magazines. What, for you, is the main difference between styling celebrities and styling models?

I think they've become simultaneous. Ten years ago it was different, but now celebrities hand themselves over to fashion. They know it's not about revealing themselves but about portraying a character. Of course, you sometimes have the difference in size. Models are usually tall, and actors have no requirements in that sense. Although if they are interested in the project, then it's a treat to work with them.

How do you prepare for a photo shoot?

You need to be open to looking at and knowing as much about culture and history as possible. I'm constantly researching photography and fashion. I go to libraries and antiques shops. I collect books. An idea might come

A WILLIAM KLEIN PHOTO SERIES SPARKED THE MOOD FOR THIS STORY IN AUGUST 2005 *TEEN VOGUE*. "IT'S SCULPTURAL WITH A SIXTIES FEEL," NICKERSON SAYS.

TEEN VOGUE TIP Surround yourself with creative, like-minded people. As a fashion assistant in London, Nickerson made friends with young photographers and designers and spent her evenings and weekends styling ad hoc shoots with them.

NICKERSON'S OWN STYLE INFORMS SOME OF HER SHOOTS. THIS FEBRUARY 2005 *VOGUE* STORY FEATURING MODEL DARIA WERBOWY "WAS WHAT I MYSELF LOVED TO WEAR AT THE TIME," NICKERSON SAYS. "SKINNY SKIRTS AND PILED-ON CHAINS—IT WAS VERY PERSONAL."

heart on the table a little bit. So it's great to build a relationship with the photographer, because the more you trust each other, the further you can explore. Then you might make something that's never been seen before.

You left Vogue *three years ago and became the fashion director at* W. *How has your work evolved there?*
It's an extension of everything Anna [Wintour] taught me. I feel lucky that I have fashion as a medium to play with my ideas. When I go to work, it doesn't feel like work at all. At *W,* I pretty much have complete freedom to explore my ideas. It's terrifying in certain respects! The only thing the creative director of *W* mandates is, "Don't bring me anything I've seen before. I would rather the shoot fail than you do something I've seen before."

In addition to magazine shoots, you've also worked side by side with various designers over the years, from Stefano Pilati at YSL to Narciso Rodriguez. How would you describe your role as stylist to a designer, and whom are you currently working with?
At the moment, I'm working with Francisco Costa at Calvin Klein and Tommaso Aquilano and Roberto Rimondi at Gianfranco Ferre. I love clothes so much, and I'm constantly changing my clothes, so I try to bring the designers things that move me, whether they be books, records, clothes, a

TWO SMALL CUBS WERE BROUGHT IN, COURTESY OF A BEAR WRANGLER, FOR THIS RUSSIA-INSPIRED STORY (*TEEN VOGUE,* SEPTEMBER 2005), WHICH WAS SHOT AT NICKERSON'S HOUSE IN UPSTATE NEW YORK. "WE WANTED TO CREATE A LOVE STORY LIKE *DOCTOR ZHIVAGO,*" SHE EXPLAINS. "IT WAS VERY DREAMY AND IDYLLIC, AND QUITE CHARMING TO HAVE THE LITTLE BEARS IN THE PICTURE."

NICKERSON LOOKED AT FIFTIES-THEMED FILMS—LIKE *EAST OF EDEN,* *GREASE,* AND *THE WANDERERS*—FOR THIS ROCKABILLY-INSPIRED SHOOT WITH MANDY MOORE. "WE WERE GOING FOR A PUNKED-OUT SCHOOLGIRL: HIGH SCHOOL SWEETHEARTS, BUT GONE WRONG! FOR ME, MANDY WAS VERY MUCH THAT NAUGHTY PREP GIRL," THE STYLIST SAYS.

rock I found on the beach, or something my kids made in school. I see the collection through, from beginning to end. You start with the colors you love. Like, I've just got to have green today, and it needs to be frayed—or, no, it needs to be perfectly finished. Or I have to have my belt on my waist. No, now I really want it on my hips. Whatever those gestures are. And I see it through to the models, the music, the lighting.

What qualities does a stylist need to be successful?
You're a member of a team, so you have to be a team player. It's not easy. You're hauling clothes around, flying all the time. It's not glamorous.

What do you wear on set?
I always wear a pair of heels! But I don't have a uniform; I'm constantly changing.

What should an assistant wear?
Look fabulous. You're trying to explain what you're thinking by what you're wearing.

Are there specific things that impress you when hiring assistants?
Someone who has stayed at a job. Someone who's done a little bit extra—anything out of the ordinary or a bit bonkers!

Any dos or don'ts for interview dressing?
I wouldn't wear a trend-of-the-moment. You want someone who leads, not follows. But you can't tell everything from an interview. I employ and then find out whether it works.

What kinds of things do your assistants do?
They do research in libraries. They pack clothes, follow up with showrooms and market editors, and make boards of the looks we've chosen, which are constantly edited and updated. They'll find extra accessories to inform the character we're trying to build. They'll tell me about their night out—who was there, what they were wearing, what music they're listening to. It's a 24-hour job. They have to be tireless. And I don't think it's something you can learn in college. You have to be out working in the field. It requires a great deal of dedication.

What's the biggest misconception about being a stylist?
When I started, I did everything. I booked models, hotels, flights, chose locations, found the accessories, picked the clothes, bagged them, packed them, unpacked them, sent them back. You work really, really hard, and it doesn't happen in a minute. I think people assume it clicks overnight and you get instant satisfaction, but it's a craft. God, if it just came from turning on the tap, that would be so boring! ★

NICKERSON CALLS THIS FANTASTICAL
SHOOT WITH COUTURE TWEEDS
AND KABUKI-STYLE FACE PAINT ONE
OF HER FAVORITES. "THERE WERE A
THOUSAND INSPIRATIONS—OSKAR
KOKOSCHKA PAINTINGS, ELSA
SCHIAPARELLI DESIGNS," SHE SAYS.
"THE SHOOT WAS QUITE DIFFERENT
FOR AMERICAN VOGUE IN THAT THE
IMAGES WERE RATHER ABSTRACT."

The Accessories Master
Elissa Santisi

WITH A REMARKABLY SHARP EYE FOR STORYTELLING WITH ACCESSORIES, THIS *VOGUE* VETERAN TURNS OUT CINEMATIC SHOOTS THAT ELEVATE MERE BAGS AND SHOES TO EPIC PROPORTIONS—AND "IT" STATUS.

How did you break in to the industry?
As soon as I graduated from college, I moved from Philadelphia to New York City. I wanted to work in magazines, so I blindly called the human resources departments at different publications. But I did not get hired. Then I heard about a job in mannequin display at Bloomingdale's. I compiled a little book of outfits styled from my own clothes, which I had pegged up on a wall in my apartment and taken pictures of. A friend of mine who was a graphic designer helped me put it together. It was a funny way of presenting my work, but I got hired because of it.

That really speaks to the importance of making yourself stand out on an interview.
Yes, it does! Then one of my sisters, who also worked in the fashion industry, heard about an opening for an accessories editor at *Harper's Bazaar.* I had no experience in a position like that, but I wore my favorite silver ball-and-chain bracelets to my interview, and that got a lot of attention. I had to go to about four interviews because they were concerned about my lack of experience. They actually hired someone else first who didn't work out. Then they called me a few months later to offer me the job.

Was there a big learning curve when you started?
It would have been a lot easier if I had been an assistant before, but that's not the way it worked out. I did my homework, though. I looked at every magazine and broke down everything I liked. I had to learn quickly.

Was that when you started styling accessories stories?
No, I was a market editor first, so I worked with stylists to get them what they needed for their shoots. I used to go to the market to look for jewelry, and if I couldn't find what I wanted, I had someone make it. I learned to be creative and not to take no for an answer. If someone doesn't have what you're looking for, then get on the phone and say, "Well, let's find something else!" I think that helped me when I transitioned into styling. I knew what to expect. I went to work at *Elle* and *Mirabella* next, still as an accessories editor. Then when Liz Tilberis took over as editor in chief at *Harper's Bazaar,* she hired me to do accessories sittings. That was the first time I styled shoots. I remember being in a panic, like, What if I can't do this well? The thing about accessories is that you have a lot more freedom with the idea, whereas with fashion it has to be shot on a model.

> "A GOOD *stylist* THINKS OF THE *big picture.* IT'S ALMOST LIKE *producing a movie.* CASTING, HAIR, MAKEUP, LOCATION—ALL THESE *ingredients* ARE *essential* TO BRING THE CLOTHES AND *accessories to life.*"
>
> —ELISSA SANTISI

SANTISI IN THE ART DEPARTMENT AT THE *VOGUE* OFFICES IN NEW YORK CITY. BEHIND HER ARE LAYOUTS FOR A FUTURE *VOGUE* BOOK PROJECT.

With accessories you can do anything, really. I started working with [photographer and longtime collaborator] Raymond Meier almost immediately. When Anna Wintour hired me at *Vogue*, Raymond came with me.

You two have created so many iconic stories together over the years. Can you describe your collaboration process?

When planning a shoot, I first come up with the fashion idea. Then I work with the photographer to decide how we want to set the stage around it. What story are we telling? There's a lot of back-and-forth to developing an idea. To spark something, I sometimes watch movies or go to the library. I did this one shoot with Raymond where we used python accessories. I had recently watched the Alfred Hitchcock film *The Man Who Knew Too Much*, and I loved it. So I sent Raymond some photos—literally, screen shots that had inspired me, including one with taxidermy. I like shoots where there's a little irony in the picture—that contrast of lightness with a dark twist, almost like a David Lynch film.

Other than cinema, where else do you look for inspiration?

I have a drawer filled with xeroxed pictures that inspire me in some way. They can come from anything, from sixties *Vogues* to art books. It might even be something I saw on the street and photographed. The drawer isn't organized, because I'm always rifling through it. Ideas have to come from a personal place, though. That's how you develop a style.

What advice would you give someone who wants to work in fashion?

I would try an array of jobs, to see what you like and what you're good at. Try to assist in different areas of the industry, from styling and market to working in a store. Training is important because that's how you get experience.

Aside from an apprenticeship, what else would you recommend?

Shop, go to galleries, watch movies, read underground magazines. I used to go to a Japanese bookstore in New York, Kinokuniya, to browse through the different things there.

What qualities do you look for in an assistant?

Well, first of all I have to like the person. I look for someone creative, but it doesn't have to be in a typical way. If someone's good at producing a shoot by going on the Internet to

SANTISI STYLED THEN-NEWCOMER JESSICA STAM FOR *TEEN VOGUE*'S FIRST ISSUE. "IT WAS FUN WORKING ON *TEEN VOGUE*. IT'S FOR A YOUNGER AUDIENCE, SO IT WAS A LITTLE FREER," THE STYLIST SAYS. "JESSICA WAS THIS QUIRKY, CUTE GIRL—NOT AS MAINSTREAM AS SHE IS NOW."

YOU'D NEVER KNOW IT WAS RAINING IN MIAMI THE DAY THIS PICTURE WAS TAKEN. "WE FLASHED IT TO MAKE IT APPEAR SUNNY AND SHOT THE MODELS AGAINST A HEDGE SO THAT YOU COULDN'T SEE THE CLOUDS," SANTISI SAYS. "WE WANTED THE PHOTO TO HAVE A HAPPY ENERGY. LOTS OF JUMPING AND MOVEMENT."

find props and then figuring out a way to get them for free, that's creative! It's not just thinking up ideas, because we all do that. I need someone who can be organized and make my job easier. Someone who can problem-solve and think independently. And someone who's curious and willing to work hard. Shoots can go on indefinitely—that's part of the deal. I don't really look at where my assistants went to school, though if they went to a fashion school, that would be a plus. They should also know how to prep clothes: steam, iron, et cetera, so that I can grab anything off the rack and have it ready to go.

Do you look for a particular sense of style?

I look for a certain sensibility; it's part of the whole package. I remember dressing for interviews—you have to think about how you want to come across. Sometimes I will ask my assistant's opinion, and you don't want someone in left field who has no sense of style. I want to know that they have an eye.

How would you describe a typical day of preparing for a shoot?

It's always a little bit of everything. At *Vogue,* when I have an idea for a shoot, I first meet with Anna [Wintour] to present it to her. It's funny, because I can say something really wacky to her, and sometimes the stranger it is, the more receptive she'll be. She'll say, "Oh, that sounds good," or even finish my thought. Once my idea is approved, I start working on story boards, tagging the accessories and clothes I like from look books or my own pictures, which I take on appointments. Then I coordinate with the market department to ensure that the clothes and accessories are coming in and that they're the right pieces. If one thing isn't available, then I find out what is. The photographer and I work on picking a location. I follow up on hair, makeup, and models. Styling a shoot is kind of like directing a movie: All the ingredients are really important. ★

teenVOGUE TIP Whether or not you have experience, find creative ways to show what you're capable of. Before her first fashion-job interview, Santisi styled and snapped pictures of her own outfits, then turned the images into a mini portfolio.

Emily Weiss, SANTISI'S ASSISTANT
AGE 24 COLLEGE NEW YORK UNIVERSITY
HOMETOWN WILTON, CONNECTICUT

it's important to build a reputation based on your work. Becoming a public figure too early on can be damaging.

At *W* I learned how to call in clothes for shoots and interact with press offices. It was a good way to segue into styling. When I made the leap, I found that the connections I had formed at *W* and *Teen Vogue* were how I got work. It's so important to keep relationships strong and solid. I met stylist Tina Chai through Jane, and she hired me to help her on several shoots. Then she recommended me to Elissa Santisi. I loved Elissa's work, but I had never met her before. By proving myself to Tina, I ended up with the job.

As Elissa's assistant, I help produce shoots. I figure out the budget—how much we can spend on hair, makeup, the location van, et cetera. There's a lot of finagling to get numbers down. I also help Elissa do research, photocopy references, and conceptualize. Then, when we get to the shoot, the first thing I do is make sure I have all the styling tools on me. I love wearing heels in the office, but on set I do jeans and flats because I'm on my hands and knees, dressing models most of the time. I keep safety pins all over my jeans, and my tool kit contains clamps that fit clothes onto the model, double-stick tape, a lint roller, cuticle scissors for unstitching pockets, thongs, bras, a watch fixer, and a first-aid kit. You have to be prepared for anything.

I think what makes a great stylist's assistant is taking as much pride in the shoot as if it were your own. You need to feel as responsible for everything as the stylist does and

Emily on "The Hills"

to think of everything through her eyes. It's important to stay calm and collected, because if you're flustered, then you make your boss flustered too. You also need to be self-sufficient. Obviously if you have questions, don't be too cool to ask. But you don't want to be texting about every little thing. You're there to make your boss's life easier, so you need to learn to think for yourself, manage your time, and manage her time. It's like a marriage. You're with this person all day. There is an X factor that can't be negotiated. A job interview is equal parts how well you get along and how confident your boss can be in you.

I love working for Elissa because she makes me feel like I'm part of her team. She's very collaborative, which is awesome. As a stylist's assistant, you're like a copilot. Every day presents a new challenge, so in order to become a good assistant—and, eventually, a good stylist—you need to absorb and learn from each experience. It's not something you can read in a book: It's literally being on set, watching a mentor, and paying close attention to how that person cultivates her ideas. It takes time, but assisting first is what makes for the best stylist in the long run."

"I don't have any family connections to the industry. When I found out the person whose children I babysat worked at Ralph Lauren, I asked if he could help me get an internship. I was only fifteen at the time, but he arranged an interview with human resources for me, and the summer after freshman year in high school I started working in the design department there. I commuted into Manhattan every day on the train with all the dads. At Ralph Lauren, I got to sit in on meetings, and I helped backstage at the show. When it came time to apply to colleges, I did early-decision at NYU so I could be in New York and keep working in fashion.

I started interning at *Teen Vogue* my sophomore year, first in the fashion closet and then with Jane Keltner in the fashion features department, where I worked until I graduated. That was my crash course in assisting. It helped me to establish a vocabulary. I helped with the administrative flow, scouting girls for personal style pages, and runway and trend research. I also assisted on some shoots and was eventually given the opportunity to write and style some smaller stories. While I was doing a semester abroad in Florence, Italy, I scouted a girl there and sent pictures of her to Jane, who said to go for it. We ended up shooting the girl, and I got to style it. I loved the experience of seeing a shoot through from beginning to end. I was like, I could do this forever!

After I graduated, I started as a fashion-market assistant at *W* magazine. I had to work extra-hard to get the job because of my involvement in *The Hills* during the last year of my *Teen Vogue* internship. Being on the show was a great opportunity to go to L.A., but in this industry

STYLIST TOOL KIT
essential items of the pros

DESIGNER LOOK BOOKS
A quick way to view the latest collections and select clothing and accessories for stories.

TOPSHOP

DIGITAL CAMERA
Records outfits before photo shoots, making them easier to re-create on set.

Nikon

COOLPIX

NIKKOR 5X OPTICAL ZOOM 5.9-29.5mm 1:3.6-4.8 **VR**

SCISSORS
For last-minute fixes, from loose threads to hems.

Johnson's baby powder

CLINICALLY **Mildness** PROVEN

Keeps skin silky soft, fresh & comfortable

Johnson & Johnson

NET WT 1.5 OZ (42g)
724362

BABY POWDER
The industry trick for squeezing in and out of tight shoes.

DOUBLE-STICK TAPE
Holds low-cut garments in place.

Fashion-Fix
www.fashion-fix.com

SHOE INSERTS
Prevent models from sliding around in too-big heels.

UTILITY BELT
Lots of pockets keep essential tools at your fingertips.

50th ANNIVERSARY EDITION

AUDREY HEPBURN   FRED ASTAIRE

Funny Face

STATIC GUARD
Keeps clothes moving freely.

STATIC GUARD

Instantly Eliminates Static Cling

Fresh Scent

NET WT 5 OZ (156g)

CAUTION: EYE IRRITANT/FLAMMABLE

CLASSIC FASHION FILMS
These form a foundation of iconic references to work from.

PINCUSHION
Keeps pins in one place.

LINT ROLLER
Clothes get a once-over
before shots and shows.

PINS
Used to create
the illusion of a
perfect fit.

**STAIN
REMOVER**
Cleans up marks.

TYLE LIBRARY
ooks provide inspiration from
e industry's heavy hitters.

BLACKBERRY
Use it to stay
connected while
on set.

SSORTED CLIPS
nch extra fabric on
odels to achieve
e desired silhouette.

Break in to the industry with these tips.

★ STUDY THE WORK OF STYLISTS YOU ADMIRE TO SEE HOW THEY SET THEMSELVES APART. THEN START DEVELOPING YOUR OWN STYLING TRADEMARKS.

★ TRY TO LAND A JOB AT A MAGAZINE BEFORE STRIKING OUT ON YOUR OWN AS A FREELANCER. THAT WAY YOU BUILD UP INDUSTRY CONNECTIONS AND AN UNDERSTANDING OF THE MARKETS.

★ DEVELOP A CULTURAL REFERENCE BASE BY SPENDING TIME IN BOOKSTORES AND ART GALLERIES, CATCHING UP ON OLD MOVIES, AND LISTENING TO NEW BANDS. FIND OUT WHAT MAKES YOU TICK AND CULTIVATE THOSE INTERESTS SO THAT YOU CAN HONE YOUR AESTHETIC.

★ PAY ATTENTION TO WHAT'S HAPPENING ON THE STREET. TRENDS DON'T START AND STOP AT THE RUNWAY, SO CHECK OUT WHAT TEENS ARE WEARING AND HOW THEY'RE WEARING IT.

★ TAKE FASHION COURSES IN YOUR SPARE TIME, INCLUDING SEWING AND BASIC CLOTHING DESIGN. FUNDAMENTAL FASHION SKILLS CAN INFORM YOUR STYLING WORK.

★ GET AS MUCH HANDS-ON EXPERIENCE WITH CLOTHES AS YOU CAN, WHETHER STYLING YOUR FRIENDS, STAGING IMPROMPTU PHOTO SHOOTS, WORKING IN A STORE, OR SIMPLY GOING TO BOUTIQUES TO STUDY GARMENTS.

★ BE RESOURCEFUL WHEN IT COMES TO REALIZING YOUR STYLING GOALS—THE INTERNET IS YOUR BEST FRIEND! AND IF YOU REALLY CAN'T FIND AN ITEM THAT YOU'RE LOOKING FOR, THEN MAKE IT YOURSELF.

MODELS

Question:

My dream is to be
How do I know if

Answer:

Discover the answer
the most of your na
models and industr

model.

have what it takes?

and how to make

tural assets from top

insiders.

teen VOGUE
Team

THE WALLS OF
BONOMO'S OFFICE,
IN NEW YORK CITY,
ARE PAPERED WITH
POLAROIDS OF
PROSPECTIVE MODELS.

The Model Scout

Lara Bonomo

THIS EDITOR WORKS BEHIND THE SCENES TO DISCOVER FRESH FACES FOR *TEEN VOGUE.*

"My mother was a model in the sixties, and when I was younger I loved looking at her portfolio. She saved everything—her model cards, negatives, receipts—and she has so many stories! I also enjoyed looking at the magazines she subscribed to: *Vogue, Glamour, Mademoiselle.* I liked reading the stories, but the models brought everything to life for me.

When I graduated from college, I wasn't sure what I wanted to do. I had interned at NBC, which was fascinating, but I realized I didn't want to be in the television world. My older sister was working at *Elle* magazine at the time, and she said that if I was interested in that industry, I should send my résumé to every publication I could think of. So I sent my résumé to about 20 magazines and followed up with phone calls; the fashion director at *YM* happened to pick up and asked me to come in for an interview. I was hired as a fashion assistant there and worked in that department for just under a year. Then the model-bookings editor suggested I apply to be an assistant at Next Models, because she knew I was looking for something full-time. I did, and I got the job. At Next, I coordinated schedules

AT THE WOMEN/
SUPREME AGENCY
IN NEW YORK CITY,
BONOMO SCOUTS
FACES FOR AN
UPCOMING SHOOT.

for the girls who were sent to New York for testing, arranged their photo shoots, made sure they were looked after and had a place to stay in the model apartment, and set up their books. Then someone I had worked with at *YM* called to let me know that a bookings-assistant position had opened at *Mademoiselle* and that I should apply for it.

At that job, I assisted the model-bookings editor, and one of my responsibilities was to book all the male models for shoots. It was a lot of fun because I was only 22 and many of them were older than me. They were so good-looking! After that I went to Ford, New Faces, and then to *Vanity Fair*, which was more of a fashion job—I assisted a stylist and a market editor—and that's where I realized I preferred working with models to working with clothes. So I became a bookings editor at *Cosmo Girl*, went back to *Mademoiselle* until it folded, and then came to *Teen Vogue*.

A typical day for me includes seeing anywhere between two and ten new models. When I look for models, I try to find someone who's young and beautiful, obviously, but also someone who has a personality. A model's job is more than just standing there and looking pretty: She's got to really jump off the page. The best part of my job is being able to launch new faces, girls whom no one has seen before but who I know will have big careers. Agents tell me that clients—like major fashion houses looking for models to cast in their ads—will ask, 'Has she done *Teen Vogue* yet?' I look at all the pictures from the fashion-show catwalks to see if there is anyone who has had a good runway season but hasn't necessarily broken out. I love finding those girls—it's like getting a scoop." ★

These models all passed through Bonomo's office before hitting the big time.

Gemma Ward

FEBRUARY 2006

"Gemma was the first-ever model on a *Teen Vogue* cover! Her wide-eyed innocence paved the way for a whole new trend in the modeling world."

MARCH 2007

Ali Michael

"Ali's combination of porcelain skin and full eyebrows is all-American and gorgeous. Ideal for *Teen Vogue!*"

Karlie Klass

"Karlie has such charm and elegance. The moment she left our office, I was on the phone with her agent, trying to book her for a shoot!"

FEBRUARY/MARCH 2003

Jessica Stam

"Jessica's piercing blue eyes and feline looks set her apart from other models. She's truly one of a kind."

***teen*VOGUE TIP** "Study modeling cycles. Each period has a look, from the *glamazon* eighties to what's going on today. It's important to be able to 'recognize' a model." —LARA BONOMO

Sigrid Ayren

JUNE/JULY 2008

"I think you could place Sigrid in any time period and she would be a successful model. Her beauty transcends time."

Kasia Struss

MARCH 2007

"Kasia is one of those rare girls with the perfect mixture of looks and personality. Photographers and stylists can't get enough of her."

The Vogue Veteran

Caroline Trentini

SPOTTED ON THE STREET IN HER BRAZILIAN HOMETOWN, THIS EDITORIAL STAR STARTED HER CAREER AT *TEEN VOGUE.*

"I didn't grow up around fashion magazines or runway shows in my small hometown of Panambi, Brazil. I had no idea I even wanted to be a model until after being approached by a scout when I was fourteen. I remember my mom having doubts, but once we realized the scout was legitimate and we visited the agency in São Paulo, she changed her mind.

I moved to São Paulo when I was fifteen. I was scared to be in such a large city, and I cried the first week I was there. It was a big change from going to school and playing volleyball every day. Yet as homesick as I was, I knew it was a great opportunity, and if it didn't work out, I could always go back home.

I came to New York in 2003 for a shoot and some castings, and I ended up moving in to an apartment with nine other models. It was difficult to be so far away from my family, but not being able to speak English was the hardest part. Because my work schedule was so full, there was no time for language classes, so I was forced to pick up English on my own.

That same year, I did my first major editorial work for *Teen Vogue.* I was lucky to be in the right place at the right time. The magazine was launching just as my career was starting. It was an important step for me.

TRENTINI GOT HER FIRST BIG BREAK POSING FOR EARLY ISSUES OF *TEEN VOGUE*: "I WAS SO YOUNG AT THE TIME, AND THE MAGAZINE WAS NEW, TOO, BUT I REMEMBER PEOPLE SAYING, 'YOU DID A SHOOT FOR *TEEN VOGUE*? THAT'S SO GREAT!'"

Hands down, my most challenging job was when Steven Klein shot me nude surrounded by raw meat in a walk-in freezer for a *Vogue* beauty story about winter skin. The experience was such an intense shock that I've been a vegetarian ever since—and that was five years ago! Yet during the shoot I had to stay poised and focused to get a great shot. These challenges are learning experiences and keep my job interesting.

It's amazing that so many girls dream about being a model. A lot of people think it's all a party, but it's a job—and it's hard. Like an athlete, a model needs to be healthy and in good shape. It's a fast-paced career, and you have to be willing to put in the work and travel all the time. It can be lonely. There was one season when I did about 110 shows in three days—part of me just wanted to run away from it all and go home, but I had to be professional.

I always remind myself that modeling is a short career. You put so much work into it, then when you're about 26 years old it stops—and you still have your whole life to think about! I am lucky and proud to have achieved so much at only 22. I don't know what the future holds for me. In 10 or 20 years I hope to have a family and be back in Brazil. But whatever I end up doing, I will always appreciate and follow fashion." ★

Shortly after I did the *Teen Vogue* story, I was booked to walk in a Marc Jacobs runway show, and then my career took off. I started appearing in Marc's campaigns, which led to more editorials, in *Vogue* and Italian *Vogue*.

I realized very quickly that modeling is so much about building relationships. When you work well with someone, he or she will book you again and again. After my Marc Jacobs debut, I met all the top designers and started walking in lots of major shows. I've now done more than ten runway seasons. I have to wear some pretty weird stuff on the catwalk at times, but part of my job is to make it work.

To be a successful model, you have to do both runway and print work. As much as I love being a part of shows, I prefer the excitement of photo shoots. There is a lot more to them than just standing and posing. It's important to understand what the photographer is trying to convey in each shot and to find the story in the styled looks. Every time I work with a photographer like Irving Penn, my job becomes a class. I learn how to dig deeper and look more closely at what he wants to express. Steven Meisel once put a mirror behind his camera so that I could see myself during a shoot! That helped teach me how to pose and move.

"THIS WAS THE FIRST JUMP I HAD TO DO ON A PHOTO SHOOT," TRENTINI SAYS OF A 2003 *TEEN VOGUE* STORY. "I THOUGHT THE PICTURE WAS GOING TO COME OUT HORRIBLY, BUT IT ACTUALLY LOOKED REALLY CUTE!"

teen VOGUE TIP A diva attitude could cost you jobs. People whom Trentini clicked with on set often booked her again for future magazine shoots and ad campaigns, which helped her career take off.

"THIS WAS A GREAT JOB TO WORK ON BECAUSE IT WAS SHOT BY ARTHUR ELGORT, WHO IS SO TALENTED," TRENTINI SAYS OF THIS PAPARAZZI SEND-UP STAGED ON THE COBBLESTONED STREETS OF NEW YORK CITY'S MEATPACKING DISTRICT. "I WAS INEXPERIENCED AT THE TIME, AND ARTHUR WAS VERY PATIENT AND KIND."

The New Supermodel
Chanel Iman

WITH LOADS OF CHARM AND A NAME THAT FORESAW FASHION GREATNESS, THIS YOUNG STUNNER IS MAKING A BID TO BRING BACK THE SUPERMODEL.

Named, as she was, after a legendary designer, and blessed, as she is, with height, high cheekbones, and an unusually fast metabolism, Chanel Iman should be forgiven for viewing a career in fashion as her birthright. She is, after all, in possession of the kind of skyscraping beauty that inspires people, again and again, to stop a girl on the street and tell her that she ought to be a model. But the genetically gifted eighteen-year-old—who got her start in the industry at the tender age of twelve, when her aunt took her to the Los Angeles office of Ford Models one day after middle school—is quick to point out that hard work has played a role in her smash success. "You have to walk into a casting with a lot of energy," she explains, "and you have to be your best. Even when you're young, you have to act like an adult: You have to be responsible and you have to be on time."

In person, Iman—clad in a Forever 21 dress and an Urban Outfitters fedora—is both smaller and younger-looking than anyone accustomed to seeing her grace the runways or the pages of *Vogue* might expect. And she acts like a typical teenager too: She claims that she and her model friends have frequent sleepovers and says that one of the biggest downsides of her job is that it so frequently takes her away from her dog, Louis Dior. ("I bought him a couple of days before I went to Paris," she says, "and when I got there, I went straight to a fitting for Dior. So I asked John Galliano if he thought Dior would be a good name for my dog. He said it would be his honor.")

Iman's career first took off after she competed in the 2006 Ford Supermodel of the World contest, a kind of launching pad for up-and-coming models, in which she placed as a runner-up. Early on, she became a favorite of magazines like *Teen Vogue*. She switched from high school to home school—she has since earned her diploma—and maintained a furious pace of shooting, attending go-sees, and walking dozens of runway shows. "There's not really such a thing as a typical day for a model," Iman says. "Today I met with my accountant, and now I have this interview. I just got back from doing the couture shows in Europe, and I've been shooting major ad campaigns and editorials." The constant, if there is one, is variety. "I'm always, always traveling, having fun, and learning a lot. When I was in school, I had a hard time with French, but I've found that if you're with French people, it's so much

FEBRUARY

teenVOGUE

SPRING PREVIEW

cool pale denim
flirty dresses
bold bags

celebrate
valentine's
day in style

fashion's new
dream girls
KARLIE, CHANEL,
AND ALI
ON THE REAL WORLD
OF MODELING

megawatt
makeup

4 BRIGHT IDEAS

slim chance THE THIN LINE BETWEEN DIET AND DANGER

FROM IMAN'S FASHION WEEK DIARY

★ **7:00 a.m.** Time to wake up! I grab a shower and some fruit for energy.

★ **8:00 a.m.** There's plenty of time before my first show, Peter Som at 11:00, but I love having the chance to catch up with all the models and stylists.

★ **11:45 a.m.** I scramble from Peter Som to my next show, Isaac Mizrahi, at noon. A crew swarms to change my hair, makeup, and wardrobe, with minutes to spare!

★ **1:30 p.m.** I have a short break, so I make some personal calls, like dialing my mom. Then I pick up a wrap for lunch at the gourmet deli around the corner.

★ **2:00 p.m.** I stop by a casting at Vera Wang, where I run into the same group of models I always see.

★ **4:00 p.m.** I arrive early for Marc Jacobs, my final show of the day, at 9:00. Listening to my iPod, I catch my second wind.

★ **8:45 p.m.** The models line up backstage to get ready to walk out on the runway. It's the calm before the storm.

★ **10:30 p.m.** Time for bed! I hope I can sleep in tomorrow.

IMAN IS NAMED AFTER COCO CHANEL, HER MOTHER'S FAVORITE DESIGNER. THE MODEL (ABOVE) TAKES A SHOPPING BREAK BETWEEN PARIS FASHION WEEK SHOWS AT, FITTINGLY, THE CHANEL BOUTIQUE.

THE MODELING INDUSTRY HAS BEEN CRITICIZED IN RECENT YEARS FOR A LACK OF DIVERSITY, PARTICULARLY IN EUROPE. BUT IMAN—WHO IS OF AFRICAN-AMERICAN AND KOREAN DESCENT—MANAGED TO BREAK DOWN RACIAL BARRIERS BY BOOKING HEAVY HITTERS LIKE DOLCE & GABBANA (LEFT) AND GUCCI, WHICH MADE HER THE FIRST BLACK MODEL TO WALK FOR GUCCI IN SEVEN SEASONS.

easier! I also know a little Italian, a little Portuguese, and a few words of Russian," she says. "Being a model has given me a chance to learn so much about how people act and how the world works. I've also learned a lot about fashion, of course, about different fabrics and how to put things together—the dos and don'ts."

Not that she adheres too strictly to the rules. "Fashion is fashion," Iman says airily. "You can wear whatever you want. I wear boots in the summer, which some people would say is a no-no but I think is fabulous." Personality, she says simply, is the key to success. "You can't be afraid to be yourself. When I walk into a casting, I like to show who I am—I want people to know that I'm a regular girl. And a model can be a regular girl," she adds. "You can be fun and have fun with what you're doing." But make no mistake—Iman is also very ambitious, and she's constantly thinking about her future: "I'm just going to keep working hard to take it to the next level," she says. "I want to make myself a brand, not just a model." ★

IMAN IN *VOGUE*

The model turns it on for the camera in a spring 2009 story highlighting the looks of the season.

Practice makes perfect—picture-perfect! "All models have to know their poses, because everybody has bad angles, no matter how beautiful they are. Spend time in front of the mirror to see what looks best." —CHANEL IMAN

Question:

What's the best way to the beauty indust

Answer:

Star hairstylists and share how they got

e break in
ry?

makeup artists
to the top.

The Minimalist
Gucci Westman

FANS LIKE CAMERON DIAZ AND KATE HUDSON ARE WILLING SUBJECTS FOR THIS MAKEUP ARTIST, WHOSE LESS-IS-MORE PHILOSOPHY IS EMBRACED BY HOLLYWOOD AND HIGH-FASHION CLIENTS ALIKE.

"I was born in California, but I grew up in Sweden and moved around Europe a lot during my childhood. At eighteen I went to Switzerland to be an au pair, and the mother I worked for was a fashion journalist. Up until that point, I thought I might want to be a translator—I love learning new languages—but she brought me to fashion shows and exposed me to a very chic world. She gave me big boxes of makeup from Guerlain, Dior, and Chanel—all of it was stuff that she'd gotten as gifts and didn't want.

When I was 23, I decided to go to makeup school at the Christian Chauveau École des Techniques du Maquillage Artistique in Paris. I attended for four months and then went to Los Angeles to take a two-month course in special-effects makeup for film. I had planned to go back to Paris, but I liked L.A. and decided to stay. At first it was very hard for me to get any paying work. I would assist people, but I was always too shy to ask for payment. At that point, the only agent who would take me on was actually the agent's assistant. But she was awesome—she really believed in me. What I learned from that is sometimes allying yourself with the junior people is best because, like you, they have to prove themselves and they share your enthusiasm.

When I moved to L.A., people told me to do a lot of test shoots—where you get together with an aspiring hair-stylist, a model, and a photographer and take pictures for your portfolio—and I did. But I have to say, I didn't feel like the resulting images were anything I could really show during job interviews. You wouldn't want to show up at *Vogue* with just a test book. Instead, I think the best way to get ahead is through assisting, getting exposure on set and doing as much as possible—even for free—to get experience and learn how it works. The most important thing isn't getting paid—it's going out there and getting a taste of what working in the industry *really* means.

Nowadays, when I look for an assistant, I try to find someone with a good personality and passion, and also organizational skills. If the person is lazy, I'm not interested. I like to think that I was a very good assistant back in the day, because I was always doing things ten minutes before anyone asked me to. I look for a similar quality in my assistants.

Being able to learn from your mistakes is important as well. I remember my first big mistake: I made up an actress for a talk show—I think it was *The Tonight Show with Jay Leno*—and I looked at the monitor and saw that her neck

HOW SHE GOT THE LOOK

Here, Westman breaks down a festive makeup look she created for Teen Vogue.

"I wanted to create a smoky eye but with a 24-karat sheen. For a makeup-heavy eye like this, be sure to use a primer first, so that the shadow lasts all night."

"At most shoots, it can take up to an hour to prep skin to be photo-ready. Not with model Ali Michael [pictured here]. Her skin is amazing—creamy, practically poreless porcelain! She barely needed any work at all."

"It's best to keep lips and cheeks light if you're working a heavy eye. Ali's lips are naturally cherry red. I toned them down by dabbing on concealer. Then I finished the look with a simple, silvery gloss."

VOGUE

JULY

COOL GIRL
KATE HUDSON's Effortless Chic (And Teflon Marriage)

Dancing With the Stars
SARAH JESSICA, J.LO, DREW, SIENNA, GISELE & CHARLIZE AT THE PARTY OF THE YEAR

SHAPE-SHIFTING FASHION
Fall's New Silhouettes
The Bustle, the Bell, the Big Shoulder

HIGH ANXIETY
Stop Worrying Yourself Sick

Barefoot Beauty
THE ULTIMATE D.I.Y. PEDICURE

OUR BODIES, HERSELF
The Abortion Battle's Fearless Warrior

"I've worked on all Kate Hudson's Vogue *covers, including this one shot by Mario Testino in 2006. The first ever was in 2002, with Herb Ritts, and I remember immediately being charmed by this beautiful bohemian girl. Now, since I've done Kate's makeup so many times, I always try to find something different to enhance. I especially love her eyes."*

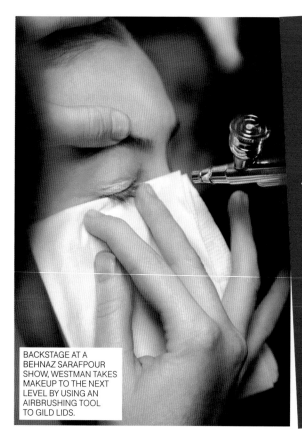

BACKSTAGE AT A BEHNAZ SARAFPOUR SHOW, WESTMAN TAKES MAKEUP TO THE NEXT LEVEL BY USING AN AIRBRUSHING TOOL TO GILD LIDS.

"WHEN YOU'RE *practicing* ON *your own* IN THE BEGINNING, TAKE TIME TO *learn* HOW TO *blend.* BUT WHEN YOU'RE ON A *shoot,* REALIZE THAT NOBODY HAS *patience.* AND *don't limit* YOURSELF. TRY *everything.* *Dare* TO GIVE YOURSELF NEW *challenges.*"

—GUCCI WESTMAN

was a completely different color than her face. I thought to myself, *Oh, my God.* Still, though, I learned—I would never do that again.

Slowly, in Hollywood, I started to meet people. I had a friend who worked as a stylist for the director Spike Jonze, and he trusted my friend enough to give me a job and see if it could work out; years later I ended up as the lead makeup artist on the movie *Being John Malkovich.* Around the same time, I met photographer Bruce Weber and started working with him. It was great to have a foot in both the movie and the fashion worlds, because they're two totally different things. A movie can take six months, and you have to do the same look every day for continuity. Whereas with fashion, every shoot, every day, is different. And the personalities involved vary as well.

I prefer to do fashion work—it's more suited to my life now. When I'm working on a show, I'll meet with the designer a few days beforehand, and we'll do a hair and makeup test. I almost never know what kind of ideas the person will have unless I run into them (though I always know what Rag & Bone is planning, because my husband is one of the

designers), so I bring my entire kit—which is all my lip and eye colors, every pigment, fake eyelashes, and everything else I could possibly need—in a big suitcase. It's the same kit that I bring to editorial shoots, where the makeup I do is influenced by the subject of the story, whether it's a tweed story, a little-black-dress story, or a fairy-tale story. Once I find out the theme of the shoot, I immediately start brainstorming. But I want to be able to give things a little variety. You don't always want things to be so literal—making it your own and giving it your touch is the best part.

The makeup is always inspired by what's happening in the fashion world: The trends end up complementing one another. I work with Revlon as a consultant, creating color collections and advising them conceptually on product development, and that is influenced by what's going on in fashion. Right now I want to bring back the iconic, sexy, all-American girl. But really I like that so many different things are considered fashionable today. It's not like in the fifties, sixties, or seventies, when there was only one look for each era. Now you have so much to choose from. It's very freeing." ★

_teen_VOGUE TIP "Don't wear too much makeup to an interview. People can be suspicious of anyone who tries too hard. You want an air of effortlessness." —GUCCI WESTMAN

Mary Clarke, WESTMAN'S ASSISTANT
AGE 25 **COLLEGE** JOE BLASCO MAKEUP SCHOOL
HOMETOWN YORBA LINDA, CALIFORNIA

"When I was little, when I wasn't stealing my mom's makeup I would be drawing with water-color markers on my brother's face. Those were the first signs that I was meant to be a makeup artist! But even so, I wasn't totally sure until high school. I used to do the makeup for all the plays. One day I asked myself whether I wanted to *work* for the diva or *be* the diva—in other words, act. That was when I realized that a career in makeup was *really* what I wanted. Doing makeup for the theater department was great practice. I got to mess around, make mistakes, and try everything.

I went to college, but whenever I was supposed to be doing homework or writing a paper I would be looking online at different makeup schools instead. Makeup was all I dreamed of. I asked myself, Why am I wasting my time? This is silly! I know *exactly* what I want to do. It fits me *perfectly*. So when I turned eighteen, I dropped out and moved to Los Angeles.

I went to the Joe Blasco Makeup School, which offered a three-month program. Being there helped me with more than just technique; it reinforced what I already knew: that this was what I wanted to do. My teachers started hiring me for films—for a lot of horror movies and special effects, which I ended up not liking because I didn't want to look at ugly things all the time. I wanted them to be beautiful! Around that time, I started working at a M.A.C. cosmetics counter at a Nordstrom. I learned a lot there. M.A.C. is like a mecca for people who love makeup. I met a few photographers there just by giving out my card

and talking to people. Some would say, 'Oh, you're interested in that? I know someone! Here's their information.'

When I turned 21, I felt like I had a good amount of experience, so I quit and started working with an agency. It took three months of e-mailing them once a week before they put me on a job. I used to vary the day and the time that I sent the e-mail—sometimes I'd send it on a Monday afternoon and sometimes on a Thursday morning—because I didn't want them to expect it. Eventually they started sending me out on jobs. And I also kept e-mailing New York agencies, asking to assist their artists when they came to L.A., because I still felt like I had a lot to learn and I wanted to pay my dues.

Now I'm 25 and I recently moved to New York, where my hairstylist-assistant friend who had worked with Gucci recommended me to her. It's been awesome. My job consists of a lot of different things: I have to make sure everything is clean—I keep Gucci's kit in perfect condition. I tissue off the lipstick pal-ettes so that you can see the white lines between the colors and organize her storage area so that I know the location of everything. I help her whenever she needs something, and she teaches me so much.

When you're an artist you think that all you'll ever have to do is be an artist, but there is more to it. There are business aspects, and as the assistant I try to take care of those details and the clerical side as much as possible, so that Gucci can just walk on the set and focus.

For me, the next five years will be about grow-ing. You don't get that many opportunities, and the field gets so narrow at the top: There are only a handful of people up there, and at the bottom there are a million. I don't want to miss my chance, so I'm going to keep assisting for a while, to learn as much as possible."

> "YOUR *girlfriends* ARE YOUR *best tool.* YOU CAN'T LEARN WITHOUT *practicing,* SO *every* TIME YOU ALL GO OUT, YOU SHOULD *put on their makeup!*"
>
> —MARY CLARKE

The Mane Man
Guido Palau

A BEAUTY-SCHOOL DROPOUT, THIS HAIRSTYLIST EVENTUALLY FOUND HIS PASSION—AND A CAREER AS ONE OF THE FASHION WORLD'S TOP EDITORIAL TALENTS.

"Doing hair wasn't a lifelong ambition for me. I wasn't one of those people who dreamed of it or who played with my mother's hair. I grew up in Dorset, a seaside town on the southern coast of England, and didn't really know what I wanted to do. I didn't get particularly good grades in school, and when I left I just wanted to experience life for a bit. I traveled around Europe—I ended up living in Denmark for about a year—then decided I had better get back to England to figure out my life. Fashion had always interested me, and a lot of my friends were hairdressers, so I thought, Oh, I'll do hair.

I was accepted for an apprenticeship at Vidal Sassoon when I was 20. But after about eighteen months I really wasn't doing that well. It was fantastic training but a very strict regime, and basically they fired me and said they didn't think hairdressing was the right profession for me. I *was* probably very bad at my job and deserved to be fired, but having that happen gave me a good push. I thought, I'll show you! I went on to numerous other salons in London, still as an apprentice. At one of them, one day, there was a girl going to work on a photo shoot, and I offered to come along and help. When I arrived at the studio, I felt really connected to what was happening: I realized that this—styling hair for photo shoots—was what I wanted to do.

I spent three more years training in salons, which confirmed that working on clients behind a chair was not my thing. So I started doing test shoots with models, photographers, and makeup artists who were all just starting out. I got an agent to take me on and began working small jobs on my own, gradually building up my experience.

In the early nineties, the grunge movement was starting to happen in England: The original supermodels, like Cindy Crawford and Claudia Schiffer, were being chased out of the spotlight by the Kate Mosses, the Amber Vallettas, and the Shalom Harlows. Those girls are big stars now, but back then they were an alternative kind of beauty. And I was riding that wave with a new group of photographers and stylists; it really catapulted my career. I came to New York with Kate Moss and British photographer David Sims, and we started working on print-ad campaigns for Calvin Klein—that pushed us all up to a very high level. It was my big break. I continued learning and doing photo shoots and fashion shows and went on to work with fantastic photographers I had always dreamed of teaming up with—like Richard Avedon, Irving Penn, Bruce Weber, and Steven Meisel—and amazing designers like Marc Jacobs."

PALAU CONSIDERS
PONYTAILS TO BE THE
PERFECT HAIRSTYLE:
"THEY'RE IDEAL FOR
EVERY DAY. LOW-
MAINTENANCE
BUT CHIC!"

PALAU IS KNOWN FOR
HIS OVER-THE-TOP
TAKE ON HAIR AND
ACCESSORIES, SEEN HERE
ON MODELS LIU WEN
(LEFT) AND CONSTANCE.

BABY
LOVE

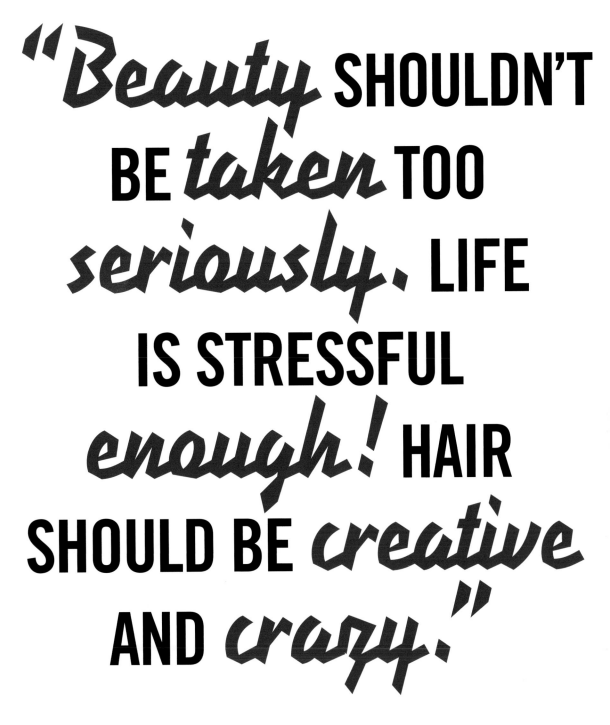

"Beauty SHOULDN'T BE *taken* TOO *seriously.* LIFE IS STRESSFUL *enough!* HAIR SHOULD BE *creative* AND *crazy.*"

—GUIDO PALAU

MODEL MANES

Palau's height-of-fashion hairstyles in Vogue.

GISELE BÜNDCHEN'S
UNDONE GLAMOUR.

COCO ROCHA'S
EXTREME VOLUME.

SLEEK AND SHINY
ON GEMMA WARD.

A TECHNICOLOR
PONYTAIL ON RAQUEL
ZIMMERMANN.

teenVOGUE TIP "Once you find your calling, really go for it. I didn't know what I wanted to do. I got fired from my first salon job, but that gave me a good push." —GUIDO PALAU

JAPANESE ANIME CHARACTERS WERE PALAU'S INSPIRATION FOR THIS SHOOT.

What's the difference between doing hair at a shoot and doing hair for the runway?

At a shoot, the hair is static and you can perfect it. Whereas when you're at a fashion show, there are so many elements that can go wrong, like girls arriving late or with dirty hair. The other day I did a show, and 20 girls arrived nineteen minutes before the start. You're under a different kind of pressure. A thousand people are backstage doing their jobs—makeup artists, photographers, journalists—and the power is being switched off or the generators are blown, and sometimes you have to let go of perfection. There are aspects that you can't control, but that's part of the excitement of being backstage at a fashion show.

Do you prefer one over the other?

It's great to do both. Once I finish the shows each season I'll have had enough and be happy to go back to the studio. But when the next season rolls around, I'll get buzzed up about it again.

How do you and the designer agree on the look for a show?

A lot of the designers I work with—like Marc Jacobs, Miuccia Prada, Nicolas Ghesquière, and Calvin Klein—I've worked with for a long time. So I understand the kind of woman they're trying to embody in their collections. They have ideas, I have ideas, we talk about it, and it's a collaboration. Some designers will call you in, and you're there for an hour and a half. With others, you're there for three days. You have to be open and unafraid of criticism,

because you're working together to reach the same point. Sometimes it comes easily, and sometimes it takes a bit of work—but that is part of the process.

How often do you end up cutting hair?

Not very often at all. Obviously, models can't have their hair cut every time you work with them. In a salon, being a hairdresser is all about cutting. My job is a different kind of thing: It's to interpret fashion for a shoot or a show, and it's knowing when to do the right thing at the right moment—knowing when to push something and create something strange and wonderful and fantastic. That fantasy is what keeps the whole industry going. It can't always be about reality—if we just put reality on the pages of a fashion magazine, there would be nothing to strive for.

What advice do you have for aspiring hairstylists?

First you have to work at a salon to get your groundwork, and then you need to move someplace where there are photographers, magazines, and designers—like Milan, Paris, London, or New York. Then you should contact someone like me, through an agency, and offer to assist on a show. If you don't live in a big city yet, go to a college where there are photography students who might need help with hairdos for their pictures, or get in touch with local modeling agencies to see if any of the models need their hair done for test pictures. You can't do it overnight. You need to build your portfolio and your reputation, and that can take a while. And you really must be passionate about hair—you have to make the decision to do it and follow through. ★

The Drama Queen
Pat McGrath

COLLABORATING WITH FASHION'S MOST CELEBRATED DESIGNERS AND PHOTOGRAPHERS FROM A YOUNG AGE PROPELLED THIS SELF-TAUGHT MAKEUP WHIZ TO THE TOP.

She's considered by many to be the world's most influential makeup artist, and it would probably be easier to enumerate the very few top designers, photographers, and fashion magazines she *hasn't* worked with than to rattle off the staggeringly long list of those she has. But Pat McGrath, superstar though she is, has a personal history that offers hope to any girl (or boy) who would like to paint faces for a living. Not only is she almost entirely self-taught—and thought by some to be all the better for it—but the Northampton, England–born former art student, who was raised by a Jamaican immigrant mother, had no particular "in" when she started making her way through the London fashion world more than a decade and a half ago.

Today McGrath spends her time shuttling between shows and editorial and advertising shoots and serving as the Global Creative/Design Director for Procter & Gamble Beauty (one of the world's largest beauty companies; it owns Cover Girl and Max Factor).

McGRATH'S NUMBERS

Each show season she uses:

- ★ 42 MAKEUP ARTISTS (ON HER TEAM)
- ★ 12 HOTEL ROOMS
- ★ 55 BAGS OF MAKEUP
- ★ 20 BAGS OF REFERENCE BOOKS AND IMAGES
- ★ 822 PAIRS OF FALSE EYELASHES
- ★ 42 DIFFERENT EYELINER PENCILS
- ★ 56 BOTTLES OF FOUNDATION
- ★ 18 TYPES OF FACIAL AND BODY MOISTURIZER
- ★ 21 PACKAGES OF 100-COUNT MAKEUP WIPES

SPRING 2008 COUTURE

SPRING 2007 COUTURE

SPRING 2004 COUTURE

When did you first realize that "makeup artist" was a job and, furthermore, the right job for you?
When I was in school, people would approach me on the street to say how much they liked the makeup I was wearing. That's when I realized I could do makeup for a living.

You're known for your ability to create a very diverse range of looks. Where do you get your ideas?
I get them from everything around me: books, films, TV, history, photographs, art exhibitions, nightlife, travel, fashion, and nature.

What are the favorite looks you have conceived over the years?
The top three are probably the Dior 2004 Spring couture show, which had an Egyptian theme; the Dior 2005 Fall couture look, which celebrated the 100-year anniversary of Christian Dior's birth; and a shoot I did for Italian *Vogue*'s March 2007 issue called Sublime, with model Sasha Pivovarova in forties style.

What's the best part of your job?
The inspiring, highly creative people I work with. We work extremely hard, but we have so much fun doing it!

What tips do you have for young people looking to break in to the business?
Consider working at a makeup counter to get lots of practice doing makeup on people of all ages and with different skin tones. This, along with the training that the company provides, will make you a better artist. Plus, your counter colleagues may just lend you a helping hand with your career in the future. Assist a working makeup artist, someone who has a lot of experience in the industry. It will be an invaluable opportunity. Build your portfolio by test-shooting with a variety of photographers. And finally, when you're confident of your work, take your book to agencies that represent hair and makeup talent.

What can an aspiring makeup artist do right now to better her odds?
Take color theory and art classes to get the basics on how to mix colors and work with light and shadow. These are the guiding principles for all great makeup artists. Second, collect makeup images you like from magazines, the Internet, and people on the street. Practice re-creating these looks so that you can hone your skills. Keep up on the latest magazine editorials and fashion shows—these are where makeup trends are created. Third, take classes on photography, lighting, and composition, so that you know what good photography entails. ★

teenVOGUE TIP "For a quick fix, wear mascara, put light concealer on dark under-eye circles, and apply color on at least one feature: the eyes, cheeks, or lips. You'll look instantly vibrant!" —PAT McGRATH

"I LIKE TO USE UNEXPECTED ELEMENTS, LIKE METALLIC ACCENTS, TO CREATE UNIQUE LOOKS," McGRATH SAYS. HERE, MODEL SASHA PIVOVAROVA SPORTS GLITTERY LIDS IN A SHOOT PHOTOGRAPHED BY STEVEN MEISEL.

ON MODEL SNEJANA
ONOPKA, McGRATH
BLITHELY (AND
SUCCESSFULLY) BREAKS
THE CONVENTION OF
HIGHLIGHTING ONLY
ONE FACIAL FEATURE,
WHILE SIMULTANEOUSLY
USING NONTRADITIONAL
MAKEUP COLORS.

McGrath's top tip:
"LOVING *makeup* IS *crucial* TO BEING A GREAT MAKEUP *artist.* BUT HAVING *innovative ideas* AND THINKING *outside the box* ARE WHAT WILL SET YOU *apart* FROM THE *rest* OF THE *pack.*"

TEEN VOGUE, 2008

"I WAS *one* OF THE *first* TO WORK WITH THIS MODEL, *Viktoriya Sasonkina.* SHE REMINDS *me of* A YOUNG *Jessica Stam.*"

—PAT McGRATH

The Wild Card
Serge Normant

THIS SUPERSTAR HAIRSTYLIST IS KNOWN FOR CREATING LARGER-THAN-LIFE LOOKS.

As one of the most versatile hairstylists in the world, Serge Normant balances his time among his signature salons (two in New York and one in Los Angeles), magazine shoots, advertising campaigns, runway shows, and a devoted celebrity following that includes Sarah Jessica Parker and Julia Roberts.

But his beginnings in the business weren't *quite* so glamorous. Normant started cutting hair when he was just thirteen; it was his mother who served, he says, as his "first victim." Growing up in a small town outside Paris in the sixties, Normant was enamored of the amazing hairdos of the era. "I loved the sculptural aspect involved in hairstyling," he explains. "For me, hair is the most ephemeral art form. I love that you can construct a whole enormous updo and two seconds later just totally destroy it. And with the right haircut, you

"GIRLS OFTEN FIGHT THEIR NATURAL HAIR TEXTURE. INSTEAD, THEY SHOULD EMBRACE IT!" NOTES NORMANT, WHO CREATED THIS IMAGE FOR *TEEN VOGUE* IN 2008.

can change the way someone feels. It can give them a new start on life for a few months at a time." With that in mind, Normant began his career by interpreting what he saw in magazines. Fortunately, his *mère* was *très* game. "I gave her a very Vidal Sassoon-ish cut," he recalls. "Although my father didn't quite understand it, she was very enthusiastic, creative, and open."

By the time he turned 20, Normant was working at a Jacques Dessange salon in Paris. There he met hairstylist Bruno Pittini, the salon's creative director. "He was my mentor," Normant says. He followed Pittini to America and worked with him for several years. Once in New York, it didn't take long for Normant to find a place in fashion. "I was living with Laura Mercier, the makeup artist, and through her I met the photographers Steven Meisel, Michael Thompson, and Walter Chin. Meeting them meant they might think of me to replace someone on a shoot—one here, one there—and that's how I got started, a little at a time. It was the era of the supermodels—like Naomi Campbell, Linda Evangelista, and Cindy Crawford—and since I had been thrown in with those people, I had to keep up with the pace. It was exciting to be part of that generation."

Normant was equally excited when he began to work with actresses in the early nineties. "I met Julia Roberts on a *Vanity Fair* photo shoot with Herb Ritts. It was after

PHOTOGRAPHED IN FRONT OF HIS L.A. SALON, NORMANT GIVES A MODEL ONE OF HIS SIGNATURE VOLUMINOUS LOOKS.

NORMANT'S BOOK WAS PUBLISHED IN 2004.

Pretty Woman came out," Normant explains. "We clicked and started working together regularly and became very close friends." (In a TV appearance, Roberts remembered their first meeting thusly: "I had been shooting all night on a movie.... I sat down for Serge to do my hair, and about three and a half minutes later I fell asleep. And he just very gently moved my head around and did my hair while I slept. And I woke up and looked fabulous.")

Nowadays, balancing celebrity styling, real women, and models is just part of Normant's day-to-day life. "When you style a model for a fashion editorial story, you can get a little bit more crazy with her hair, whereas if you do an actress for the red carpet, she has to look contemporary and cool but not overdone," he says. "A lot of women and girls want to experience what they see on the red carpet, in movies, or on the catwalk. The truth is, I always like to mix in everything. Regardless of where I'm working or who I'm working on, I'm still doing the same job—styling hair. But being able to do it in so many different situations and for different reasons makes it exciting." ★

teenVOGUE TIP "Once a door is opened, make sure it stays open by always being reliable. I got started a little bit at a time; photographers here and there remembered me for shoots, until my reputation was finally proven." —SERGE NORMANT

"WITH EACH LEARNING
EXPERIENCE I
BETTER MYSELF,"
SAYS NORMANT, WHO
GAVE MODEL NATALIA
VODIANOVA A DEMURE
BUT DARING DO.

The Beauty School Knockout
Jemma Kidd

THIS ENTREPRENEUR GAVE UP MODELING TO FULFILL HER DREAMS OF OPENING A BEAUTY SCHOOL THAT TRAINS FUTURE MAKEUP ARTISTS AND CREATING THREE COSMETICS COLLECTIONS TO CALL HER OWN.

The saying goes that necessity is the mother of invention. No one knows this better than makeup artist Jemma Kidd. A short stint as a model sparked her fascination with the beauty world—and helped her realize the need for make-up education. Soon enough, she opened an eponymous school in London. Three lines of products (a luxury one sold at Neiman Marcus, a line intended for use by makeup professionals, and a mass-market collection sold at Target) followed. What's next for this budding beauty mogul? "More products," Kidd says. "And more schools! I love teaching girls and women how to look their best."

How did you break in to the beauty business?
I started my career as a model, but I never felt comfortable in front of the camera. I found that I was more interested in what the makeup artists were applying to my face than what was happening on the catwalk. But it's not like I always knew that I would work in the beauty industry—I used to be a real tomboy!

Who taught you to apply makeup?
I was lucky to have makeup artist Mary Greenwell as my

mentor. I also did basic training at a school in London called Glauca Rossi School of Makeup.

Do you have a beauty-biz role model?
Estée Lauder is my all-time favorite. I also think Pat McGrath and Stéphane Marais are the most talented makeup artists in the industry today.

What is the inspiration behind the Jemma Kidd Makeup School?
Millions of women wear makeup, but so few of them have been taught exactly how to apply it. I founded the school seven years ago as a place where people could go to learn how to put on makeup, whether professionally as a makeup artist or just to look their best. I love working with girls and women who come to my makeup school for lessons. They teach me as much as I teach them, and I always get great ideas for new products!

What makes your products different from all the other ones on the market?
I wanted to create my own line right from the start of my

"NO MATTER WHAT LOOK YOU'RE CREATING, SKIN SHOULD BE AT ITS BEST," SAYS KIDD, WHO FASHIONED AN INTENSE VIOLET EYE FOR *TEEN VOGUE* IN 2006.

KIDD ENCOURAGES PLAYING WITH SHEER COLORS FOR A PRETTY DAYTIME LOOK.

career. It was always my dream, but it just took a long time to get off the ground. The products are meant to be really user-friendly—we provide step-by-step guides, tips, and tricks with all of them.

What's a typical day in your life like?

There's one word you could use to describe my typical day: *manic*. I usually have meetings at the school, then meetings with my team to discuss new product development, press events, or writing my beauty column for *You* magazine, which comes with *The Mail on Sunday* [a newspaper in the United Kingdom]. I do try to get up early to ride my horses—it's a real passion of mine, and I have both show-jumping and dressage horses. And I try to do yoga a couple of times a week. Normally, I am so exhausted that I'm in bed early!

What are some common mistakes that women make when it comes to makeup?

Foundation always seems to be the problem. The key is to use it only where it's needed. If you have good skin, don't cover it up! Apply a small amount of foundation, blending well around the hairline and the jaw, then layer on more where needed. Women often tend to use the wrong shade of foundation. I always buy two, one slightly lighter than my natural skin tone and one slightly darker. Then I mix them

to coordinate with my skin tone. Make sure that you apply foundation in a natural light, to get the best color match.

Do you find there's a big difference between runway and real-life makeup?

I love working backstage! The energy is just amazingly creative. One thing women don't realize, though, is that just because it's on the runway doesn't mean it's unattainable—it doesn't always have to be complicated couture looks. Plenty of runway makeup is relaxed and glowy, like what you typically see at Chloé or Stella McCartney. Just mix a skin illuminator with foundation to create soft, dewy skin, and brush a touch of powder along the nose and chin. Use a camel-colored eye shadow on lids and a warm blush on cheeks in a cream formula so that it blends well into the skin for a natural finish.

What kind of advice would you give aspiring beauty entrepreneurs?

You have to be 100 percent dedicated. The makeup world is evolving so fast that it's important to keep up with all the products and formulations on the market. Get as much experience as you can by working on people of different ages, with different features and face shapes. And be patient: It takes years to make a living! ★

BEAUTY AT WORK

From runway gigs to product development, Kidd is developing her own brand.

LIQUID EYELINER FROM HER LOWER-PRICED JK LINE, AVAILABLE AT TARGET.

"MY SISTER, MODEL JODIE KIDD [RIGHT], IS MY MUSE."

BARGAIN-HUNTING AT RICKY'S, THE FAMOUS BEAUTY EMPORIUM IN NEW YORK CITY.

BACKSTAGE AT LONDON FASHION WEEK WITH HER SISTER.

***teen*VOGUE TIP** "Take a makeup lesson with a professional—the knowledge will last your whole life. And drink plenty of water. If your skin is dry, you'll look unfinished no matter how much makeup you have on." —JEMMA KIDD

BEAUTY TOOL KIT
essential items of the pros

HAIR PICK
Gives definition to bangs.

SHARPENER
Keeps pencils in perfect condition for fine lining.

KLORANE DRY SHAMPOO
Instantly adds texture to hair.

ROUND BRUSH
For soft, loose waves.

T3 HAIR DRYER
Favored by stylists for its quiet power.

LITTLE SCISSORS
Safely trim false lashes.

Q-TIPS
Used to apply makeup and skin treatments.

HAIR ROLLERS
Add lift to the crown.

FALSE LASHES
A must-have for defined eyes.

BRUSHES
Makeup artists always have a collection.

M.A.C. CLEANSING TIPS
Premoistened to erase eyeliner errors precisely.

KIEHL'S LIP BALM SPF 15
Provides sun protection and sheen.

NAIL FILE
A manicure essential.

BOOKS
A compendium of references is important.

CLIPS
Separate sections of hair while styling.

BANDS AND BOBBY PINS
Makeup artists and hairstylists keep these on hand.

BEAUTY BLENDER SPONGE
A favorite among makeup artists.

SHU UEMURA CURLER
Considered the gold standard in lash curlers.

ELNETT HAIR SPRAY
Stylists bring back this beloved product from Europe.

WEDGE SPONGES
Disposable for hygienic blending.

LINEA PRO FLAT IRON
Ceramic plates ensure even straightening.

MASON PEARSON BRUSH
Indispensable for backstage blowouts.

Break in to the industry with these tips.

★ START A KIT OF BEAUTY MUST-HAVES—HAIRBRUSHES, CLIPS, AND EXTENSIONS FOR HAIRSTYLISTS; BRUSHES, MAKEUP, AND SKIN CARE FOR MAKEUP ARTISTS.

★ KEEP SUPPLIES ORGANIZED. YOU'LL NEED TO KNOW EXACTLY HOW TO ARRANGE EVERYTHING AT A SHOOT, WHICH IS A HIGH-PRESSURE ENVIRONMENT.

★ WORK AT A MAKEUP COUNTER OR A SALON WHILE YOU'RE IN HIGH SCHOOL OR COLLEGE. YOU'LL GET TO PRACTICE ON PEOPLE WITH DIFFERENT HAIR TEXTURES AND SKIN TONES.

★ MOVE TO A MAJOR FASHION CITY, LIKE MILAN, PARIS, LONDON, OR NEW YORK. THEN CONTACT SOMEONE YOU ADMIRE THROUGH HIS OR HER AGENCY (DO THE RESEARCH ONLINE) AND OFFER TO ASSIST AT A SHOW OR A SHOOT.

★ WATCH MOVIES FROM DIFFERENT ERAS SO THAT YOU AMASS A WIDE RANGE OF BEAUTY REFERENCES AND INSPIRATIONS.

★ MAKE FRIENDS WITH FELLOW ASSISTANTS—THEY'LL HAVE THE BEST JOB LEADS, AND AS YOU ADVANCE IN YOUR CAREER, THEY WILL TOO.

★ AT INTERVIEWS AND WHILE ON THE JOB, WEAR CLEAN, NATURAL MAKEUP AND KEEP YOUR HAIR SIMPLE. YOUR LOOK SHOULD APPEAR EFFORTLESS, TO KEEP THE FOCUS ON THE WORK YOU DO.

★ MISTAKES ARE INEVITABLE, AND TASTES CONSTANTLY CHANGE. TAKE TIME TO REVIEW YOUR WORK AND BECOME STRONGER.

Question:

How can I become a photographer?

Answer:

Here, twelve renow their stories and tips related professions.

fashion

ned lensmen tell

Plus, discover

The Industry Icon

Patrick Demarchelier

DEMARCHELIER FOUND HIMSELF ON THE OPPOSITE SIDE OF THE CAMERA WITH HIS CAMEO IN THE *SEX AND THE CITY* MOVIE IN 2008. (REAL-LIFE *VOGUE* EDITORS, FROM LEFT, LAWREN HOWELL, PLUM SYKES, AND ANDRÉ LEON TALLEY ALSO TOOK STAR TURNS.)

THIS FASHION-WORLD FAVORITE HAS THE ULTIMATE INSIDER ACCESS.

In his decades-long career, world-renowned photographer Patrick Demarchelier has focused his lens on everyone from Diana, Princess of Wales, to Britney Spears. He has worked extensively for *Vogue* and *Vanity Fair,* among numerous other publications, and has created ad campaigns for Dior, Chanel, L'Oréal, and Louis Vuitton. And while he's famed for his facility with the camera as well as the subject, Demarchelier's first jobs in his chosen field were, he says, instructively humble.

"I started by working in a photo shop in Normandy, France, where I grew up," he recalls. "I did portraits for weddings and took pictures for passports, and that's where I learned how to print. Then I moved to Paris and started working in a photography lab." Mindful of his ultimate goal, he managed to wrangle a job taking test photos of models for a local school and agency—"I did their books," he says, "about 20 girls a month"—and then, after a six-month stint assisting photographer Hans Feurer, Demarchelier went out on his own. "My first big job in France was for American *Vogue,*" he says, "and in 1975 I moved to New York City."

Despite his obvious mastery of the form—he recently released a monograph titled *Patrick Demarchelier*—he insists that he is still, on some level, a student. "Photography is something you learn more about every day," he explains. "Even me—I'm still learning. It's a vast form of art." ★

"TAKE PICTURES *all the time.* *Don't worry* IF YOU TAKE A *bad photograph;* YOU *learn more* BY TAKING A BAD PICTURE THAN A *good* ONE. IF YOU *don't like it,* *study it* AND FIGURE OUT WHY YOU DON'T LIKE IT. *You'll learn* FROM YOUR *mistake."*

—PATRICK DEMARCHELIER

A favorite of celebrities and models alike, Demarchelier is the go-to lensman for high-wattage cover shots. In his work for Teen Vogue, *he has shot a who's who of young Hollywood.*

"There are many stories that showcase just designers or models. But I wanted to show the people at the couture ateliers who work so hard for months before the show. The workers I shot weren't at all nervous—they were very proud to be part of the picture and to be involved with the creation of Natalia's dress."

"Keeping the balloon from flying away in the wind took great team-work—everyone was trying to capture it!"

"Natalia is one of the best girls in the world. She's not just a great beauty, either; she is also a terrific person and wonderful mother. Every model is different—they each have their own charm that makes them unique."

A TEAM OF THIRTEEN—INCLUDING MAKEUP ARTIST CHRISTIAN McCULLOCH (LEFT) AND HAIRSTYLIST TEDDY CHARLES (RIGHT)— TRAVELED TO MIAMI TO SHOOT TEEN MODEL GEMMA WARD FOR THE FEBRUARY ISSUE.

teenVOGUE TIP Start small. "I took wedding portraits and even passport pictures before I started assisting. Every little thing can help you grow." —PATRICK DEMARCHELIER

> "*Photography* IS *something* YOU *learn* MORE ABOUT *every day*. EVEN ME—I'M STILL *learning*. IT'S A VAST FORM OF *art*."
>
> —PATRICK DEMARCHELIER

Victor Demarchelier,
PATRICK DEMARCHELIER'S ASSISTANT
AGE 24 COLLEGE VASSAR COLLEGE
HOMETOWN NEW YORK, NEW YORK

LEIGHTON MEESTER'S FEBRUARY 2009 *TEEN VOGUE* COVER STORY WAS HER FIRST SHOOT WITH DEMARCHELIER.

"When I was very little, I would sometimes travel with my father on jobs. I don't remember much about the shoots, except that all the people were so nice and it was such a relaxed atmosphere. I thought everyone was my father's friend, just hanging out; I didn't think it was work.

At the start of college, I wanted to work in finance, so I decided that economics would be something practical to study. But by my sophomore and junior years, I began focusing more on studio art: printmaking and, eventually, photography. As soon as I graduated, I started working with my father as an assistant.

There are certain aspects of photography that are good to learn in school, like printing and other technical things, but there are others that you can grasp faster as an assistant. Of course, it's very important to be on time and work hard, but when you're an assistant you shouldn't forget that you are there to soak things in. Keep your eyes open.

The more people you talk to, the more you understand, so at shoots I ask everyone a lot of questions. I want to understand different points of view, the ways people think.

Now I'm starting to publish my own pictures in magazines including *Cream, Glitterati,* and *Inked.* I love fashion because I enjoy working with a team of people—hairdressers, makeup artists, models—and the outcome, I think, is really nice. The people in this business are just so great, and that's a big part of why it's something I want to be involved with."

The Young Vibe
Frederike Helwig

AN EARLY START AND STRONG TECHNICAL TRAINING WERE THE KEYS TO SUCCESS FOR THIS PHOTOGRAPHER.

Photography is a very democratic form of art. As frequent *Teen Vogue* and *Vogue* contributor Frederike Helwig points out, "There's no formula. You just pick up a camera and start." And although Helwig got her first paying gig with British magazine *i-D* before she had even graduated from art school, she says that it's important to begin slowly, to learn how to feel comfortable with a camera before attempting a big fashion shoot. "There's a lot of insecurity at the beginning of a career," she explains. "Suddenly, people—the stylists, the models—are watching you. Photography is something you do by yourself at the beginning, but in fashion you work as a team."

How did you first become interested in photography?
I grew up in Germany and started taking pictures in school when I was sixteen. I was in a youth photography club, which was very low-key, and then at eighteen I said, "Okay, I'd like to do this for a living." So I went to a two-year photography school in Munich, which was very technical—learning everything about how it works, from A to Z—followed by two years at an English art college that was very creative. Those two experiences were a good combination.

What was your first professional assignment, and how did you get it?
While I was still in college, I rang up the creative director of *i-D* and asked if I could show him my work. He liked it, so he commissioned me to shoot an "underwear directory," lots of different pictures of the latest fashions in underwear. The story was three pages, but my budget was only £50 [about U.S. $75] per page. They said, "You better shoot the whole story on three rolls of film, because with printing, £150 isn't going to get you very far!" I used a few models and a few of my friends, and we just tried to have fun. But truthfully, it was a bit scary: You photograph your friends all the time, but all of a sudden you have to shoot them for a purpose, to feature clothes, and it's a different approach. It's not just about capturing a moment. But *i-D* loved the results, and from then on I was doing directories for them on a regular basis. I spent about three years working for the magazine, building up my name and reputation and fine-tuning my style.

How does a photographer develop her own style?
You have to find out what you like within the pictures you

"DON'T *conform.* THE BEST WAY TO *take a picture* IS TO STICK TO WHAT *you like,* NOT TO WHAT YOU *think someone else* MIGHT LIKE."

—FREDERIKE HELWIG

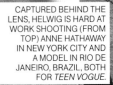

CAPTURED BEHIND THE LENS, HELWIG IS HARD AT WORK SHOOTING (FROM TOP) ANNE HATHAWAY IN NEW YORK CITY AND A MODEL IN RIO DE JANEIRO, BRAZIL, BOTH FOR *TEEN VOGUE.*

take. You start off by shooting loads of pictures, and then if you're lucky there will be one that really appeals to you, that tells you a bit more than the others. You look at it longer, you notice it, and then you try taking pictures like that more often. Really, I think *language* may be a better word for it than *style,* because it's not taking the same picture over and over again—it's feeling comfortable with a way of working.

So many aspiring photographers start out as assistants. Why didn't you do that?
Honestly, back then I think being female made it more difficult to find an assistant position.

What do you look for in an assistant?
Somebody who's really keen and willing to help out, adaptable, and charming. My agency will sometimes find people for me, so that's one way to get your start: by approaching an agency.

So what did you do after your three years with i-D?
I went over to *The Face,* and I started doing advertising jobs with companies like Nike. And now I work for *Teen Vogue,* American *Vogue,* British *Vogue, The New York Times Magazine,* and many others.

What are the differences between editorial work and advertising work?
With editorial, you have more freedom—you're often the art director as well as the photographer. With ads, it's a bit stricter: The bottom line is that you're there to sell. But you get paid more to do the advertising jobs.

What is your job like on a day-to-day basis?
I travel a lot, so I'm often away from home for two weeks of every month, shooting and scouting. And when I'm in London I do office work—editing film, overseeing the digital retouching, taking meetings, and prepping for the next shoot.

Do you prefer to shoot digital or with film?
I'm mainly digital now, but I still use film for smaller jobs. You're more independent with film—you can just turn up with your camera. Whereas when you shoot digital, you need a computer and a digital technician to operate it.

Can you share any simple tips about how to take a better picture?
Have integrity and stick to your own taste. Be as free as possible, experiment as much as you can, and surprise yourself. ★

teen VOGUE TIP "When you're just beginning, don't start with fashion. Find your language in basic photography first, and then you can apply that language to fashion." —FREDERIKE HELWIG

HELWIG'S WORK IN *TEEN VOGUE*

From celebrity portraits to fashion shoots, Helwig takes a colorful approach.

ISSUE: October 2004
THE CONCEPT: "We shot this while Kirsten Dunst was in the middle of filming her movie *Elizabethtown* with director Cameron Crowe and actor Orlando Bloom. We wanted to get outdoor shots of her in the beautiful cornfields of Kentucky."
THE SCOOP: "It was a very hot summer day, so Kirsten wasn't too sure about shooting outdoors—but she did it anyway. And she loved the pussycat so much that she wanted to keep her."

ISSUE: October/November 2003
THE CONCEPT: "This was my second fashion shoot for *Teen Vogue*. We wanted to shoot bright, sporty winter clothes."
THE SCOOP: "We were only meant to shoot for two days in Squaw Valley, California, but had to stay an extra day because there was supposed to be a nasty snowstorm. But we woke up and were greeted with the most beautiful, snowy morning! It was great fun to zoom around on those snowmobiles."

ISSUE: November 2006
THE CONCEPT: "We wanted to capture Hay-on-Wye in Wales. It's this wonderfully tiny village with a beautiful, old, decrepit castle in the city center."
THE SCOOP: "Each year, Hay-on-Wye hosts an international book fair, with journalists and authors coming from all over the world. The town is full of books for that reason. Nearly every shop is a bookshop—it was exactly the right background for the *Teen Vogue* story."

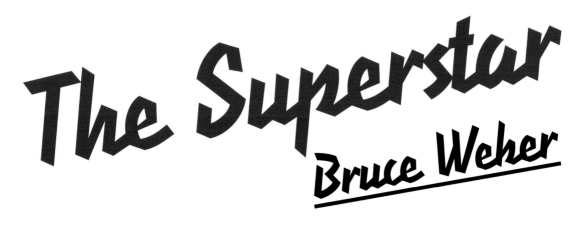

The Superstar
Bruce Weber

HIS EASY, INTIMATE IMAGES OF BEAUTIFUL YOUNG PEOPLE (ABERCROMBIE, ANYONE?) HAVE ESTABLISHED THIS LENSMAN AS ONE OF THE FASHION WORLD'S MOST CELEBRATED TALENTS.

For more than four decades, Bruce Weber has been one of the most influential photographers in the world, working for magazines like *Vogue, GQ,* and *Vanity Fair* and creating countless iconic images for advertising clients like Calvin Klein and Ralph Lauren. His aesthetic also informs the (sometimes controversial) campaigns he has shot for Abercrombie & Fitch since 1993. Aspiring photographers interested in familiarizing themselves with his style should start by checking out any of his 25-plus published books. Although one can learn a lot simply by scrutinizing Weber's work, he was also willing to spend a little time sharing his accrued wisdom.

How did you first become interested in photography?
I was a lonely kid growing up in a farm town—my parents traveled a lot and I didn't play any sports. So I began to use photography as a means to communicate with other people and to showcase my adventures out in the world.

Whose work has inspired you?
Today it could be Diane Arbus, yesterday it could have been Richard Avedon, and two weeks ago maybe it was Edward Weston. Tomorrow my favorite photographer could be someone who's hungry enough to save their money to buy their first camera and photograph something that they hold dear.

As one of the world's top talents, what tips do you have for aspiring photographers?
Well, I read a lot of books. I believe that words open your world and help you to see each day as if you've never seen anything before.

Are there any rules an amateur can follow to take a better picture?
Stay close to home. Remember: Your backyard studio can be the city of Paris.

Do you feel that it's important for a young photographer to go to art school?
Yes. Meet with your teachers and feel comfortable enough with them that you can show them the worst photograph you ever took. You will learn something from those experiences.

THIS STORY, STYLED BY GRACE CODDINGTON FOR *VOGUE* IN 1998, CAPTURED THE OFFBEAT NUPTIALS OF TWO DOGS.

How about assisting a working photographer? What can one expect to learn from that experience?

My assistants stay for a few years and then go on to become photographers or cinematographers or to work in other ways where photography is still a large part of their lives. It's definitely important to work with someone who has a big life.

Of the shoots you've done for **Teen Vogue**, *which stands out as your favorite?*

Kristen Stewart for the March 2007 issue [left]. I shot her before *Twilight,* and at that point she hardly ever wore dresses. But she trusted me enough to do so for the pictures. We just had a good time together being friends. I hope the photos show that happening. ★

"Be flexible. No matter how much you plan, you can never be sure that everything will turn out the way it's supposed to. Make sure you're always able to change things at a moment's notice." —BRUCE WEBER

PAPARAZZI FOLLOWED ZAC EFRON—PHOTOGRAPHED IN MONTAUK, NEW YORK—TO THIS SHOOT.

THE JOURNALS OF DAN ELDON
THE JOURNEY IS THE DESTINATION

"I FIRST SHOT NATALIE PORTMAN WHEN SHE WAS FOURTEEN YEARS OLD," WEBER SAYS. THE PICTURES OF HER ARE "A RECORD OF A BEAUTIFUL PERSON."

PRETTY-PUNK FASHION, SHOT IN BRIDGEHAMPTON, NEW YORK, IN 2008 FOR *TEEN VOGUE*.

MISCHA BARTON IN A 2006 *TEEN VOGUE* SHOOT INSPIRED BY FOLKSINGER JONI MITCHELL.

Sherri O'Connor, WEBER'S ASSISTANT
AGE 28 COLLEGE THE UNIVERSITY OF THE ARTS HOMETOWN TRUMBULL, CONNECTICUT

"As an artist, I have always been very influenced by what I see in magazines. When I was a teenager, I was inspired by the images and used to draw from them. When I went to art school I realized that the kind of photography I liked to do was well suited to fashion. After college I started working at a photo studio, where I met photographers and networked with their assistants, which helped me get assistant jobs. Now, in addition to being a digital technician, I'm also a full-time freelance assistant, working with photographers like Bruce Weber and William Abranowicz. I organize the cameras, lenses, and equipment; set up the backdrops and lights; and operate the digital cameras and the software that goes along with them.

Being on set with a professional photographer is a fantastic way to learn about the business and also a great preparation for your own career. I've been with Bruce on several of his biggest advertising jobs, for Abercrombie & Fitch and Ralph Lauren, and even though the set may seem chaotic, he is totally in the moment. For him, it's almost like breathing. He's very intuitive, and it has been educational for me to see that. Assisting is not essential—lots of photographers haven't done it—but I think it helps so much in the long run. You can also get started simply by sending your résumé to photographers' studios and explaining why you want to work with them. Then, once you have your foot in the door, the best way to get jobs is through word of mouth. In the meantime, you can prepare by taking pictures and studying photography and art history in school. You need passion to be good at photography. That's the way to make real art."

Straight Shooters

WITH CAMERAS IN HAND, THESE UP-AND-COMING PHOTOGRAPHERS ARE TURNING A FRESH EYE TO FASHION.

FROM A BUSINESS MAJOR TO A
FORMER TEEN MODEL, THESE
YOUNG WOMEN BROKE IN TO THE
ART AND FASHION INDUSTRY FROM A
VARIETY OF BACKGROUNDS.

Hilary Walsh

Tina Tyrell

HOMETOWN: PHILADELPHIA, PENNSYLVANIA
STAR SHOTS: RACHEL BILSON, ED WESTWICK
BIG BREAK: DKNY PURE AD CAMPAIGN

"I was a business major in college, but I started working in photography when a friend of mine who had been hired to assist a photographer couldn't do it and recommended that I go in his stead. I took the job, and it was a great experience. From there I assisted lots of big-name photographers over the next seven years, including Tierney Gearon, Ellen von Unwerth, Steven Klein, and Mark Seliger. Being an assistant taught me that treating others kindly on the set—as opposed to acting arrogant or nasty—goes far in helping a shoot go well.

My first paying gig was for Betsey Johnson, and it didn't quite go as planned. The store hired me to take some advertising pictures, but I didn't know how to use a four-by-five camera, which was the best model for the shot I needed to get. So I read the instruction manual and learned on the spot. Unfortunately, the lab cross-processed my film! I had to reshoot the whole job and didn't make any money.

Now, as a working photographer, I prefer to shoot without using a lot of equipment; I can't get the picture if there's too much stuff lying around. Lately I've started making videos, too, but I'm not putting any pressure on myself about it. I just want to learn."

HOMETOWN: LOS ANGELES, CALIFORNIA
ART SCHOOL: ART CENTER COLLEGE OF DESIGN
EDIT JOBS: *TEEN VOGUE, THE NEW YORKER, NYLON*

"When I was twelve, I saw the music video for George Michael's song 'Freedom 90,' which featured supermodels Linda Evangelista, Christy Turlington, Naomi Campbell, Cindy Crawford, and Tatjana Patitz. I thought it was the coolest video ever, and I became very interested in fashion and began cutting pictures of models out of magazines and putting them up in my room. Over time, I realized that it wasn't the clothing or the models I was responding to—it was the photographs themselves.

I studied at the Art Center College of Design in Pasadena, California, for four years. My first shoot for *Teen Vogue* was a Style A to Z fashion story (I did 'Z is for Zippers'), and I clearly remember not being able to get the model to smile. In hindsight it was funny, because much of my book up to that point was very somber, and the one thing I was told when I got the job was that there absolutely had to be smiles in the photographs!

I think there's something within a person that drives him or her to become a photographer and develop a unique aesthetic—some people call it a photographer's eye. While shooting techniques and photography trends may come and go, that essence should always remain intact."

TIP "Have your own vision. Don't reference your contemporaries too much in your work."

TIP "Give yourself time to develop as an artist. As the saying goes, 'Rome wasn't built in a day.'"

Ahbey Drucker

Glynnis McDaris

HOMETOWN: BELLMORE, NEW YORK
STAR SHOTS: BRITNEY SPEARS, CIARA
AD JOBS: CAPITOL RECORDS, STILA

"I studied photography at the Fashion Institute of Technology and the School of Visual Arts, both in New York City. After graduation, I looked up Ellen von Unwerth's number in the phone book, called, and asked if I could intern for her. I wanted to get hands-on experience and see what it was like for a woman working in this industry. Thankfully, she said yes! As her intern, I handled photography assignments for some of the top modeling agencies in the city, which helped me build my portfolio and gain valuable insight into the fashion world.

Once, at a job interview with the creative director of *Nylon,* I mentioned my interest in doing a behind-the-scenes story with model Carmen Kass during Paris Fashion Week. She liked the idea and sent me a list of all the runway collections she wanted me to cover. In Paris, I spent many hours following Carmen to fittings, interviews, dinners, and shows. In the end, *Nylon* ran a 20-page story! Shortly thereafter I got a contract with *Teen Vogue* and began shooting backstage at fashion shows regularly—just me with my backpack, no gear, no assistant. It was an eye-opening experience, and it led me into the world of commercial photography."

HOMETOWN: MEMPHIS, TENNESSEE
FAVORITE PHOTOGRAPHER: MARIE COSINDAS
BIG BREAK: 2005 SOLO SHOW IN NEW YORK CITY

"I was originally a film major at Pratt in New York City, but I quit for a semester to work on a movie. That experience helped me decide that I wanted to major in photography instead. When I went back to school I began shooting portraits and showing them at galleries, and I made CDs of my work and dropped them off with photo editors. That's how I started booking jobs at small art and fashion magazines like *Self Service.* Today I work for *Teen Vogue, Art Review, Details, i-D,* and *Wired.*

I never assisted anyone—mainly because I didn't know that's how most people get started in this industry. But it's probably a great thing to do as an aspiring photographer, because you're rarely on set with other photographers. It can be educational to watch how they work and get their images.

Luckily, I've never had anything go drastically wrong on a shoot. Sometimes little things happen, like the rental equipment breaks, but I always bring along backup supplies. Be prepared for anything: For example, you might plan on shooting in artificial light, but beautiful afternoon light may spill in. I always have a bounce, or several speeds of film, on hand so that I can capture exactly what I want."

TIP "Believe in yourself and your work, but keep your ears open to advice at the same time."

TIP "When starting out, shoot your friends and what's going on around you. It's a good way to define your style."

Poppy de Villeneuve

Isabel Asha Penzlien

HOMETOWN: WEST SUSSEX, ENGLAND
DREAM CAMERA: DIGITAL HASSELBLAD
AD JOBS: NANETTE LEPORE/ELIZABETH ARDEN

"My dad is a photographer [he discovered sixties model Twiggy], so I was always against doing it, because it was what he did. But then, during art school, I picked up a camera for a project, and it just felt natural and made sense.

I got to spend one day assisting Juergen Teller, who was perfectly wonderful—I admire how inspiring and free he is with his work. But I ended up going the fine art route with my photographic style: I decided to jump in a car, drive around, and shoot. I took my fine art book with me to meetings at fashion magazines, and soon thereafter I began working for *The Daily Telegraph*. Then *Teen Vogue* hired me to do a shoot with my sister, illustrator Daisy de Villeneuve.

My mother was a model and I modeled in my teens, and that experience really helped me understand the dynamic between photographer and subject. I never ask people to perform; I prefer to make them feel comfortable. The more you can explain something to someone or connect with them, the better your shot will be.

To be a great intern, you need to understand that a shoot can be stressful, so stay positive. And always ask the photographer what you can do to help before, during, and after the shoot."

TIP "Don't rush when you're shooting. Take your time; work out what you want to do and how to do it. It's not a race."

HOMETOWN: HAMBURG, GERMANY
FIRST CAMERA: NIKON F-3
STAR SHOTS: LIL MAMA, FAT JOE

"I remember taking lots of pictures with my first camera and experimenting and learning how to shoot with it—I felt like a little professional! My dad runs a photo-printing lab, and I enjoyed spending time there with him as a child and as a teen, printing out my own work. I also got the chance to assist a photographer in Hamburg, which is where I'm from. Then I came to New York City, to attend the International Center for Photography, and I decided to stay after graduation and start working as a freelance assistant for commercial and fine art photographers. I also made sure to set aside time to continue doing my own personal projects.

I handle both editorial and advertising projects. I really like shooting for *Teen Vogue* because everyone on the set is always so nice and inspiring. When you're on a job, remember to be professional and diligent at all times, because one project can lead to others simply through the contacts you make.

The unfortunate reality is, some photographers do not want to hire a female assistant. So when you're starting out in the industry, it's all the more important that you show people how serious you are about the work."

TIP "Don't take no for an answer. Prove to people that you're empowered, strong, and extremely hardworking."

Skye Parrott

HOMETOWN: HOBOKEN, NEW JERSEY
FAVORITE PHOTOGRAPHER: HELMUT NEWTON
BIG BREAK: MENSWEAR STORY FOR *10 MEN*

"I didn't start taking pictures until I was seventeen years old, right around the time I saw Nan Goldin's show 'I'll Be Your Mirror' at the Whitney Museum of American Art. That exhibition had a huge influence on me. I later worked as her studio manager in Paris, and I was also the managing editor at *Self Service.* I remember sitting around one day, thinking, What would I do if I had my own magazine? So a couple of years ago I started *Dossier,* an arts and culture journal, with several friends.

I learned a lot early in my career by freelance assisting for photographers like Mario Sorrenti and Pamela Hanson. I was also Horst Diekgerdes's full-time assistant. Horst told me that when he was starting out, someone said it would take him ten years and about $140,000 to become a photographer. That sounds right to me. When you're young, you may not realize what a commitment it is to be a freelancer in photography—or in any creative field, for that matter. You never know when a job will pop up and interrupt your plans; you might make lots of money one month, and then very little the next. I find it inspiring to work in different places all the time, but it's not for everyone. It can be manic. You need to have the temperament for it." ★

TIP "Be a good listener and admit when you don't know something. That's the best way to learn."

Shoot Checklist

★ BRING ALONG SOMETHING THAT INSPIRES YOU, WHETHER IT'S A PIECE OF CLOTHING, A PAGE FROM AN OLD BOOK, OR A FORTUNE-COOKIE NOTE. IF YOU GET STUCK CREATIVELY, LOOKING AT IT CAN HELP YOU REGAIN YOUR FOCUS.

★ KEEP A COLLECTION OF YOUR FAVORITE MUSIC ON SET. PLAYING GOOD SONGS GOES A LONG WAY TOWARD MAKING YOUR SUBJECT FEEL COMFORTABLE IN FRONT OF THE CAMERA.

★ USE SUNSCREEN IF YOU'RE SHOOTING OUTDOORS; IT'S AN ABSOLUTE MUST. WEAR A WIDE-BRIMMED HAT FOR EXTRA PROTECTION AND TO SHIELD YOUR EYES FROM THE SUN'S GLARE.

★ INVEST IN A LIGHTWEIGHT, WATER-RESISTANT BACKPACK WITH MULTIPLE POCKETS TO CARRY SUPPLIES. LOWEPRO MAKES BAGS WITH A HIDEAWAY TRIPOD HOLDER.

★ WEAR A CAMERA NECK STRAP THAT IS LIGHTLY PADDED TO ENSURE YOU STAY COMFORTABLE DURING THE ENTIRE SHOOT.

★ KEEP EXTRA BATTERIES FOR YOUR CAMERA AND FLASH ON HAND, JUST IN CASE.

★ PACK A MICROFIBER LENS CLOTH. IT REMOVES DIRT AND OIL WITHOUT CAUSING SCRATCHES OR STREAKS.

The Glam Man

Mario Testino

THIS PERUVIAN POWERHOUSE HAS BECOME THE MOST SOUGHT-AFTER PHOTOGRAPHER OF THE CELEBRITY SET—FROM MEMBERS OF THE BRITISH ROYAL FAMILY TO HOLLYWOOD'S BRIGHTEST STARS.

His career as a fashion photographer may span three decades, but superstar Mario Testino still clearly remembers the thrill of experiencing his first big-break moment. "British *Vogue* published a small, postage stamp–sized picture of mine, and it was beyond amazing," he recalls fondly.

It's hard to believe that as a young kid growing up in Lima, Peru, Testino wasn't really that interested in photography. He didn't even major in an art-related field during his college years, when he studied economics, law, and international relations. It was only after he moved to London, in 1977, that he fell in love with taking pictures and began training to

become a photographer—and he hasn't looked back since.

Testino was catapulted to worldwide fame in 1997 for his portrait images of Diana, Princess of Wales, which appeared in *Vanity Fair*. Today he remains celebrated for his mega-glam, high-energy photos of A-list entertainers and other VIP subjects, from Madonna and Jennifer Aniston to England's princes William and Harry. Testino's talent is in greater demand than ever, and he shows no sign of slowing down. "Photography is still so exciting for me after all these years," he says, "because in this job, there are always changes and surprises."

TESTINO CHECKS HIS SHOT ON THE SET OF A MARCH 2009 *ALLURE* BEAUTY SHOOT.

KATIE HOLMES, PHOTOGRAPHED
AT A LONG ISLAND, NEW YORK,
BEACH RESORT FOR THE
DECEMBER/JANUARY ISSUE.

DURING HER COVER SHOOT IN
MIAMI FOR THE JUNE/JULY
ISSUE, KATE BOSWORTH WAS
EXCITED ABOUT THE EXPERIENCE
OF BEING PHOTOGRAPHED BY
TESTINO. SHE SAYS, "IT'S ONE OF
THOSE THINGS WHERE YOU THINK,
IS THIS REALLY HAPPENING?"

PALS JAKE GYLLENHAAL AND ALISON LOHMAN TRADED JOKES ON THE SET OF THEIR OCTOBER/NOVEMBER COVER SHOOT.

'She's free of the restrictions. Certainly you can see that.'

TESTINO SAYS THAT HIS 1997 VANITY FAIR SHOOT WITH DIANA, PRINCESS OF WALES, IS HIS FAVORITE WORK TO DATE.

You've photographed many talented, young celebrities for **Teen Vogue.** *Which shoot stands out as your favorite?*

The cover shoot I did with Kate Bosworth in 2003. It was my very first job for *Teen Vogue* and a great start to my future with the magazine.

What qualities do you look for in an assistant?

Hardworking, humble, funny, and well-mannered. I want someone who puts no limit on the number of hours he or she is willing to give to a project.

What types of duties can a young photographer expect to handle as an intern?

You'll be responsible for running all sorts of errands—everything from archiving shoots to making tea. I trained for three months when I started out. Internships are by far the best way to learn about the industry. ★

teenVOGUE TIP "If you want to be a photographer, never give up! But also be open to other job possibilities, as we never know what life has in store for us." —MARIO TESTINO

Lucy Lee, GLOBAL PRODUCTION MANAGER
COLLEGE BABSON COLLEGE
HOMETOWNS HONG KONG AND GUAM

"I came to the United States from Guam to attend college in Boston, and at around the same time my mom and aunt opened a clothing boutique back home. They started to take me along on their buying trips to Paris, and it seemed like the best job in the world! So after graduation, I got an interview with the department store Neiman Marcus, and they offered me a position in their buying program, which is based in Dallas. I was set to start in September.

Over the summer, I worked at a greeting card company, just to make a little extra money, and my boss sat me down one day and asked, 'Do you really want to move to Texas?' I didn't, but what could I do? The job was there. She ended up getting me an internship at KCD [a fashion PR and production firm] in New York City, where she used to work as a receptionist. So I wrote a letter to Neiman Marcus, asking if I could start the program in January instead. They agreed.

Working at KCD opened my eyes to all the things that fashion could be. The company produced runway shows, events, and parties—aspects of the business that I never knew existed! I spent most of my time filing model cards, because photo casting is a big part of fashion-show production. Eventually they offered me an assistant position, and even though the pay was much lower than what I would have gotten in Dallas, I didn't even blink. I wrote Neiman Marcus a letter declining their offer, and I took the KCD job.

I traveled to Milan to produce shows and had a lot of fun, but I was working so hard, nonstop, that I ended up getting sick. Afterward, I realized that while this was an awesome life, it wasn't for me. A friend of mine was working as an assistant photo editor at *Harper's Bazaar* at that time, and we basically traded jobs.

I assisted the photo editor at *Bazaar*, produced every photo shoot in the magazine, and did photo research, which involved finding and pulling all the paparazzi images that we used. At that job, I learned a lot about photography, why a certain photographer is best suited for a particular project, and how to speak to photographers. In just a few years I was thoroughly prepared for my next job, which ended up being photo editor, in charge of the entire department, at *Teen Vogue*. I worked there for three years and then became a producer at an agency called Art Partner.

I produce shoots for Mario Testino, am a junior agent for David Sims, and manage the entire production department. Mario is a major photographer, and since I deal with the production for all his U.S. clients, I spend a lot of time responding to e-mails. When he gets a job, I have to option the team members—stylist, hair and makeup people, assistants, prop stylist, and location scout. I also book the hotels, flights, and catering, and then I run all the details by Mario. He gives me his feedback, and I'll make changes if necessary.

If you're interested in a job like mine, you need first and foremost to be prepared to work really hard. Internships are always a great place to start, but make sure you treat them like a real job. Perhaps you're not getting paid—but if you don't take it seriously, there's no point in being there. If you do work hard, people will see that and hire you when a position opens up. And as I learned early on, just because a job is great for someone else, doesn't necessarily mean it's great for you too."

TESTINO PHOTOGRAPHED MISCHA BARTON FOR THIS JUNE/JULY 2004 *TEEN VOGUE* COVER SHOOT, PRODUCED BY LEE. SHE SECURED THE MALIBU, CALIFORNIA, LOCATION AND ORGANIZED ALL THE DETAILS, INCLUDING THE CASTING OF A CREW OF SKATER BOYS.

"I TELL BEGINNERS TO LEARN WITH A FILM CAMERA, NOT DIGITAL," SAYS ELGORT, PHOTOGRAPHED IN CALIFORNIA. "THAT WAY, YOU KNOW HOW TO FOCUS AND READ LIGHT."

The Storyteller

Arthur Elgort

THIS GLOBE-TROTTER STRESSES PRACTICE AND PERSONALITY AS THE KEYS TO SUCCESS.

"My first camera was a Polaroid 100. I was studying painting, graphics, and art history at Hunter College in New York City, and I bought the camera because I wanted to take pictures of my own artwork. But when I started to shoot, I didn't understand why my pictures didn't look as good as the ones I saw in books and magazines. I asked a fellow I knew, and he said, 'Well, you've got to have a *real* camera.' And I said, 'A real camera? That's interesting, what's the difference?' He gave me an issue of *Pop,* a fashion magazine, and told me to figure out which pictures I liked and then see what kind of cameras took them. More often than not it was a Nikon 35 mm. The art department at school had one, and they needed someone to take pictures of artwork for the teachers, so I started doing that. And at the same time, I was working as a waiter, so I saved up to buy a camera of my own.

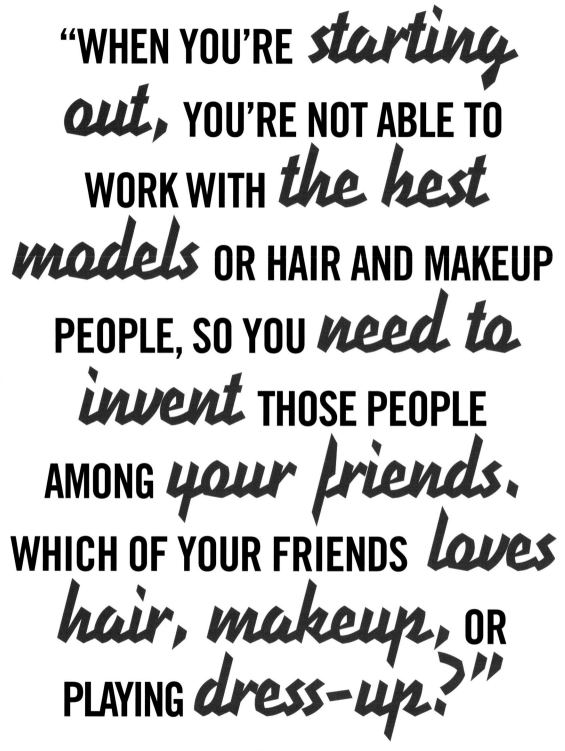

"WHEN YOU'RE *starting out,* YOU'RE NOT ABLE TO WORK WITH *the best models* OR HAIR AND MAKEUP PEOPLE, SO YOU *need to invent* THOSE PEOPLE AMONG *your friends.* WHICH OF YOUR FRIENDS *loves hair, makeup,* OR PLAYING *dress-up?"*

—ARTHUR ELGORT

ELGORT'S SON ANSEL
MODELED FOR THIS
BLUES-INSPIRED
SHOOT IN MISSISSIPPI.

HOW I GOT THIS PICTURE

who: MODELS JAC, CAMERON, AND COLTON
what: WESTERN-INSPIRED FASHION FOR *TEEN VOGUE,* SEPTEMBER 2008
where: RED ROCK CANYON, CALIFORNIA

"This shoot was fun because there was so much action. The models had to pretend they were actors making a film. Generally, I like shooting models over celebrities, because with stars, there are always a lot of people on set."

"Due to magazine schedules, we typically shoot fall clothes like these during the summer. This was shot in May, and it was so hot. I like this canyon very much—I've had good luck there! Jac [below] is a terrific young model who is strong and creative. And the stylist, Jillian Davison, has really great ideas."

"To get a model to move a certain way, I demonstrate exactly what I want her to do. It helps, of course, if the model is naturally graceful—and long-legged—to start out with!"

ELGORT CAPTURED BOTH THESE IMAGES—IN THE PETERHOF PALACE (LEFT) AND IN FRONT OF A FAMOUS CHURCH (RIGHT)—IN ST. PETERSBURG, RUSSIA.

In those days you got back a contact sheet and looked at it with a magnifying glass, and film processing was very expensive. So before I knew it, I was learning how to process film in the dark of my kitchen in the middle of the night, and I had an old enlarger and all the stuff that went with it. I always tell people who want to do photography that, if they can stand it, they should learn how to do it the hard way. You know, with film and a light meter and a camera that you have to focus and adjust yourself, just so you know what you're doing. It's almost like learning to drive with a clutch instead of an automatic: It feels different, and you're more in control.

And, of course, technical skill is only a part of it; photography is also about personality. For example, a few years ago I was taking pictures of this skinny little girl named Ali Lohan for *Teen Vogue,* and I brought my son Ansel, who was about her age, along on the shoot. He's been around photography and has been in pictures, so I said to him, 'Why don't you take some photos of her too?' And his were almost as good as mine! He's a pretty good photographer for his age—he was eleven at the time. The magazine wound up using my shots, but to be honest I could have snuck a few of his in there. He did so well because he was charming, handsome, and could speak her language. That's important. When I'm interviewing people to be my assistant, I like if they're sociable. And it also helps if they're musical, polite, and know a foreign language—Spanish, French, and Italian are good! One of my first paying photography jobs was taking head shots—I posted an ad at a famous acting school. It was excellent practice for me, to photograph people who were normal-looking and to get a good picture of them in a short period of time.

Keep in mind that when you're learning, you obviously won't be able to work with the best hair and makeup people or the biggest models. So you need to invent those people among your friends. Figure out which of your friends loves to do hair or makeup or play dress-up, and pick the ones who will make the bravest subjects, and then just do it. In any field, you want to find your contemporaries and learn how to collaborate with them and come up with something new." ★

teenVOGUE TIP "Some of the people who've assisted me went to the Brooks Institute in California or the School of Visual Arts in New York. But school doesn't make you a better idea person; it just teaches you technique." —ARTHUR ELGORT

teenVOGUE

MARCH

TAYLOR SWIFT:
"I never expected all this to happen to me"

the clash

what to do when your parents hate your friends

GET A NEW LOOK

28 BRIGHT BEAUTY IDEAS TO TRY

+

WIN A TOTAL MAKEOVER
AT TEENVOGUE.COM
DETAILS INSIDE

BRING IT ON!

SPRING FASHION AT EVERY PRICE

"THE WEATHER WAS VERY COLD IN NASHVILLE THE DAY WE SHOT TAYLOR," ELGORT SAYS. "SHE WAS A GOOD SPORT FOR WEARING SHORT SLEEVES!"

"TAKE *photo* CLASSES. WITH EXPERIENCE, YOU CAN *look out the window,* SEE THE LIGHT, AND *know* WHAT TYPE OF *film* YOU SHOULD USE AND WHAT KIND OF *exposure,* ALL THAT STUFF. YOU ALREADY HAVE THE *ideas,* BUT YOU *need to know* HOW TO MAKE *sure* YOUR *pictures* DON'T COME OUT BLURRY OR OUT OF *focus.*"

—ARTHUR ELGORT

A 1991 *VOGUE* SHOOT BY ELGORT, FEATURING TARTAN-CLAD SUPERMODEL LINDA EVANGELISTA.

The Illusionist
Shona Heath

THIS SET DESIGNER'S IMAGINATIVE HAND ENLIVENS SOME OF FASHION'S MOST ENCHANTING RUNWAY SHOWS AND PHOTO SHOOTS.

The job of a set designer is difficult to describe, even when you ask a set designer herself to explain it. As Shona Heath—a London-based 35-year-old who has worked extensively with _Vogues_ American, British, Italian, and _Teen_—says: "I do lots of different things. I work with photographers to produce interesting or slightly fantastical fashion pictures. So that means I paint, build sets, and sort out everything with regard to props, whether we're talking about millions of white rabbits, a giant fishhook, or lots of balloons." And her work isn't limited to editorial spreads; Heath has designed sets or directed art on advertising campaigns for such brands as Cacharel, Dior, Hermès, and Juicy Couture. "I also do store windows and interiors, T-shirt designs, and stages for fashion shows," she says.

Her vocation draws on a wide array of talents—one assignment might call for her to paint a complicated trompe l'oeil backdrop, while another could find her screwing broken records into a rec-room wall. And it isn't technically a necessary element of fashion photography—not every photo or magazine shoot involves a set designer. But even the most cursory glance at a story on which Heath has worked will leave you convinced that her contribution was invaluable.

When did you discover this line of work, and how did you get your start?
In England, during high school, anyone who wants to go to art school must first do what's called a foundation course, a yearlong class in which you try a bit of everything: sculpture, graphics, pottery, fashion, and painting. Then you choose an area to specialize in. After my foundation year, I enrolled in the fashion and textile design program at the University of Brighton.

Work placements are a big part of the program at that school, which helped me figure out what I did and didn't want to pursue. One of the companies I worked for was in charge of costumes and styling for pop-music videos and commercials, and I loved it. I just thought it was brilliant. I was making clothes, as well as painting, and I found it to be a very crafty, multimedia way of working with fashion. The company offered me a job when I graduated, and I was there for two years before I went freelance and started working with friends who were photographers in the fashion industry. I did a shoot for _Dazed & Confused_ magazine for which I made a paper set—my mother used to make me paper sculptures when I was little—and from there my career just snowballed. I wasn't

> **"** I built a skateboarding ramp. Since it's all made out of wood, I needed to punch it up with color, so I painted these swirly patterns on it. **"**

> **"** I wanted to create a seventies vibe for this shoot by photographer Dusan Reljin, so I included these retro TVs. They have a lot of bright color to them, which helps make the whole photograph pop. **"**

HOW I GOT THIS PICTURE

when: AUGUST 2004 *TEEN VOGUE* FASHION FEATURE
what: THE SET CONCEPT WAS A SKATER CHICK'S ULTIMATE DREAM HANGOUT
where: A NEW YORK CITY PHOTO STUDIO

"When I was young, I hung a lot of cassette tapes on my bedroom wall and pulled out the ribbons. With that in mind, I decided to create this miniature tree of tapes with their insides falling out. It adds to the eclectic look of the room."

ZOË KRAVITZ (FAR LEFT) AND LORRAINE NICHOLSON PHOTOGRAPHED IN NEW YORK CITY. EVERY ELEMENT OF THIS SET—INCLUDING THE GLASS VANITY TABLE, THE DECORATED WALLS, AND THE WINDOW—WAS ASSEMBLED BY HEATH IN AN EMPTY STUDIO SPACE.

expecting all the jobs that followed, but I made up for it by being a capable, hard worker.

Please describe your process.

As an example, let's take a particular story I did with stylist Camilla Nickerson for *Teen Vogue:* It was a fashion portfolio with a series of double spreads, each one themed around a specific gang or tribe—young aristocrats, skate kids, and rockabillies. About five weeks in advance, someone rings up my agent and books me. Then Camilla calls to tell me her initial ideas and sends me images for reference—say, for the rockabilly spread, a picture of a smashed-up guitar—and I flip through rockabilly books, do some research on the Internet, go through my scrapbook, and send her back some images. I draw a sketch of the set I have in mind and show it to her; either she says, "Great," or "No, horrible."

Usually she likes it, and then I work out a budget. There are loads of costs—you can't even imagine! I have to build things from scratch, which means I need to hire a van to transport the materials, as well as hire someone to drive the van. I also need to find a place to park the van. At the end of the job I have to get rid of the stuff, and that often costs a lot of money too—I can't just throw away an entire set. I present the budget, and normally there's a big fight and everybody says, "We don't have that kind of money!" Then we negotiate and it all turns out fine.

Next I start sorting the ideas into categories. There are things I have to buy, like lightweight props—in this case, a bunch of records from a charity shop or tires from eBay—and things I have to rent, which are slightly more expensive items, like an electric guitar. I wanted the environment for the rockabilly spread to feel like a rock 'n' roll dance in a basement, so we built what looked like an underground bunker with corrugated iron and brickwork, and I got an

teenVOGUE TIP "It's important to learn how to paint, sew, and build basic structures. Be interested in everything: Look at the finishes on furniture or the odd materials you see in shops." —SHONA HEATH

FROM THE TORN NEWSPAPER ON THE WALLS TO THE GIANT RED ROSE SCULPTURE, HEATH CREATED A ROCK-INFUSED BEDROOM FIT FOR A PUNK PRINCESS IN THE AUGUST ISSUE.

old sofa from a secondhand shop and painted an eagle on it, like one you might see on the back of a leather jacket. I get builders to construct the basics, if needed, and I put on the finishing touches myself.

And is the process for an advertising shoot similar?

It's very similar. The only difference is that editorial work doesn't pay as much as ad shoots. But the designers or PR directors of big fashion brands look at what you did for *Vogue* and think, We want this team for our ad. So the payoff is quite obvious.

Do you have any thoughts on how a young person might get in to set design?

Well, I was very lucky that the *Dazed* shoot came my way when I was starting out. If you are a fan of looking through magazine stories, and you always look to see who does the set design, then choose someone whose work you like. Contact the person and say you'd like to intern with them.

Is it important to go to art school?

You'd have to be a genius not to need a bit of formal training. I find that people who have been to art school seem to have extra discipline, and they're not frightened of painting. If you say to them, "Can you paint green spots on that?" they just get on with it. Having that kind of confidence is important, and art school helps you develop it.

What else do you look for in an intern or assistant?

It's such a mix. The people who are star workers are strong in different areas. Some are good at making costumes, others are skilled at creating graphic backgrounds on a computer, and still others are great with clients and intuitively know what I need. I like the person who, if there's nothing to do, will tidy up or offer to make a cup of tea. I can't bear it when someone just stands around.

Is there anything that a teenager can do right now to prepare for a career in set design?

It's important to learn how to paint, sew, and build basic structures. Be interested in everything: Look at the finishes on furniture or the odd materials you see in shops. If it's fashion photography you're interested in, educate yourself about fashion, because the set should reflect the clothes. And be prepared to work hard, because you'll always be the last person to leave the set after a job. ★

The Design Guru
Lina Kutsovskaya

THIS ADVERTISING DIRECTOR USES HER ART SCHOOL BACKGROUND TO WORK WITH BUYERS, SET DESIGNERS, PHOTOGRAPHERS, AND MODELS TO CHANNEL A LEGENDARY STORE'S UNIQUE AESTHETIC.

"When I was a little girl growing up in Kiev, Ukraine, I thought I wanted to be an animator. We had our own Soviet version of Mickey Mouse called Cheburashka—he's this really cute animal with big ears on the side of his head rather than the top. When I watched the cartoons I felt very inspired. As a result, I started taking drawing classes when I was seven years old. There, a teacher spotted me as having extra talent and advised my parents to look into a specialty school. So I began attending art school full-time in the fourth grade.

It was pretty intense, and it exposed me to the world of fine art—I remember traveling to Moscow with my classmates to see a Salvador Dalí exhibition when I was fourteen. I thought I would go to art school in Russia and become a painter, but when I was seventeen my parents decided we should move to the United States. I had to figure out a new plan: Running around, painting canvases is not the kind of thing immigrants do, and I knew that I had to study *something* that could lead to a job. I had always been very influenced by Russian Constructivism, so that drew me to the idea of studying poster design, typography, and layouts. I decided to go to Parsons the New School for Design in New York City and major in communication design.

In Russia, we didn't really have any fashion magazines. Every so often we would get a magazine from Germany, which had maybe one dress pattern in it. But there was no high fashion to speak of, and what style was there was improvised. When I came to New York, I found that I loved to read magazines. Once I graduated, a teacher suggested that I drop off my portfolio at Condé Nast Publications because they were looking for people to do paid internships. I spent six months at *Vogue*, doing all kinds of things: scanning, bringing coffees to people, and designing little pages like the table of contents. Then a position opened up at *Allure*, and I ended up getting a job there. I was still doing small things, but I was on the masthead, which meant a lot, and had a few sections that were entirely my responsibility. After a few years I was ready to move on, so I went back to *Vogue* as a senior designer, which was the perfect next step. I stayed for a year and then agreed to be the art director at *Nylon*, which had recently launched.

It was a big job, and I was scared. But I also knew that it was a great opportunity. Suddenly, I was working with photographers, planning shoots, scouting locations, picking models.

"PHOTOGRAPHER NICK HAYMES TOOK THIS PICTURE OF ME IN TOKYO, WHERE WE HAD TRAVELED TO SHOOT FOR *TEEN VOGUE*," KUTSOVSKAYA SAYS. "THIS WAS OUR FIRST DAY IN THE CITY, AND IT WAS POURING RAIN! WE HAD TO COME UP WITH CREATIVE SOLUTIONS—LIKE USING THESE BRIGHT WHITE UMBRELLAS—TO GET THE IMAGES WE NEEDED."

"WE HAD THE MURAL BY NAOKO MACHIDA [BEHIND MODELS ALI MICHAEL AND HARDY McCALL] COMMISSIONED ESPECIALLY FOR THIS SHOOT," KUTSOVSKAYA RECALLS OF THIS SPREAD BY PHOTOGRAPHER NICK HAYMES. "ALI AND HARDY HAD THE CUTEST CHEMISTRY—THEY WERE REALLY SHY. IT WORKED WELL WITH THE IDEA BEHIND THE SHOOT, WHICH WAS SUPPOSED TO EVOKE A JAPANESE LOVE STORY."

THE BARNEYS CATALOG DOES MORE THAN HIGHLIGHT EACH SEASON'S CHICEST CLOTHING—IT TELLS A STORY, WITH THE HELP OF CREATIVE TALENT LIKE THE VIRGINS (SECOND FROM TOP) AND TOP MODEL COCO ROCHA (LEFT).

I was making decisions! I learned so much. And then one day, when I was just beginning to want to try something new, I got a call from Amy Astley, asking me to help her launch *Teen Vogue.* It would be another challenge, so I took the job.

I was the first person in the office, before we really started, working on the logo. It was funny, because I had different versions of the letters all over the walls, and at one point *teen* didn't seem like it was even a word anymore. It felt as though those two e's were looking at me like a pair of eyes—like I was being watched!

Now I'm a vice president of advertising for Barneys New York, which means that I'm in charge of all the creative imagery—the catalogs (which we call mailers), the ads, and the billboards—that comes out of the store every season. We do 22 mailers a year, and each of them is almost like a magazine or a small book. I conceptualize everything, from the photo shoots to the layouts; I work with photographers, stylists, set designers, models, and, in the office, my team of art directors and designers. It's a completely different perspective from the work I did in the magazine world, because magazines have a more personal relationship with their readers, whereas an advertisement really needs to stand out. I think very hard about what I can do that's different, that's interesting, that will make people take notice. But in some ways it's actually a very similar kind of involvement—now, instead of working with editors, I meet with the store's buyers to get a sense of the direction for the coming seasons. I also go to the fashion shows so that I can see things for myself, and I find it useful to stay current with what's going on in the art world.

You need to educate yourself about the history of fashion and culture in order to be able to do this kind of work. Visually, I think *Citizen Kane* is the top film of all time. I also like *Don't Look Now, Fellini's Roma,* and *The Deer Hunter.* Recently, a girl who didn't know who Jackie O. was came into my office—when people don't have these basic references, they can't work effectively. Obviously, when I arrived in the U.S. from Russia, I had a lot of catching up to do. I had to cover the years that I'd missed, and fast. But I did it, and it has helped.

It's so hard to know from a young age what you want to do or be. Parents ask, of course, but you really don't know until something happens—at the theater, the ballet, or on the bus—and then it just clicks. It's such a personal experience, where it all starts. Once you figure it out, though, you should do as many extracurricular activities as you can to build a foundation. And go above and beyond what's expected. If someone tells you to read a particular article, why not read the whole newspaper? When I'm hiring, I look for people with that level of enthusiasm, people who have the curiosity to go to galleries over the weekend, or the movies, and can bring what they've seen back to their work." ★

***teen*VOGUE TIP** "Go above and beyond what's expected. If your boss tells you to read a particular article, why not read the whole paper? When I'm hiring, I look for people with that level of enthusiasm." —LINA KUTSOVSKAYA

GLOBE-TROTTER

As Teen Vogue's *former creative director, Kutsovskaya traveled around the world and back. Here's how she got these pictures.*

ISSUE: December/January 2009
THE CONCEPT: "We wanted the story to be romantic, of course, because it was Venice, Italy. We parked our boat near the Piazza San Marco and just started walking when all these pigeons gathered around us!"
THE SCOOP: "The model wasn't wearing an outfit that was supposed to be shot; it was just something to keep her warm. But the photographer quickly snapped all these shots, which turned out to be amazing!"
PHOTOGRAPHER: Nick Haymes

ISSUE: September 2007
THE CONCEPT: "The goal with this story was to capture the idea of new China and old China colliding."
THE SCOOP: "The production team did location-scouting for beautiful, unique places, like the bridge, which would evoke that feeling. We shot these pictures in a village north of Beijing. The road there was a tiny, winding, bumpy gravel path. But it added to the experience of the shoot."
PHOTOGRAPHER: Nick Haymes

ISSUE: October 2007
THE CONCEPT: "This story was part of our Young Hollywood feature. The three teen actors—Taylor Momsen, Jake Miller, and Gabe Nevins—were the stars of Gus Van Sant's movie *Paranoid Park*."
THE SCOOP: "We strung up thousands of bulbs. There are even more, which you can't see in the picture. It was so hot, and as the pictures were being taken, the bulbs kept overheating and breaking."
PHOTOGRAPHER: Nick Haymes

PHOTO TOOL KIT

essential items of the pros

MUSIC
Cool tunes inspire lively shots.

TAPE
Marks locations for models to stand.

GLOVES
For handling delicate prints.

GELS
Light filters available in a variety of colors.

WAX PENCILS
Used to highlight selects on negatives.

CLAMPS
Help keep backdrops in place.

LOUPE
For a magnified view of prints and slides.

CLIP
Keeps lights, gels, or other equipment in place.

DIGITAL CAMERA
Provides quick turnaround time and on-the-spot editing of images.

LIGHT
Fakes a bright day or creates special effects like shadows.

MICROFIBER CLOTH
Removes dirt and oil from equipment without scratching.

FILM CAMERA
Some photographers prefer the quality of light captured on film.

DUST SPRAY
Keeps equipment spotless.

FISHING LINE
Suspends objects and binds electrical cords.

BOOKS
Get inspired by the works of photographers from different eras.

LEVEL
Ensures that props and backdrops are perfectly aligned.

Break in to the industry with these tips.

★ GET GOING! IN PHOTOGRAPHY, PRACTICE TRULY CAN MAKE PERFECT, SO TAKE AS MANY PICTURES AS POSSIBLE OF FRIENDS, FAMILY, AND THE LANDSCAPE AROUND YOU. AND LEARN HOW TO SHOOT ON A FILM CAMERA SO THAT YOU KNOW HOW TO FOCUS AND READ LIGHT.

★ STUDY THE PHOTOS YOU'VE TAKEN THAT YOU *DON'T* LIKE. ANALYZE WHAT WENT WRONG—THE LIGHT, COMPOSITION, OR POSES—AND APPLY THAT KNOWLEDGE TO YOUR NEXT PROJECT. IF YOU'RE IN SCHOOL, SHOW YOUR TEACHERS THE PICTURES AND ASK FOR CONSTRUCTIVE CRITICISM.

★ BE CREATIVE. ASK YOUR FRIENDS TO HELP STYLE, DO HAIR AND MAKEUP, AND ASSIST. THEY'LL ADD A FRESH PERSPECTIVE TO YOUR PICTURES.

★ TAKE WHATEVER WORK IS OFFERED TO YOU WHEN YOU FIRST START IN THE INDUSTRY. PLENTY OF BIG STARS BEGAN WITH SMALL JOBS LIKE FAMILY PORTRAITS OR CATALOG WORK.

★ HIT THE MUSEUMS. IT'S IMPORTANT TO HAVE A WIDE RANGE OF VISUAL REFERENCES. AND SEEING THE WORKS OF PAST MASTERS CAN HELP YOU PINPOINT IDEAS TO EXPERIMENT WITH.

★ SHOW THAT YOU'RE SERIOUS ABOUT ASSISTING ESTABLISHED PHOTOGRAPHERS BY RESEARCHING THEIR CAREERS. READ THEIR BOOKS, KNOW WHERE THEY'VE EXHIBITED, AND LEARN WHO THEIR INFLUENCES ARE.

★ BE PATIENT. YOU NEED TIME TO DEVELOP AS AN ARTIST. IT CAN TAKE YEARS TO LAUNCH A CAREER, BUT REMEMBER: PURSUING YOUR PASSION IS THE ULTIMATE PATH TO SUCCESS.

APPENDIX

Question:

How do I take the ne
pursuing a fashion

Answer:

Finding schools that
field and becoming
industry will help pr

xt step in
career?

specialize in the
familiar with the
epare you for success.

CONCLUSION

PARTING WORDS OF WISDOM
FROM THE PROS....

"INSTEAD OF *being jealous* OF YOUR PEERS, *be inspired* BY WHAT THEY DO."

—SERGE NORMANT, *HAIRSTYLIST*

"*Take pictures* ALL THE *time.* IF YOU *don't like* ONE OF THEM, *study* IT TO *figure* OUT WHY."

—PATRICK DEMARCHELIER, *PHOTOGRAPHER*

"ARRIVE AT WORK *before your boss* AND STAY UNTIL AFTER SHE LEAVES. THE PEOPLE I WANT TO *promote* ARE *enthusiastic* AND EAGER TO TAKE ON MORE WORK AND *responsibility.*"

—AMY ASTLEY, *EDITOR IN CHIEF,* TEEN VOGUE

"BE AS *free* AS POSSIBLE, *experiment* AS MUCH AS YOU CAN, AND *surprise* YOURSELF. DON'T *conform.* YOU NEED TO HAVE *integrity* TO BE *yourself.*"

—FREDERIKE HELWIG, *PHOTOGRAPHER*

"KEEP *in mind that* YOU *can't* PLEASE EVERYONE EVERY *single* TIME."

—LAZARO HERNANDEZ, *DESIGNER, PROENZA SCHOULER*

"BE NICE."

—REED KRAKOFF, *CREATIVE DIRECTOR, COACH*

"DON'T *be too* **picky:** YOU CAN LEARN FROM WHATEVER *situation you're* IN."

—LEE ANDERSON, *INTERN, THAKOON*

"STAY *close* TO *home.* REMEMBER: YOUR *backyard studio* CAN BE THE CITY OF *Paris.*"

—BRUCE WEBER, *PHOTOGRAPHER*

"IF YOU *want* TO BE A FASHION *blogger,* WHAT'S *stopping* YOU? *Start your* OWN BLOG *tomorrow!*"

—NATALIE HORMILLA, *EDITOR, FASHIONISTA.COM*

"ASK *yourself,* ARE YOU SURE THIS *world* IS FOR YOU? ARE YOU SURE YOU ARE THE *right person* TO *survive* IN THIS WORLD—THE WORLD OF *fashion,* A WORLD WITH NO *rules,* NO *laws?*"

—KARL LAGERFELD, *DESIGNER, CHANEL*

"DON'T GO *too fast.* BECAUSE OF *reality television, everyone* IMAGINES THEY CAN JUST BE A FASHION *designer, photographer,* OR MODEL. THAT'S NOT THE *way* THINGS GO. LEARN YOUR *craft.*"

—ANNA WINTOUR, *EDITOR IN CHIEF, VOGUE*

Design Schools

A CAREER IN THE FASHION INDUSTRY REQUIRES A SOLID EDUCATIONAL FOUNDATION. THESE ESTEEMED SCHOOLS, LOCATED ALL OVER THE WORLD, CAN GIVE YOU THE TOOLS FOR SUCCESS.

ACADEMY OF ART UNIVERSITY

79 NEW MONTGOMERY ST., SAN FRANCISCO, CALIFORNIA 94105
ACADEMYART.EDU **TUITION:** $16,080 PER YEAR
UNDERGRADUATE ENROLLMENT: 11,500

The Academy of Art University in San Francisco advertises that it was "built by artists for artists," and with an 80 percent–plus job-placement rate at companies such as Azzedine Alaïa, Nike, and Pixar, this communal approach seems to be working. The academy was founded in 1929 in a rented loft at 215 Kearny Street and is now the largest private art university in the country, providing a wide assortment of majors—from animation and visual effects to multimedia communications—and occupying more than 30 buildings in downtown San Francisco, all of them accessible by a free morning-to-night shuttle. The school also offers summer study-abroad programs to Belgium, France, Italy, and the Netherlands.

CALIFORNIA COLLEGE OF THE ARTS

1111 EIGHTH ST., SAN FRANCISCO, CALIFORNIA 94107 *CCA.EDU*
TUITION: $31,032 PER YEAR **UNDERGRADUATE ENROLLMENT:** 1,383

Cited as one of the world's best design schools by *Business Week* in 2007, California College of the Arts was founded in 1907 by German cabinetmaker Frederick Meyer. Meyer had envisioned a "practical arts school"—so classes like Body in Motion Drawing and Art & Society combine artistic ideals with everyday applicability. CalArts is composed of two campuses set twelve miles apart—the San Francisco branch houses the architecture and design programs and connects by shuttle to the Oakland campus, which is home to the undergraduate art programs—and has lately been making good on Meyer's mission by engaging in eco-friendly projects. For example, jewelry and metal-arts students are participating in a national program dedicated to repurposing old, donated jewelry into unique, newly fashioned pieces.

Editor's note: Tuition enrollment is subject to change. For the most recent numbers, visit each school's home page.

CENTRAL SAINT MARTINS COLLEGE OF ART AND DESIGN

SOUTHAMPTON ROW, LONDON, ENGLAND WC1B 4AP
CSM.ARTS.CO.UK **TUITION:** $14,464 PER YEAR
UNDERGRADUATE ENROLLMENT: 2,929

Situated in the heart of London, Central Saint Martins is a stone's throw from Savile Row, a street with significant influence on British fashion. One of the most competitive art and design colleges in the world, the School of Fashion & Textiles encourages students to concentrate on a fashion pathway such as menswear, womenswear, or fashion marketing. Born when two art schools combined in 1989, the school has produced some of the smartest designers on today's runways, including Stella McCartney and Zac Posen, and graduates have gone on to work at venerated companies like Dior and Prada. Applicants from the U.S. should apply through the international office, which helps students from more than 90 countries adapt to their new setting.

CRANBROOK ACADEMY OF ART

39221 WOODWARD AVE., BLOOMFIELD HILLS, MICHIGAN 48303
CRANBROOKART.EDU **TUITION:** $24,960 PER YEAR
GRADUATE ENROLLMENT: 150

Named number one on *U.S. News & World Report*'s 2009 list of master's of fine arts programs, the highly selective Cranbrook Academy of Art (which accepts only about 75 of its 600 applicants) is situated within the 315-acre Cranbrook Educational Community campus, adjacent to an

art museum with works by Donald Judd and Andy Warhol. The academy—20 minutes outside of Detroit—comprises ten departments, including the two-year 2D Design program, all stressing independent learning. There are no classes; rather, students are assigned to a studio during orientation and are expected to produce designs on which they receive input from their fellow students and an annual faculty critique. Prospective students must prepare a comprehensive portfolio and display the ability to work independently in a graduate-level environment, in addition to holding a B.A. from an accredited university or college.

DREXEL UNIVERSITY

3141 CHESTNUT ST., PHILADELPHIA, PENNSYLVANIA 19104
DREXEL.EDU **TUITION:** $35,100 PER YEAR
UNDERGRADUATE ENROLLMENT: 8,318 FULL-TIME; 2,196 PART-TIME

Located near downtown Philadelphia, Drexel University prides itself on its Cooperative Education program, which allows students to alternate studying with full-time employment related to their career interests. The school's Antoinette Westphal College of Media Arts & Design offers subjects like music industry and fashion design, and it mandates that attendees spend at least six months working in their chosen career fields to gain real-world experience. Companies such as Oscar de la Renta, Saks Fifth Avenue, and Target have participated in the Co-Op program; firms like Bergdorf Goodman and Chanel have hired Drexel students.

ÉCOLE NATIONALE SUPÉRIEURE DES ARTS VISUELS DE LA CAMBRE

21 ABBAYE DE LA CAMBRE, BRUSSELS, BELGIUM *LACAMBRE.BE*
TUITION: $1,034 PER YEAR **UNDERGRADUATE ENROLLMENT:** 650

With a student body consisting of people from 30 different countries, La Cambre—named for the sixteenth-century abbey that houses the classrooms—is an international destination for serious design students. Founded in 1927 by artist and architect Henry van de Velde and a group of avant-gardists, the school encourages its students to push the boundaries of art, architecture, and design in illustration and performance-and-art classes—a curriculum that helped foster fashion designer Olivier Theysken's innovative vision. The school offers programs at the European bachelor's and master's levels, so most students graduate with a master's degree in five years. French is commonly spoken at La Cambre, so be prepared to converse with admissions officers *en français*.

ICON LEGEND

BUDGET FRIENDLY

TEEN VOGUE SCHOLARSHIP

COMMUTER FRIENDLY

OFFERS STUDY ABROAD

LOW ENROLLMENT

HIGH ENROLLMENT

SUBURBAN

URBAN SETTING

STUDENT HOUSING

PARSONS THE NEW SCHOOL FOR DESIGN.

FASHION INSTITUTE OF TECHNOLOGY

SEVENTH AVE. AT 27TH ST., NEW YORK, NEW YORK 10001
FITNYC.EDU **TUITION:** $2,284 PER SEMESTER FOR RESIDENTS;
$5,570 PER SEMESTER FOR FULL-TIME NONRESIDENTS
UNDERGRADUATE ENROLLMENT: 6,601

FIT benefits from the same enriching New York City setting as Parsons (see opposite page) does, but the two schools are certainly not synonymous. Founder Mortimer C. Ritter, a tailor and educator, set out to create an "MIT for the fashion industries," so the public institution's curriculum focuses on the technical aspects of fashion in addition to a core liberal arts education. The campus boasts an impressive museum whose permanent collection includes 50,000 garments and accessories from the eighteenth century to the present, with pieces by Azzedine Alaïa, Balenciaga, Halston, and Paul Poiret. FIT—which has more than 40 undergraduate programs such as packaging or accessories design, and business majors like cosmetics/fragrance marketing—is best known for its merchandising program. However, the design program is nothing to sneeze at: Francisco Costa, Calvin Klein, and Michael Kors are alums.

KENT STATE UNIVERSITY

KENT STATE UNIVERSITY, KENT, OHIO 44242 *KENT.EDU*
TUITION: $4,215 PER YEAR FOR RESIDENTS; $7,931 PER YEAR FOR
NONRESIDENTS **TOTAL UNDERGRADUATE ENROLLMENT:** 29,227;
SCHOOL OF FASHION DESIGN AND MERCHANDISING: 1,100

Students at Kent State's the Shannon Rodgers and Jerry Silverman School of Fashion Design and Merchandising experience all the excitement a large public school offers—strong athletics, a diverse student body, Greek life—yet receive the personalized attention of a small program. Classes—such as Fashion Fundamentals or the History of Costume—boast an eighteen-to-one student-teacher ratio. The Midwestern location—Cleveland is the nearest major city, at 40 miles away—doesn't seem to deter companies in New York from hiring: KSU students have completed internships at design houses like Michael Kors and Zac Posen, and graduates have been offered jobs at Abercrombie & Fitch and Kenneth Cole. (Pop trivia: Suede, from the fifth season of *Project Runway,* is a KSU fashion school alum.)

MARIST COLLEGE

3399 NORTH RD., POUGHKEEPSIE, NEW YORK 12601 *MARIST.EDU*
TUITION: $25,100 PER YEAR **UNDERGRADUATE ENROLLMENT:** 4,851

Situated on 180 acres about 90 miles north of New York City in the scenic Hudson River Valley, Marist College started

ÉCOLE NATIONALE SUPÉRIEURE DES BEAUX-ARTS

14 RUE BONAPARTE, 75006 PARIS, FRANCE *ENSBA.FR/ENGLISH*
TUITION: $440 PER YEAR **UNDERGRADUATE ENROLLMENT:** 570

Perched on Paris's enchanting Left Bank (or Rive Gauche), across the Seine from the Louvre, École Nationale Supérieure des Beaux-Arts was founded in 1648 and has produced the likes of Hubert de Givenchy. Best known as a school for aspiring artists and architects, ENSBA serves as an appropriate setting for someone interested in a cerebral, artistic approach to design. The five-year curriculum is divided into two parts: The first cycle lasts three years, during which time students learn the technical aspects of their craft. The second cycle lasts two years, involves a professional internship and seminars, and culminates in a *Diplôme national supérieur d'arts plastiques* (roughly comparable to a master's degree). International applicants, who constitute about 20 percent of the student body, must prove they have a good command of French to be considered. *Bonne chance!*

as a seminary a little more than a century ago and has since evolved into a highly respected liberal arts college: In 2009, *U.S. News & World Report* named Marist one of 70 "schools to watch," based in part on the 2000 construction of several state-of-the-art facilities including an 83,000-square-foot library. Students at the School of Communication & the Arts take career-specific classes and electives, such as knitwear design or digital layout and design, in conjunction with a core liberal arts education. In addition, the campus is only two minutes from a train that runs to Grand Central Station, allowing Marist students to intern at the New York City outposts of companies like Chanel and MTV.

MARYLAND INSTITUTE COLLEGE OF ART
1300 MOUNT ROYAL AVE., BALTIMORE, MARYLAND 21217
WWW.MICA.EDU TUITION: $31,640 PER YEAR
UNDERGRADUATE ENROLLMENT: 1,644

Nestled in the heart of Baltimore's cultural district, just a quick train or bus ride from downtown, MICA boasts fifteen bachelor's of fine arts programs. Nearly one-third of the students pursue degrees in the design and illustration departments, where they can work alongside students in the graduate program, which is ranked fourth on *U.S. News & World Report's* 2009 list of master's of fine arts schools. In addition to liberal arts and foundation courses, students choose from electives like publication design and experimental typography, and recent students have taken advantage of the school's proximity to New York (a three-hour train ride) with internships at companies like Brooklyn Industries, Puma, and Urban Outfitters.

MASSACHUSETTS COLLEGE OF ART AND DESIGN
621 HUNTINGTON AVE., BOSTON, MASSACHUSETTS 02115 *MASSART.EDU*
TUITION: $7,900 PER YEAR FOR RESIDENTS; $14,000 PER YEAR FOR OTHER NEW ENGLAND RESIDENTS; $23,000 PER YEAR FOR NONRESIDENTS UNDERGRADUATE ENROLLMENT: 1,653

Founded in 1873, MassArt is one of the most selective colleges, in terms of undergraduate admissions, of the nation's 39 independent schools of art and design—only 50 percent of its applicants are accepted in the fashion and graphic design concentrations. Once admitted, attendees choose from 22 programs of study and show their work at nine campus galleries. The college also stresses a well-rounded education: Forty percent of every program's requirements are in the liberal arts. Recent students have put their MassArt education to good use by interning for Tommy Hilfiger and Marc Jacobs, and graduates have gone on to work at companies like DKNY and Nicole Miller. Located in the cultural district that includes the Museum of Fine Arts, MassArt has on-campus nighttime bus stops and is walking distance from the subway, so that students can enjoy Boston in its entirety.

OTIS COLLEGE OF ART AND DESIGN
9045 LINCOLN BLVD., LOS ANGELES, CALIFORNIA 90045 *OTIS.EDU*
TUITION: $30,415 PER YEAR UNDERGRADUATE ENROLLMENT: 1,200

Southern California's influence on fashion and the arts expands each year, as Otis spreads through the increasingly cultivated Los Angeles area. The main campus branch, in L.A.'s West Side neighborhood, features a 40,000-square-foot fine arts center. The Fashion Design Department is located in the heart of the downtown garment district, and the graphic design studios are in El Segundo, a beach community. All are a quick drive from one another and to area museums such as the Museum of Contemporary Art and the J. Paul Getty Museum. To develop a strong arts core, Otis freshman take a foundation year with classes like Principles of Design, and Form and Space. Majors, such as digital media or fashion design, are declared sophomore year. Fast-growing action/sports brands Hurley, Quiksilver, Roxy, Vans, and Volcom, among others, have made L.A. their home base in recent years and employ many Otis graduates. Likewise, the school's proximity to Hollywood means it's on the pulse of the digital-design industry. Musician-artist Kim Gordon of Sonic Youth is an Otis alum, and the legendary costume designer Edith Head took classes on campus.

PARSONS THE NEW SCHOOL FOR DESIGN
55 WEST THIRTEENTH ST., NEW YORK, NEW YORK 10011
PARSONS.NEWSCHOOL.EDU TUITION: $33,700 PER YEAR
UNDERGRADUATE ENROLLMENT: 3,815

Located in New York City's Greenwich Village, many of Parsons's alumni have ascended to the top of the industry's most refined high-fashion houses. Parsons boasts 26 degrees among its five thematic schools, but the world-renowned department of fashion design, which serves as the setting for *Project Runway,* has put the school on the map. Founded in 1906, the first-ever fashion design program in the U.S. has continued to produce the industry's most illustrious designers—including Tom Ford, Marc Jacobs, Donna Karan, and Isaac Mizrahi—thanks to a combination of mandatory courses such as Concept Development and impressive faculty members like designer Salvatore Cesarani and former fashion design chair Tim Gunn. Parsons also offers a four-week summer intensive-studies program, which gives high school juniors and seniors the chance to experience art school and build a strong portfolio. (Heads up: Registration starts in November, and spots fill quickly!)

PHILADELPHIA UNIVERSITY

SCHOOL HOUSE LANE AND HENRY AVE., PHILADELPHIA, PENNSYLVANIA 19144 *PHILAU.EDU*
TUITION: $26,630 PER YEAR **UNDERGRADUATE ENROLLMENT:** 2,760

Philadelphia University's name is a bit misleading: The school is actually sited on 100 acres fifteen minutes away from the heart of the city. A convenient train station and a public bus service running through the center of campus ensure that students can enjoy the proximity of a busy city along with the comforts of a quiet college campus. Two schools in particular make the private university a design hub: the School of Engineering and Textiles and the School of Design and Media, which both offer degrees geared to fashion and graphic-design careers. Students also benefit from the collection at the university's Design Center, a nationally recognized resource for the study of textiles and costumes, and a thirteen-to-one student-teacher ratio. With an 87.5 percent career-placement rate and alumni like season one *Project Runway* winner Jay McCarroll, that abundance of attention seems to be paying off.

PRATT INSTITUTE

200 WILLOUGBY AVE., NEW YORK, NEW YORK 11205 *PRATT.EDU*
TUITION: $31,700 PER YEAR **UNDERGRADUATE ENROLLMENT:** 3,109

Pratt may not be the most well-known design school in New York City, but *U.S. News & World Report* named the school's graduate interior-design program the best in the country in 2009. The School of Art and Design, which counts the late photographer Robert Mapplethorpe among its alumni, offers a variety of degrees—including media arts, industrial design, and fine arts—and is located in Brooklyn's historic Clinton Hill neighborhood, a 20-minute subway ride from Manhattan. Pratt hosts a fair every year for intern-seeking New York City–area businesses, and companies like Fisher-Price and Sony BMG have participated. Pratt's perks are appealing: In 2007, the institute received more than 4,000 applications for 586 freshman spots, the most of any other design school.

RHODE ISLAND SCHOOL OF DESIGN

2 COLLEGE ST., PROVIDENCE, RHODE ISLAND 02903 *RISD.EDU*
TUITION: $34,665 PER YEAR **UNDERGRADUATE ENROLLMENT:** 1,920

RISD is widely regarded as the best fine arts school in the country; in fact, in 2009, *U.S. News & World Report* ranked the school number one for masters's in fine arts programs. Located in Providence, a vibrant, diverse midsize city that's only a train ride away from Boston and New York, the school offers a strong liberal arts education in conjunction with art and design programs—many students cross-register at nearby Brown University. Highly selective RISD, which counts Nicole Miller and curator Yvonne Force Villareal as alumni, offers foundation courses in drawing and two-dimensional design and is well suited for those considering a career in graphic design or photography. Like Parsons, RISD offers a pre-college program that gives approximately 550 sixteen- to eighteen-year-olds the chance to strengthen their artistic techniques and get a taste of the art school experience.

SAVANNAH COLLEGE OF ART AND DESIGN

342 BULL ST., SAVANNAH, GEORGIA 31401 *SCAD.EDU*
TUITION: $27,765 PER YEAR **UNDERGRADUATE ENROLLMENT:** 9,000 (COMBINED CAMPUSES)

Located south of the Mason-Dixon Line, SCAD benefits from a quirky mix of Southern gentility and Northern sensibility (picture art students sketching below gnarled oak trees dripping with Spanish moss). The historical setting houses cutting-edge technology, such as state-of-the-art Mac labs and industry-standard software, making SCAD a leader in graphic design—alumni have advanced to companies like ESPN and Saatchi & Saatchi. The school also offers programs like dramatic writing in its various buildings, all within walking distance of one another. Every year the college lures industry giants such as Marc Jacobs and *Vogue* Editor at Large André Leon Talley (who is a member of the school's board of trustees) to Savannah for SCAD Style, a monthlong series of workshops and lectures that culminates in a fashion show in May. Students can also elect to attend the more urban Atlanta campus.

SCHOOL OF THE ART INSTITUTE OF CHICAGO

37 SOUTH WABASH AVE., CHICAGO, ILLINOIS 60603 *SAIC.EDU*
TUITION: $1,025 PER CREDIT HOUR **UNDERGRADUATE ENROLLMENT:** 2,259

Set in the heart of the Windy City, SAIC is surrounded by world-renowned museums and galleries like the Field Museum of Natural History and the Museum of Contemporary Art. But the college's unique interdisciplinary curriculum is what really sets it apart from other schools. Students do not declare a major: Instead, they are encouraged to explore several artistic disciplines with an emphasis on a chosen field, which allows students the freedom to take classes from various departments. Targeted undergraduate classes like fashion illustration and three-dimensional animation help SAIC alumni (like Cynthia Rowley) enter the workplace with a fundamental arts education and specialized skill sets.

RHODE ISLAND SCHOOL OF DESIGN.

CENTRAL SAINT MARTINS COLLEGE OF ART AND DESIGN.

SCHOOL OF VISUAL ARTS

209 EAST 23RD ST., NEW YORK, NEW YORK 10010
SVA.EDU **TUITION:** $25,500 PER YEAR
ENROLLMENT: 3,415

Although New York City's SVA offers a total of eleven areas of undergraduate study, including graphic design and advertising, its photography program is what put the school on the map. The program boasts a 100-plus faculty, a five-to-one student-teacher ratio, and guest lecturers like famed lensman David LaChapelle. The department was recently renovated with new studios, darkrooms, and four digital labs. Photography on Assignment is one of the classes offered to instruct students on how best to use the industry's latest technology. Located just north of New York's East Village, SVA lies near famed Chelsea galleries and the New Museum, and the work of recent graduates has been featured in *Details, The New York Times,* and *W.*

SYRACUSE UNIVERSITY

SYRACUSE UNIVERSITY, SYRACUSE, NEW YORK 13244 *SYR.EDU*
TUITION: $30,470 PER YEAR **TOTAL UNDERGRADUATE ENROLLMENT:**
11,796; THE COLLEGE OF VISUAL AND PERFORMING ARTS: 1,950

Located about five hours north of Manhattan, in upstate New York, Syracuse has a lot to offer those considering a career in fashion or publishing. In addition to the College of Visual and Performing Arts (VPA), which boasts alums Betsey Johnson and Aaron Sorkin, the university is home to the S.I. Newhouse School of Public Communications, which includes magazine journalism, advertising, and broadcast journalism majors. (Newhouse, for whom the school is named, founded Advance Publications, the parent company of Condé Nast Publications and *Teen Vogue.*) Anchored by a core liberal arts education, the VPA's School of Art Design also offers sixteen different art and design programs. Syracuse alumni have gone on to work at publications like *New York* magazine and companies like Ralph Lauren.

UNIVERSITY OF CINCINNATI

2600 CLIFTON AVE., CINCINNATI, OHIO 45221 *UC.EDU*
TUITION: $9,399 PER YEAR FOR RESIDENTS; $23,922 PER YEAR
FOR NONRESIDENTS **TOTAL UNDERGRADUATE ENROLLMENT:**
27,000; COLLEGE OF DESIGN, ARCHITECTURE, ART, AND
PLANNING: 1,901

Situated just north of downtown Cincinnati, the university is a 20-minute bus ride (free with student ID) from the Cincinnati Arts Association, the Contemporary Arts Center, and Taft Museum of Art. In addition to its rich cultural setting, the school boasts the highly regarded College of Design, Architecture, Art, and Planning (DAAP), which offers fashion design, fashion-merchandising, and graphic design programs and was on *Business Week*'s "A-List of D-Schools" in 2007. As part of the five-year curriculum, DAAP attendees alternate classroom work with paid professional practice through the college's Co-op Program; in recent years, students have gone on to work at companies like Abercrombie & Fitch and J. Crew. ★

GLOSSARY

AD CAMPAIGN A group of images created by a business to showcase a new collection and promote sales.

AGENCY A company authorized to negotiate bookings and fees on behalf of a photographer, stylist, producer, writer, model, or other creative entity. The agency usually charges a commission for its participation.

ASSOCIATE DEGREE An academic degree granted after completing two years of study, or about 20 classes (approximately 60 credits); available at public community colleges, private two-year colleges, vocationally inclined academic institutions, and many four-year colleges and universities. An associate degree can also transfer to a bachelor's degree.

BEAT A specialized topic—such as politics, sports, or fashion—on which a reporter focuses.

COLLECTION A line of clothing. The term also refers to seasonal ready-to-wear or couture presentations.

COMPOSITION Refers to the art and practice of arranging and presenting visual elements.

CONTACT SHEET A collection of photographs on a printed sheet that catalogs digital images or rolls of film. See also *proof*.

COUNCIL OF FASHION DESIGNERS OF AMERICA A not-for-profit trade association that aims to support the American fashion industry. Founded in 1962, the council is a sponsor of the CFDA/*Teen Vogue* Scholarship, the CFDA/*Vogue* Fashion Fund, and other awards and professional development programs. Diane von Furstenberg has been the group's president since 2006.

DRESS FORM A limbless mannequin that gives a three-dimensional view of a garment. Used by seamstresses, stylists, and designers for fittings and often made of papier-mâché and covered in linen.

FASHION CLOSET A room stocked with clothing and accessories that is located within the editorial headquarters of a magazine. Stylists pull from the fashion closet when prepping for photo shoots.

FREELANCER An independently employed contractor commissioned to work on a for-hire basis. Stylists, writers, art directors, and editors often choose freelancing over staff positions because the arrangement allows freedom to work on various projects for different organizations.

GO-SEE An audition or interview during which a casting director meets models considered for upcoming photo shoots or gigs.

GOTH A macabre youth subculture that evokes images of rebellion, death, and destruction. The contemporary goth movement is rooted in the Victorian cult of mourning. Icons include illustrator Edward Gorey and bands such as Siouxsie and the Banshees and the Cure.

HAUTE COUTURE A French term that translates into "high sewing" and refers to the creation of custom-made, handcrafted garments. The principle was first developed in Paris in the mid-nineteenth century. Also known as couture.

INSPIRATION BOARD The starting point for a fashion shoot or collection. An inspiration board may include photos of fashion shoots or runway looks that capture the mood of a collection and inspire editors and stylists when sourcing clothes or accessories in the market.

LE BOOK An encyclopedia of names, companies, and contact information for everyone in the fashion industry, including hairstylists, set designers, model agents, photographers, and stylists.

MARKET The labels and designers that stand as the main resources when planning a photo shoot. An editor may oversee a market that is linked to a specific city or type of clothing, such as Italian designers or junior apparel.

MARKET EDITOR A fashion editor who chooses clothing or accessories for photo shoots and sometimes styles looks on models or celebrities.

MASTHEAD The listing of editorial and advertising staff at a magazine.

MODEL APARTMENT An apartment that an agency leases to house models who are traveling on assignment. Major agencies may have apartments in London, Los Angeles, Miami, Milan, New York City, or Paris so that models can live in a reliable, safe place while working away from home.

MODEL CARD An eye-catching card featuring strong images of a model along with her measurements, sizes, and eye and hair color.

MONOGRAPH A nonfiction book on a specific topic.

MOOD BOARD A collection of sketches, fabric and color swatches, drawings, quotes, movie stills, or other cultural ephemera that inspire a photo shoot or collection.

NEGATIVE A strip of film that captures an original image in its inverted form—shadows appear light and highlights, dark.

PALETTE An array of colors.

PANTONE The corporation known for the Pantone Matching System, a vast collection of colors used by, among others, the publishing, fashion, and cosmetics industries.

PATTERN-MAKER A person who creates the patterns that will eventually be used as garment blueprints.

PORTFOLIO A collection showcasing a person's work, emphasizing achievements, growth, and skill.

PRODUCTION DEPARTMENT The team responsible for managing, or trafficking, copy and art flow at a publishing or other media organization.

PROOF A collection of photographs on a printed sheet that catalogs digital images or rolls of film. See also *contact sheet.*

PULITZER PRIZE A prestigious annual award administered by Columbia University in honor of achievements in journalism, literature, drama, and music. The journalism category includes public service, breaking news coverage, investigative reporting, and a number of photography awards.

RACK The rack on which clothing is presented for review during run-throughs and merchandise returns.

READY-TO-WEAR The opposite of haute couture. Ready-to-wear is not made to measure; instead, these collections are purchased off the racks. Also known as prêt-à-porter.

RE-SEE A follow-up appointment scheduled after a designer's original presentation so that a fashion editor can take a closer look at accessories and clothing.

RETAIL Selling directly to consumers.

ROCKABILLY A style based on 1950s Americana and a hybrid of music rooted in country, R&B, and rock 'n' roll. Staples of rockabilly style include plaid shirts, denim, leather jackets, and classic tattoos.

RUN-THROUGH An appointment during which a stylist presents clothing to be considered for inclusion in a photo shoot.

SAMPLE A prototype for a garment based on an item from a designer's collection.

SHOWROOM Office space where a designer displays—for editors, stylists, and retailers—clothing samples from the current collection. A showroom can be run by a designer or a public relations firm.

SITTING, SITTINGS EDITOR A photo shoot, and the person who works with the photographer to help oversee the look and feel of the pictures.

SOURCING Finding materials for a shoot, often exhausting all the resources for a desired item. Market editors and stylists are responsible for sourcing.

Word Play

HERE'S A GUIDE TO TALKING THE TALK AT MAGAZINES.

BOB: "Back of book." The magazine's final section, which includes credits, any runover from well stories, and often a trademark one-page feature that ends each issue.

book: The magazine or publication itself.

caption: Or "cap," an explanation of an image.

COB: "Center of book." A magazine's main editorial section, with cover and fashion stories but usually without advertising. See also *well.*

dek: A few sentences that summarize an article.

dummy book: A book containing the working layouts for a magazine or other publication.

dummy text: Text that is not "live," acting as a placeholder in design layouts until the final text is edited and flowed in.

first-bound: An almost-final version of a magazine, received in the office for review prior to newsstand date.

FOB: "Front of book." A magazine's first section, which comes before the feature well.

graf: "Paragraph."

hed: "Headline."

line edit: To edit a piece of text carefully for repetitions, clarity, length, and flow.

slug: A short phrase or title used to describe the contents of a page or story.

well: See also *COB;* also known as the feature well.

STILL LIFE A photograph of an arrangement of objects that illustrate a story or idea.

TRADE SHOW An industry event often held at a convention center so that designers selling the same type of merchandise can convene for a few days to introduce new products.

TREND BOARD A story presented on a board that combines similar trends from different designers.

TROMPE L'OEIL French for "trick the eye," this term refers to imagery that creates the illusion of photographic reality through the use of light and shadow. Used in paintings, murals, and textiles.

VINTAGE Old-fashioned or secondhand clothing. The term can be applied to anything from Victorian-era dresses to 1980s concert T-shirts. Vintage designer pieces often become collector's items. Stylists sometimes use vintage pieces to add character to photo shoots that are otherwise filled with contemporary clothing.

WHOLESALE The sale of products to a retailer for resale to the public. ★

NOTES

NOTES

VERY *special thanks* TO:

AOIFE WASSER, *Meghan Sutherland,* NICOLE STUART, *Corey Towers,* JANE KELTNER, *Eva Chen,* EVONNE GAMBRELL, JANE SHIN PARK, *Candice Ralph,* JANICE YU, *Liz Higgins, Zan Goodman,* AND LENE DAHL; *Ben Schrank,* DANIELLE KANIPER, *and Julianne Lowell at Razorbill;* ANNA WINTOUR, *Christiane Mack,* CASSIDY ELLIS, *and Ivan Shaw at Vogue;* FLORENCE PALOMO AT THE CONDÉ NAST LIBRARY; *Jennifer DiPreta,* ANDREW AVERY, *and Brian Cross.* THIS BOOK WOULD NOT HAVE BEEN *possible* WITHOUT THE *extraordinary contributions* OF ALL THE *designers,* STYLISTS, *editors,* WRITERS, *and photographers* INCLUDED *in these* PAGES. *Thanks also to* ELEANOR BANCO; *Amy Beecher;* LEIGH BELZ; *Mia Berg;* ANDREW BEVAN; *K. Emily Bond;* DIANA ESTIGARRIBIA; *Elizabeth Gall;* STEVE GEORGE; *Keith Grieger;* PHILIPPE HOFFMANN; *Susan Kowal;* VINCENT LaSPISA AT SABIN, BERMANT & GOULD; *Lauren McGrath;* MARGARET MEEHAN; *Mardi Miskit;* MARNI OKUN; *Mariel Osborn;* JENNIFER PASTORE; *Jackie Randell;* ROBIN REETZ; *and Lindsay Talbot.*

Lauren Waterman
COLLEGE UNIVERSITY OF VIRGINIA
HOMETOWN BURKE, VIRGINIA

"I got the chance to talk to so many inspiring people while working on this book," Lauren Waterman says. "If there's one thing I've learned, it's that there is no single secret to success. The constants, if there are any, are passion for what you're doing and a willingness to work very hard at it." Waterman herself demonstrated these traits when she started working at *Vogue* magazine a decade ago, only days after graduating with a degree in English literature from the University of Virginia. As one of two assistants to the managing editor, she may have been at the bottom of the masthead, but she never lost sight of the bigger picture.

"At first I answered phones and processed freelancer payments and contracts. But I understood that if I didn't do a good job at those things, then I would never get the chance to do what I was really interested in. And when I did start getting small writing assignments, I took them very, very seriously." In short order, Waterman advanced to features assistant, staff writer, and then contributing editor at *Vogue.* In 2002, she joined the founding staff of *Teen Vogue* as a senior writer. Now a contributing editor at the magazine, she has interviewed celebrities including Scarlett Johansson and Rihanna, has written more than 50 cover stories, and is, in her off-hours, pursuing an M.F.A. in fiction writing at Sarah Lawrence College.

PHOTO CREDITS

All credits are clockwise from top left, unless otherwise noted.

FRONT COVER

Arthur Elgort; Daniel Jackson; Margaret Gibbons; Thomas Schenk (2); Arthur Elgort; Isabel Asha Penzlien; Jason Kibbler; Thomas Schenk; Johansen Krause/courtesy of Jillian Davison; Jason Kibbler; Arthur Elgort; Stephane Cardinale/People Avenue/courtesy of Corbis; Thomas Schenk; Jason Kibbler; Jason Bell.

END PAPERS

Left to right, top to bottom: Patrick Demarchelier (2); Bruce Weber; Patrick Demarchelier; Bruce Weber; Carter Smith; Patrick Demarchelier; Arthur Elgort; Mario Testino; Richard Bush; Arthur Elgort; Patrick Demarchelier; Arthur Elgort; Patrick Demarchelier; Norman Jean Roy; Mario Testino; Patrick Demarchelier; Mario Testino; Alasdair McLellan; Patrick Demarchelier (5); Norman Jean Roy; Herb Ritts; Patrick Demarchelier (3); Carter Smith; Patrick Demarchelier; Nathaniel Goldberg; Patrick Demarchelier (3); Mario Testino.

INTRODUCTION

Page 1: Marion Curtis for StarPix.

RODARTE

Page 5: Arthur Elgort. Page 6: Marcio Madeira/courtesy of FirstView.com. Page 7: CN Digital Studio/Craig McDean; WireImage.com.

MARC JACOBS

Page 9: Margaret Gibbons. Page 10: Steven Meisel. Page 11: CN Digital Studio/Sofia Coppola/courtesy of Wilson/Wenzel Inc.; CN Digital Studio/Juergen Teller (2); CN Digital Studio/Paul Jasmin/courtesy of Wilson/Wenzel Inc.; CN Digital Studio/Juergen Teller (2); CN Digital Studio/Michael Thompson/courtesy of Jed Root. Page 13: Walter Chin/Marek & Assoc./TrunkArchive.com. Page 14: Patrick Demarchelier. Page 15: Greg Kessler/courtesy of FirstView.com (3); WireImage.com; courtesy of FashionPhile.com; courtesy of Louis Vuitton; Mitchell Feinberg.

THAKOON PANICHGUL

Pages 16–17: Mario Testino. Page 18: GettyImages.com (2). Page 19: courtesy of Lee Anderson; courtesy of Dylan Kawahara.

STELLA McCARTNEY

Pages 20–21: Annie Leibovitz. Page 22: Stephane Feugere. Page 23: Patrick Demarchelier; Doug Peters/PA Photos/AbacaUSA.com; Thomas Schenk; courtesy of FirstView.com (2).

ALEXANDER WANG

Pages 24–25: David X. Prutting/PatrickMcMullan.com/courtesy of Alexander Wang. Page 26: Marcio Madeira/courtesy of FirstView.com (3). Page 27: Hannah Thomson; Norman Jean Roy; Robert Fairer.

TORY BURCH

Page 29: courtesy of Tory Burch. Page 30: GettyImages.com; courtesy of Tory Burch; WireImage.com. Page 31: Nick Haymes.

PHILLIP LIM

Page 33: Skye Parrott. Page 34: Frederike Helwig; Thomas Schenk. Page 35: Marcio Madeira/courtesy of FirstView.com; GettyImages.com; courtesy of Asia Ragland; Michael Baumgarten.

PATRICK ROBINSON

Pages 36–37: Sebastian Kim. Page 38: Steven Meisel; CNP Digital Studio/Mikael Jansson. Page 39: Norman Jean Roy.

REED KRAKOFF

Pages 40–41: Reed Krakoff/courtesy of Coach. Page 42: Reed Krakoff/courtesy of Coach. Page 43: courtesy of Reed Krakoff; Inez van Lamsweerde and Vinoodh Matadin/The Collective Shift ™/TrunkArchive.com.

PROENZA SCHOULER

Pages 44–45: Mario Testino. Page 46: Marcio Madeira/courtesy of FirstView.com (2). Page 47: Arthur Elgort.

JUSTIN GIUNTA

Pages 48–49: Norman Jean Roy. Page 50: Melissa Hom. Page 51: Norman Jean Roy.

BLAKE MYCOSKIE

Pages 52–54: courtesy of TOMS Shoes. Page 55: courtesy of TOMS Shoes (2); Thomas Schenk; courtesy of TOMS Shoes.

KARL LAGERFELD

Page 57: Stephane Cardinale/People Avenue/courtesy of Corbis. Page 58: Chesnot/Sipa. Page 59: Steven Meisel.

DESIGNER TOOL KIT

Pages 60–61: Lucas Visser; styling, Keiko Visser.

AMY ASTLEY

Page 65: Isabel Asha Penzlien. Page 66: Dave Allocca/Star Pix; Sara Jaye Weiss/Star Pix; Abbey Drucker; courtesy of MTV; PatrickMcMullan.com. Page 67: Jeremy Balderson. Pages 68–69: Corey Towers. Page 70: WireImage.com; Donato Sardella for WireImage.com; Marion Curtis/Star Pix. Page 71: Clint Spaulding/PatrickMcMullan.com.

TEEN VOGUE FASHION MARKET TEAM

Pages 72–73: JD Ferguson. Page 74: courtesy of Garance Doré. Page 75: no credit; Jason Kibbler (7). Page 76: courtesy of JakAndJil.com; JD Ferguson. Page 77: © Scott Schuman; Susanna Howe.

JANE KELTNER

Page 79: © Scott Schuman. Page 80: Louise Enhörning; © Scott Schuman; Clint Spaulding/courtesy of PatrickMcMullan.com; Barnsley, Breeden/courtesy of PacificCoastNews.com. Page 81: Mardi Miskit (2).

EVA CHEN

Page 83: Raymond Meier. Page 84: Horacio Salinas; James Wojcik. Page 85: Thomas Bannister; James Wojcik.

AOIFE WASSER

Pages 86–87: Arthur Elgort. Page 88: Jason Kibbler (2); Corey Towers. Page 89: Mardi Miskit; Thomas Schenk. Page 90: Alasdair McLellan; Dan Forbes (2).

TRUC NGUYEN & BLAKE ENGLISH

Page 93: Tina Tyrell. Pages 94–95: Justin Kay (11).

INTERN TOOL KIT

Page 96: Cathy Crawford, Lucas Visser. Page 97: Tina Tyrell.

ROBIN GIVHAN

Pages 98–99: courtesy of *The Washington Post*. Page 100: Douliery/Hahn/courtesy of AbacaUSA.com. Page 101: courtesy of Columbia University.

NATALIE MASSENET

Page 103: © Scott Schuman. Page 104: Nick Harvey/WireImage.com. Page 105: courtesy of Net-a-Porter.com (4).

CLAUDIA WU
Page 107: Glynnis McDaris. Pages 108–109: courtesy of Claudia Wu/*Me Magazine.*

NATALIE HORMILLA
Pages 110–111: courtesy of Natalie Hormilla/Fashionista.com. Page 112: Isabel Asha Penzlien.

ANNA WINTOUR
Page 115: Greg Kessler/courtesy of FirstView. com. Page 117: Billy Farrell/PatrickMcMullan. com; Greg Kessler/courtesy of FirstView. com; © Ellen von Unwerth/Art + Commerce; WireImage.com (2). Page 118: Peter Lindbergh/courtesy of CNP Archives. Page 119: Greg Kessler/courtesy of FirstView.com; courtesy of *Vogue.*

EDITOR TOOL KIT
Pages 120–121: Lucas Visser, Cathy Crawford, Travis Rathbone, Karineh Gurjian-Angelo; styling, Anne Cardenas, Keiko Visser.

JILLIAN DAVISON
Page 125: Johansen Krause/courtesy of Jillian Davison. Pages 126–127: Patrick Demarchelier (2). Page 128: Peter Lindbergh/courtesy of Jillian Davison. Page 129: Arthur Elgort; Jason Kibbler; Raymond Meier (2).

ANDREA LIEBERMAN
Pages 130–131: Pete Black/courtesy of Andrea Lieberman. Page 132: GettyImages. com; WireImage.com; GettyImages.com; WireImage.com. Page 133: WireImage.com.

HAVANA LAFFITTE
Page 135: Danielle Nussbaum. Pages 136–137: Bruce Weber (2). Page 138: Frederike Helwig. Page 139: Nick Haymes; Thomas Schenk; Bruce Weber (2).

CAMILLA NICKERSON
Page 141: Inez van Lamsweerde and Vinoodh Matadin/The Creative Shift ™/ TrunkArchive.com. Page 142: Thomas Schenk (2). Page 143: Steven Klein; Nick Haymes. Page 144: Mario Testino. Page 145: Steven Meisel.

ELISSA SANTISI
Page 147: courtesy of Elissa Santisi. Page 148: Raymond Meier; Steven Meisel. Page 149: Thomas Schenk. Page 150: Inez van Lamsweerde and Vinoodh Matadin/The Creative Shift ™/TrunkArchive.com. Page 151: Barrett Roman; courtesy of MTV.

STYLIST TOOL KIT
Pages 152–153: Lucas Visser; styling, Keiko Visser.

LARA BONOMO
Pages 156–157: Corey Towers. Page 158: Glynnis McDaris. Page 159: Lara Bonomo; Arthur Elgort; Lara Bonomo; Thomas Schenk (2). Page 160: Lara Bonomo; Patrick Demarchelier; Lara Bonomo; Nick Haymes (2). Page 161: Lara Bonomo; Nick Haymes; Lara Bonomo; Thomas Schenk (2).

CAROLINE TRENTINI
Pages 162–163: Patrick Demarchelier. Page 164: Thomas Schenk (2). Page 165: Arthur Elgort.

CHANEL IMAN
Page 167: Thomas Schenk; Patrick Demarchelier (inset). Page 168: Elin Hörnfeldt; Marcio Madeira/courtesy of FirstView.com. Page 169: David Sims (4).

GUCCI WESTMAN
Page 173: Jason Bell. Page 174: Arthur Elgort. Page 175: Mario Testino. Page 176: Robert Fairer. Page 177: courtesy of Mary Clarke.

GUIDO PALAU
Pages 179–180: Daniel Jackson. Page 182: David Sims; Steven Meisel; David Sims (2). Page 183: Nick Haymes.

PAT McGRATH
Pages 184–185: Norman Jean Roy. Page 186: Daniele Oberrauch/courtesy of FirstView. com; Olivier Claisse/courtesy of FirstView. com; Alfred/Sipa. Pages 187–188: Steven Meisel. Page 189: Raymond Meier (2).

SERGE NORMANT
Pages 190–191: Raymond Meier. Page 192: © Steven Simko; CN Digital Studio. Page 193: Michael Thompson/courtesy of *W.*

JEMMA KIDD
Pages 195–196: Ben Hassett. Page 197: courtesy of Jemma Kidd for Target; Robert Fairer; Rex USA; Jason Bell.

BEAUTY TOOL KIT
Pages 198–199: Lucas Visser; styling, KeikoVisser.

PATRICK DEMARCHELIER
Pages 202–203: Patrick Demarchelier. Pages 205–208: Patrick Demarchelier. Page 209: courtesy of Demarchelier Studio; Patrick Demarchelier.

FREDERIKE HELWIG
Page 211: Nicole Vecchiarelli; courtesy of Frederike Helwig. Pages 212–213: Frederike Helwig (6).

BRUCE WEBER
Page 215: courtesy of Little Bear/Bruce Weber. Pages 216–218: Bruce Weber. Page 219: Bruce Weber; courtesy of Sherri O'Connor; Bruce Weber.

UP-AND-COMING PHOTOGRAPHERS
Pages 220–225: Sebastian Kim.

MARIO TESTINO
Pages 226–227: Sam Faulkner. Pages 228–230: Mario Testino. Page 231: Glynnis McDaris; Mario Testino.

ARTHUR ELGORT
Pages 232–233: Carlos Ruiz/Arthur Elgort Studio. Pages 235–239: Arthur Elgort.

SHONA HEATH
Page 241: Jennifer Livingston/courtesy of Shona Heath. Pages 242–243: Dusan Reljin. Page 244: Jonas Fredwall Karlsson/courtesy of Vernon Jolly Inc. Page 245: Dusan Reljin.

LINA KUTSOVSKAYA
Pages 247–249: Nick Haymes. Page 250: courtesy of Barneys New York (4). Page 251: Nick Haymes (4).

PHOTO TOOL KIT
Pages 252–253: Lucas Visser, Cara Howe; styling, Keiko Visser, Anne Cardenas.

DESIGN SCHOOLS
Page 260: © Richard B. Levine/NewsCom. com. Page 263: Erik Gould/courtesy of RISD; no credit.

LAUREN WATERMAN
Page 275: Andrei Kallaur.

BACK COVER
Daniel Jackson; Arthur Elgort; Horst Diekgerdes; Thomas Schenk; Arthur Elgort; Patrick Demarchelier; Daniel Jackson; courtesy of Frederike Helwig; Isabel Asha Penzlien; Raymond Meier; Nick Haymes; Arthur Elgort; Nick Haymes; Arthur Elgort; Daniel Jackson; Frederike Helwig.

BUSINESS REPLY MAIL
FIRST-CLASS MAIL   PERMIT NO. 107   BOONE IA

POSTAGE WILL BE PAID BY ADDRESSEE

TEEN VOGUE
PO BOX 37754
BOONE, IA 50037-2754